GOLF ON THE EDGE

Triumphs & Tragedies Of Q School

First published in Great Britain in 2008 by Ultimate Sports Publications

© Ross Biddiscombe

A CIP catalogue record for this book is available from the British Library.

www.golfontheedge.co.uk

ISBN 978-0-9545199-7

Typeset by PDQ Digital Media Solutions, Bungay.

Printed in Great Britain

Ultimate Sports Publications Ltd, London, England

Contents

Introduction

"Golf is like a grindstone – whether it grinds you down or polishes you up, depends on what you are made of" – Anon.

This is a story about struggle, not of the life-threatening kind, but the type that shapes sportsmen, their self-respect, their relationships, their careers.

For journeymen golfers with everyday problems like mortgages to pay, wives and children to care for, with parents who loan them money, securing a regular place on the European Tour is the one thing that drives them all. This book is about seven players' journeys to try to fulfil the dream of a place among golf's elite.

Some of the seven have never played on that Tour at all, others want to return after a painful absence and a few are trying to hang on to their place. But all of them understand that the road to the Tour is rugged and one of sport's ultimate instruments of torture can stand in their way: the Qualifying School aka Q School or, more formally, the PGA European Tour School.

The 14-round, three-stage Q School is both a blessing and a curse: succeeding at the School gives players a Tour Card, the passport to playing in some of the most prestigious tournaments and a prospective jet-set lifestyle of fame and fortune. Failing at the School can leave a player in golf's equivalent of the twilight zone.

The tension at Q School makes it one of sport's most gut-churning events; it is where careers can either be launched in a single moment of glory or extinguished by a single mistake.

Only players in the top 30 at the very end of the Q School marathon receive a Tour Card. Of the players who attempt this feat, 97% fail; the odds of success at Q School are long, but the players keep returning because the potential rewards are huge.

The seven professionals in this story all know Q School intimately. Sion Bebb, James Conteh, Phil Golding, Euan Little, Andy Raitt, Martyn Thompson and Guy Woodman all have different backgrounds and different ranges of ability. They are each at a crossroads in their careers and to fulfil their dream of that regular European Tour place means another trip to Q School, a place that is not just a barrier but also a lifeline..

The seven can take heart because some of the world's best players have passed through the School: Colin Montgomerie, Jose Maria Olazabal, Padraig Harrington, Retief Goosen, Vijay Singh, Sandy Lyle, Ian Woosnam as well as today's younger superstars like Henrik Stenson, Lee Westwood, Justin Rose, Ian Poulter, Nick Dougherty and many more. And not all these players sailed through the Q School examination first time: for example, Poulter was a four-time visitor before he secured a Card.

What every Q School graduate recognises is that the event is a golfing beast that can chew up even the best players and spit them out bewildered and badly damaged.

If there was any doubt about how tough life can be on the fringes of the Tour then listen to a man like Paul Broadhurst who has seen the best and the worst of it as well as having been a multiple European Tour winner and Ryder Cup player.

Paul first got through Q School in 1988 at the age of 23, the year he turned pro and he went on to enjoy a great five years. The West Midlander won tournaments, played in the Ryder Cup and in all the major championships; he even got married and started a family. Life was good. But then his golf game deserted him and he found himself back at Q School aged 36; that was 2001 and he failed to win back a Tour Card. Suddenly, Paul saw the end his life at the top table of European golf flash before his eyes.

The following year, 2002, Paul returned to Q School again with his confidence at its lowest ebb, his life was in turmoil. Paul – a multiple Tour Winner – felt he was under a grotesque kind of pressure, a feeling even worse than trying to win a Tour title. But somehow he succeeded "When I got my Card back in 2002 I shot 67 and 66 on the weekend and that 66 is one of the best rounds I've ever had, probably not the best, but under the circumstances it's right up there. To play six under when you know your livelihood is on the line, I took a lot from that. Maybe Q School is not as much pressure for someone who's just starting out because they have plenty of other chances, but for someone like me it is. I'd been out on Tour for nearly 15 years by then and I had nothing to fall back on."

For Paul and many of his counterparts, the Q School symbolises the professional golfer's most profound struggle. Of course, trying to win a major championship is fraught with nerves, but the Q School is different. This strange tournament of extremes represents both hope and hopelessness and the players who succeed there are worthy of the total admiration of anyone who has ever swung a golf club. And for those who fail, there is always next year.

The idea of an end-of-season Q School for the European Tour first came about in the 1970s as the pro game looked for a better system than Monday qualifiers at each different event. Why not place the players in a ranking system so that the best would get first pick of all the tournaments and so on. Entry to tournaments became predicated on a golfer's category or his exemptions based on past performances, prize money earned, Tour titles won or his position at Q School.

The first European Tour Q School took place in 1976 and pro golf on this continent suddenly had a more manageable structure. Back then there were only a few hundred players who craved the life of a tournament pro because there were relatively few events (around 20) and prize money was small (even the Open champion won just £62,000.

It took a while for the ranking system to develop into the one we recognise today. By 1984, an elite group of 125 pros was established by the end-of-season money list; they all received a Tour Card for the next season while the Q School gave Cards to 50 players. Nowadays, the numbers have changed (Tour Cards are given to the top 115 players at the end of each season and Q School Cards go to the top 30 and ties) but the basic system remains: the Q School is open to a whole range of players, from the club pro and the golfing journeyman tournament player meet the aspiring young amateur or even the ex-Tour champion. The only major change to Q School is that it is now a huge event in itself; 11 separate tournaments staged over a three-month period in five different countries.

The PGA European Tour is not the only pro golf with an end-of-season Q School, but Europe's version is the most cosmopolitan (golfers from more than 40 countries normally enter) and is therefore arguably the toughest. The focus of this story is the European Tour Q Schools of 2006 and 2007 and the 12 months in between; both tournaments involved over 850 players and the competition was fiercer than ever before.

The seven players in this book were living their European Tour dream during this period, but it was not without risk either to their marriages, their relationship with parents, their future financial security, the risk of long-term injury or even – so it seems at times – their sanity. All the players were willing to suffer this distress because of the immense potential value of a Q School Tour Card.

All they have to do is turn up at the most important tournament of their season and, under severe, relentless pressure, play some of the best golf of their lives. The only problem is, of course, that 800 other pros are trying to do just the same thing.

The Cast of Characters

The story starts in December 2006, the month after the 2006 European Tour Q School has taken place.

The seven featured golfers would love to find a way to somehow play regularly on the Tour without having to suffer another Q School torture session, but they know that this is highly improbable. Nevertheless, as another new season dawns, hope still springs eternal.

Sion Bebb – Sion almost retired from tournament golf in 2006, the struggle – for both financial and domestic reasons – was becoming too onerous. But at the end of that season, he won a Tour Card for the very first time after 20 years as a pro and it gave him new hope. However, if he thought getting to the summit was difficult then he would spend 2007 finding out how hard it was to stay there. Sion has a self-effacing nature and probably needs to recognise just how good he actually is if he is to succeed. *Career status at December 2006: Q School Tour Card winner; 2007 prospects: regular on the European Tour.*

James Conteh – When your father was a boxing world champion (John Conteh), you have a lot of sporting heritage to live up to and it can get lonely out there even when your mum is your caddie. James is an accomplished player who is battling his own demons as a young golf pro with his own dream rather than his father's expectations. But the problem remains that James is stuck on the mini tours and his nightmare is that this is all there is to his career. *Career status at December 2006: eliminated from Q School at Second Stage; 2007 prospects: EuroPro & Jamega Tours.*

Phil Golding – No British golfer has been to Q School more often than Phil, he is Mr Persistent with 17 visits. In 2003 he shattered talk of an unfulfilled career by actually winning his first European Tour title; the years of struggle seemed to be behind him. However, three years later (2006) he found himself back at Q School and failed again to gain a Card. Now in his forties, Phil has to wonder if his best years are behind him. If he fails again at Q School 2007, his Tour career may be over for good. *Career status at December 2006: eliminated from Q School at Final Stage after four round cut; 2007 prospects: occasional European Tour invites & Challenge Tour.*

Euan Little – Euan is a charming, unassuming Scot uniformly liked by his fellow pros, but he is still waiting for the glorious golf career that was predicted for him as a teenager by his famous coach Bob Torrance. He has yo-yo'd around the edge of the Tour for several years and in November 2006 suffered one of the most painful Q School heartbreaks, missing an 8ft sliding putt on the very final green at Final Stage to leave him one shot short of a Tour Card. Euan vows to improve in the next 12 months so that such torture will not happen again. *Career status at December 2006: eliminated from Q School after six rounds of Final Stage; 2007 prospects: Sunshine Tour, Challenge Tour & occasional European Tour.*

Andy Raitt – A freak injury to his left hand over a decade ago meant Andy has already lost his career once as well as his first wife, virtually all his money and the hope of a glorious golfing future. In the last few seasons he has spent almost as much time in an operating theatre or a re-hab facility than on the golf course. Somehow he has also found the courage to fight his way back, and his Tour Card win in November 2006 was one of the great fairy stories of recent Q Schools. But his battle with the injury is not over and it could still be the cause of a shortened career. Andy will spend the year trying to prove that he can still play with the big boys. *Career status at December 2006: Q School Tour Card winner; 2007 prospects: regular on the European Tour.*

Martyn Thompson – Martyn is a solid family man, he's very successful as a traditional club pro, and life has been good to him. But there is still a stone in his golf shoe – he believes that there is a chance that a 43-year-old naturally-athletic golfer could yet break onto the European Tour for the first time. It would be one of the most romantic stories in golf if it happened – the long-time club pro who becomes a member of golf's elite – and Martyn is prepared to risk his quiet life at home to chase the dream and the riches of the Tour. *Career status at December 2006: eliminated from Q School at Second Stage; 2007 prospects PGA regional events and pro-ams.*

Guy Woodman – Guy's dream since he was 12 has been to become a top tournament golfer, but his struggle has been almost overwhelming at times. His life changed when The Golf Channel made him a star of their reality show The Big Break in 2005. Suddenly Guy was a celebrity and tasted the big time. This is a young player who has given up so much to be the best he can be, but will his TV appearance be the high-point of his career or can he use that unique experience to create something else – a life on the PGA European Tour. *Career status at December 2006: eliminated from Q School at Second Stage; 2007 prospects: EuroPro Tour.*

– December 2006

Another New Beginning

"There is more pressure in Tour School without a doubt than trying to win on Tour...second most pressure is a putt to make the cut and everything else falls in after that." – Robert Lee, five times Q School graduate from seven attempts.

Modern-day sport can be very confusing. It might say 2006 on the calendar, but this is in fact the first full month of the 2007 PGA European Tour season. Golf never seems to take a breather these days. A reduced field, champions-only event has already been and gone in China as well as a regular tournament in Australia and New Zealand. And all before the first day of December dawned.

For the Q Schoolers who won their Tour Cards just a couple of weeks ago in November, there has been little time to catch their collective breath; this month is when most will look to get their seasons underway. While the majority of the seasoned Tour players will take a proper golfing holiday and emerge some time next year, Q School graduates need to make the most of the form that won them this chance. Their dream is to play regularly on Tour and now is the time to live it.

Sion Bebb is much like all 34 of his fellow 2006 Q School graduates – the first thing on his mind is to win enough money as quickly as possible to retain his Tour Card. Like football teams promoted to a higher division, Q Schoolers initially want to consolidate their newly-won position to avoid immediate relegation.

But Sion feels under more pressure than most to consolidate his position; that's because it has taken him 20 years to get his Tour Card. That said, Sion is the definition of a self-effacing pro golfer. He paid his dues during a steady rise up the pro ranks and is untouched by the obvious ego or pretentiousness that sometimes overwhelms sportsmen when they reach the heights of their profession. Call his mobile on a non-tournament day and he is likely to be found washing his car in the driveway of his home in south Wales or spending time with his two young daughters. You will not find him in meetings to discuss high-interest stock investments or worrying about the fuel costs for his private jet. He is calm and courteous and has an underlying dry sense of humour. He is a family man who just happens to be a very good golfer.

Sion finally conquered the Q School for the first time after 20 years of playing professional golf. He had very nearly given up on his dream of a Tour Card last year, but now at 38, has arrived at the summit of tournament golf and faces a different test – staying there.

It is just three weeks since his triumph and although he has tried to rest, his first tournament comes round pretty quickly. A small celebration with his family, some sessions with coach Terry Hanson and he is now in South Africa, head still slightly spinning. But Sion is finally a full Card-carrying European Tour player, and that fact alleviates some of his tiredness.

Perhaps not surprisingly, Sion is nervous at the Alfred Dunhill Championship, which is held at the Leopard Creek Golf Club, a spectacular venue for a golf tournament next to Kruger National Park in the northern part of South Africa. He has just left chilly 5° centigrade temperatures in South Wales for a South African summer where the temperature is a sapping 40°.

Sion hits the very first ball of the tournament at 6.15am on 7 December, a landmark day in his career. In the end, only the date proves memorable. He hits a poor drive and is soon taking a penalty drop. This sets a tone that results in a disappointing 76. His second round is little better (74), but he crashes out of his first tournament of the season. The pattern continues the following week at the South African Airways Open. He finishes the opening round with a 78. A second-round 68 provides a glimmer of hope, but he misses the cut again. Sion is finding out very quickly that the European Tour is just as tough as its reputation.

To make matters worse, the winner of the Leopard Creek tournament is Alvaro Quiros of Spain, a man who had finished 20 places behind Sion at Q School. While the Welshman does not earn a bean, the Spaniard's win means full exemption for the rest of the 2007 season and the two seasons that follow. Although Sion sees Quiros's triumph as proof that any Q School graduate can win on Tour, there is also an element of "why not me?" in the back of his mind.

Sion's 68 is closer to the form that he showed to win his Card. He just has to learn how to peak against the world's best. The excellent show he put on at the

Q School pales once the season begins. The standard in Tour events rises every year, and Sion will have to use all his experience and knowledge to keep up with his new rivals.

After 20 years as a pro and 11 visits to the Q School, Sion always had the skills to play regularly on Tour. Simply possessing the ability isn't enough – literally thousands of other players have claimed they have what it takes to compete on the Tour over the last few decades and never achieved it. The occasional start in a European Tour event – usually by invitation – is never enough to sate the desires of pros like Sion. To taste the Tour only momentarily is almost more frustrating than never playing there at all.

Ascending to the top of a sporting tree is something that the Bebb family knows all about. Sion's father, Dewi Bebb, was one of Wales's leading rugby union players and twice a British Lion in the 1960s. He was also well known for his extensive work as an analyst on Harlech TV. It is never easy for a son or daughter to emerge from under the shadow of a celebrity parent, but Sion made it easier on himself by choosing a different sport from that of his father.

Sion began to love golf at the age of 11. Of course, he had already played some rugby at school and had both watched and admired his father's talent, but as a pre-teen, Sion was sneaking onto the fairways and greens of Llantrisant Pontyclun Golf Club in mid-Glamorgan, a course that bordered the Bebb family's garden.

Rugby was still a possibility for teenage Sion, who grew to over six feet tall and weighed 13 stones. But the professional revolution in the sport had yet to take place in the mid-1980s, and both father and son knew that there was no money in rugby union at that time. There was, however, a vacancy for an assistant pro at Radyr Golf Club in nearby Cardiff. It was the obvious choice; Sion's older brother already had a job there and the alternatives were the police force, the fire service or working in a bank.

Working at the club meant 12-hour days – 8am to 8pm – in the shop, looking after the club members, taking green fees and selling Mars bars, but there was always time for the 17-year-old to hit some golf balls. In south Wales at this time, golf was not the big business it is today. True, a Welshman had won the Masters at Augusta and even ruled the world, coming in at the top of the Sony World Rankings when they first began. But the Ian Woosnam effect and the general growth of golf had yet to occur. Sion was simply another hopeful kid hitting balls on the range. For him, golf was a means to another end, a way of leaving school early and getting a job where he could be with his brother.

"I never thought about playing on any Tour in them days. No one ever told me I was good enough; no one praised me really – just mum and dad, I suppose." And so the story of Sion's life could easily have been a more prosaic one, simply one culminating in his passing the PGA exams to become a fully qualified pro. He took a head pro's job at Mountain Lakes in Caerphilly. At 25, he met a local girl, Rita, who worked as a tax inspector ("That didn't go down very well when she told me.") and began thinking about settling down. His relationship with his wife-to-be was the start of a profound change. Sion began to grow up.

"For about 10 years, I'd been playing no more than just regional golf and some pro-ams. I thought the entry fee and the expenses were too high, even on the smaller Tours. You had to finish [in the] top five just to win some money. The day-to-day pro-ams were very little expense up front, so I stuck to them. I was about 24 or 25 when I realised I was getting better; these days they say that at 15 or 16. I just never practiced. But when I met my wife, I knuckled down and started to see a coach. It just took me a while, I suppose."

Sion Bebb, the PGA European Tour Player, was still some way off. Sion went to Q School for the first time in 1994 and then returned almost every year, but never got close to his Card. His moment of clarity was on the horizon, though.

"My friends were playing on things like the Hippo Tour (today's EuroPro Tour equivalent) and they were doing well. I thought if they could do it then so could I. I started getting good results there, playing three- or four-round tournaments. The first big event I did well in was the European Club Pros tournament in Hungary. Four of us from Wales, we were invited by the PGA. It sounded like fun; it was a week away, an adventure. It was about £700 in costs but I finished second. I just played the same as I always did and I showed some form. I won about £6,000 and thought 'I should play more of these.' That was a lot of money to win. I played in it again in Sardinia the year after and was second, then I won it the next year, 1999. I was the first Welshman to win it. There was a £10,000 prize, a Peugeot car to use for the year and I qualified for the PGA Cup team to play in America. That was a turning point."

Finally, a young pro from an inauspicious golfing background could see a new future. And it wasn't just any old future. Sion now believed he had the ability to play at the top level. But there would have to be another turning point.

Sion had married Rita in 1996 and by 2001, their first child, Alys, was born. The couple sat down to decide if Sion's dream of the full European Tour was worth pursuing. His young family needed feeding, but Sion was making progress and they decided to give it four or five years. This decision resulted in Sion trekking around the world on the Challenge Tour in 2002. A top-15 finish at the end of the season on this tour, a subsidiary to the European Tour, would mean a full Tour Card.

Sion would usually return home from a week on the Challenge Tour with some winnings, but often they were less than the weekly £800 he spent on tour travel and accommodation. The Challenge Tour prize money is notoriously low (often only 10% of even the smallest full Tour event) to incentivise the players to graduate to the full European Tour. Without this incentive, the average Challenge Tour player might stay just that: average. Despite a little sponsorship, it was costing the Bebbs a lot of money to keep Sion's dream alive.

Sion's first year finish of 53rd was bettered in year two by an 18th-place but neither season delivered a Tour Card. Seasons 2004 and 2005 were worse, with Sion finishing 40th and 34th. Q School visits were equally fruitless. By now, it was almost time to give up; 2006 would be Sion's last chance and the early prospects were not good, but golf is the strangest of sports. The Welshman was about to find out just how strange.

Sion had spent much of the winter looking for work rather than practicing. His form had been ordinary and in July, his second child was born. Luckily for her father, young Madeline was delivered into the world at 2am on a Tuesday; for Sion it was also the week of the North Wales Open and if his daughter had appeared any later, he would have missed playing in one of his favourite tournaments.

"The wife came home on Wednesday afternoon and I looked after her for a while and then phoned up the tournament office to see if I could have a late start on Thursday; they said 'no problem,' so I drove up on Thursday morning. I walked six holes in preparation and was last off in the first round. If the tournament hadn't been in Wales, I wouldn't have played, and if I didn't do well there then I probably wouldn't have played any more Challenge Tour events. I went there without a care in the world. No pressures or worries about how I was going to play and I was very tired, I'd had not much sleep and then had to drive five hours to North Wales. I can't believe how it happened now. A sports psychologist would have a field day. I just relaxed, didn't really care if I hit good or bad shots; I was happy with the family back home. And the course is in Nevis, a lovely place, great views. I concentrated on the views; it was like playing a friendly game with my mates."

Sion phoned home each night and the news kept getting better; by Sunday evening, he had won the tournament. "I can't remember if Rita was happy with me being there or not, but winning changed my life. The week after was another Challenge Tour event in Ireland but I'd already decided not to go. Instead, there was a regional event in St Pierre, the Welsh Masters. I drove home from Nevis on Sunday, stayed the night, said 'Hello, baby' and went to this local tournament and won again. That was £17,000 in two weeks; it kept me going through the year. You just never know when your good week's going to be."

After being on the point of giving up on his dream, Sion's European Tour plans were back on track. Another trip to Q School was inevitable, but surely his luck had turned. At 38, Sion would be one of the older competitors, yet now he had fresh impetus. His Challenge Tour ranking meant no First or Second Stage dramas; he went directly to San Roque and Final Stage. Six rounds of the highest pressure golf would secure that Card.

Sion's 11th Q School visit started as many of the others had finished, with disappointment. In the worst of the opening round weather at the southern Spanish resort, he shot a 74 and followed it with a 76. He was six over par and tied for 110th position, absolutely nowhere near the top 30. In fact, no one who eventually won a Tour Card in 2006 got off to a worse start. Two more poorly-played rounds and he would miss the four-round cut and face an early trip home to Wales.

However, only one of the other 155 players beat the 67 Sion shot in round 3. He was now tied for 44th place. A two under par 70 in round 4 further lifted him to a tie for 29th. From a disastrous start, he was sitting in position for a Tour Card with two rounds to go. Somehow there were no nerves in round 5 when he shot a 68 and moved to a joint 10th place.

The final day was beset by high winds and lashing rain that exaggerated the usual round six dramas. Sion certainly felt the tension when he bogeyed four holes in a row from his 5th. Shortly afterwards, an enforced bad weather break gave him some breathing room. "The break happened at a good time for me. I had to rush back to the apartment to decide if I was still going to take a flight home that night or the next day. Once I decided to stay the night, I relaxed." Sion returned to the 13th hole and shot level par for the final six. His 74 was enough for a 14th place finish and a Tour Card.

Not an overtly emotional man, Sion's pride at finally achieving his lifelong ambition was tempered by the absence of the one man he wanted to share it with most: his father. Dewi Bebb died of a brain tumour in 1996 at the age of 59. "Before he died, I was only playing in local competitions and not showing any of form I have now. It's only since he died I've reached the level I'm now playing at. It would've been fantastic for him to see me play. My mother always mentions that Dad would've been proud. I did well up inside when I got home and I'm sure he's watching me. I think you have to keep on trying and believing in yourself. It was just perseverance that got me through Q School this year."

The achievement of another thirtysomething pro at San Roque last month also prompted lavish congratulations from his fellow pros – a sure mark of a legitimate triumph chiselled out of persistence and adversity. The story of Andy Raitt's return to the Tour at the November 2006 Q School is almost the stuff of Hollywood screenplays.

Andy is a solid professional, liked by his peers and neither brash nor cocky. He looks a little like Nick Faldo's younger sibling and has the appearance and manner of everyone's favourite big brother, the one you always wanted to have as a best mate. Andy is large in the shoulders and usually moves no faster than treacle. He laughs easily, knows when it's "beer o'clock", but can also narrow his eyes and focus when necessary.

The drama in Andy's life started in 1995. He was 25 years old and had just turned pro after shining brightly during four years on a golf scholarship in America at the University of Nevada. Andy was already being hailed as a new young hope for the future of English golf; he had been voted the number one U.S. junior college golfer; and won four college titles from the likes of Phil Mickelson and Jim Furyk. It was in his first year as a pro that he innocently arranged nine holes of golf with a friend at the Surrey club St. George's Hill. Andy brought his Staffordshire bull terrier Nikki to the course with him, but left his friend in charge of the dog while he checked their tee time. On his return, he was horrified to see another dog, an Alsatian, fighting with Nikki and sinking its teeth into her neck. Andy tried to separate the two dogs. It was a decision that has clouded the rest of his life.

The Alsatian, named Zomba, removed his teeth from Nikki, and instead sunk them into the little finger of Andy's left hand. The top of the finger and the fleshy part of its front was almost totally bitten off; the damaged sections were joined only by a few strands of skin. With blood spurting, Andy detached the damaged part of his finger, wrapped it in some toilet paper and sped to the nearest hospital where surgeons were luckily able to rebuild the finger. But that's where most of his luck would run out for the next decade.

Such an injury would be alarming for any sportsman. For a golfer, there was immediate uncertainty that Andy would ever play again, especially as the injured finger turned black, became swollen and was septic for weeks. But after several months of anxiety, a healing process began. The main problem was that the left hand little finger was now five millimetres shorter than before and all of its upper padding had been lost. In addition, there was severe scarring and numbness.

Andy could easily have given up professional golf at this stage, but he was set for a fabulous pro career, so he fought to overcome this painful obstacle despite no-one knowing what the consequences of the injury would be. Although early indications were that the damage would repair over time, there was no precedent. Andy's golf future was totally uncertain.

Amazingly, he started playing again after three months and attended his first Q School in 1995. He failed to win a Tour Card, but he had demonstrated his potential at times during the season and still looked forward to climbing the professional ladder.

However, secondary effects from Andy's injury slowly began to manifest themselves. The more Andy played, the bigger the problems became because a whole network of muscles in his left hand, arm, shoulder and even the left side of his body were activated in a new way as a result of the injury. Top pro golfers hold the golf club with the lightest of grips, they use their fingers rather than the main part of the hand to hold the club. Andy's grip on the golf club was now different and became increasingly more difficult as the pains in the other parts of his body grew.

Despite continuing with his career as best he could, Andy eventually decided to sue Zomba's owner. His case initially looked to be of the open-and-shut variety. The owner had stood aside and let the two dogs fight, and no one argued that it was the Alsatian who bit Andy's hand and was the cause of him almost losing the top of his finger. There was talk of £1 million or more in compensation.

The legal case continued in the background of Andy's life as he kept playing. He made further unsuccessful trips to the Q School in 1996 and 1997 before finally achieving his dream in 1998 at the School in Sotogrande. He then spent the next three seasons as a classic journeyman pro bouncing between Q School and the fringes of the Tour. He still shot some good rounds, but there had also been warning signs that all was not well.

In one instance, Andy was vying for the Scottish PGA title at Dalmahoy, but in the middle of two swings in the last few holes, he "lost" the club-head on his downswing and the ball shot miles off-line. The shots came out of the blue, Andy had no idea what was happening. For the top pro to "lose" his feel for the golf club is the ultimate nightmare; it is like a skater suddenly losing his balance for no reason. Pro golf is a game of control and Andy was now uncertain where once there was no doubt in his mind about what his body could do on the course. Many pros voiced their concerns about his future career on the Tour.

Andy's injury case finally came to the High Court in December 2002 just one month after he had won his Tour Card for the third successive time. Andy's life, however, was in turmoil - he had suffered other injuries (particularly to his shoulder) and his marriage was under intense strain. His legal team provided expert testimony from a number of golf experts, including top coach Denis Pugh and one of Europe's finest-ever players Colin Montgomerie. They were unequivocal in saying the loss of the top part of a little finger would hamper any professional golfer.

However, at the last minute, the legal team defending Zomba's owner found a single expert witness of their own, a fellow professional who said Andy should be able to cope with the injury. To Andy's amazement, the court took the defence's argument to heart and the anticipated £1 million in compensation dwindled to a meagre £4,900, while Andy had to pay the costs of the defence. It was a financial gut-punch and, not only that, the case had taken over six years to settle during which time Andy's golf game had spiralled downwards. In 2002, he earned less than £35,000 in prize money – far less than his expenses for the season.

An appeal was set up, but to no avail, merely adding to the legal bill. In the ultimate indignity, Andy was forced to pay £250,000 in costs.

In December 2006, the words "a total nightmare" are the best Andy can do to describe 12 years of physical, emotional, financial and legal pain. He's tired of telling the story and yet it runs his life. He can't find closure because the bills for legal costs keep arriving and negotiations to pay off the dog's owner continue. His marriage disintegrated soon after and he now finds solace on the golf course. But instead of giving up his dream of being a top class Tour pro, Andy has battled back.

At a pro-am event in 2001, he met an eminent Brazilian surgeon, Jose Luiz Pistelli who specialises in hand surgery. The physician could hardly believe Andy's story and agreed to try and help. The surgery would be costly, but Andy still believed he would win damages to cover the expense. Pistelli performed two operations on Andy's left little finger and, although, the digit was still short in comparison to his other fingers, progress seemed to be made. However, another surgery would be required.

The next stage of the process was highly risky for Andy because Pistelli would attempt techniques he had never tried before. The revolutionary surgery would mean lengthening the finger by cutting it open and inserting a vice in which a couple of screws would be turned each day in order to stretch the bone. Andy was hesitant, but once the court ruled against him, he found another level of strength to fight for his golf career. The final operation took place in the summer of 2005.

"I could've gone off and done something else, but I had already lost almost everything and I thought 'Right, I'll give this guy a try'. I went to Brazil, had the surgery and had two flesh grafts. I saw the surgeon every day for over 90 days; he put two screws and two bits of hip bone in the finger so that it's long enough to get some traction. Anything like a door handle, a kettle, a saucepan or a gear stick was difficult [before the surgery]. At one time, I couldn't even hold onto a beer glass and I still struggle to hold something like that even now."

The £35,000 Andy spent trying to cure his problem was a large amount of money for a Tour pro still attempting to make his mark, but he had to hope it was worth it. Afterwards, the surgeon said it was the best bit of surgery he had performed in 40 years.

Post-operation, Andy became a slave to physiotherapy. This was either performed by an expert or by Andy himself using simple exercises like squeezing plasticine or opening and closing a clothes peg. The training strengthened the muscles in the left side of his body in general and the finger muscles in particular.

By late 2006 – just over a year after the surgery – Andy is still trying to come to terms with the possibility that his old golf game may never return. He tries not to talk about the injury but it springs back into the conversation unconsciously on a regular basis. Andy admits to no longer being the happy-go-lucky young pro he was in 1995 when he was fresh out of US college and with the golf world at his feet. The trauma has changed him, he has lived for more than a decade under a cloud that was largely not of his own making.

Andy's last full year on Tour was in 2004 when he amassed €110,000 and finished 135th on the money list. In November 2006, he was making his comeback, playing in his first Q School event in three years and he did so with a sense of relief. Being in the locker room again was like coming home; there was the *craic* and just the golf to concentrate on. He put aside the fact that he had played almost no tournament golf in over 12 months and lined up in Catalunya for Q School Second Stage in good spirits. For two rounds he performed well, but on day three Andy found himself in trouble. He was six over after 10 holes of the round and he needed a "go-to" swing to grind him through the rough patch, maybe not the prettiest swing, but something he could totally rely on. However, this was his first serious tournament since the final surgery and he was caught between his new way of playing - with his newly-lengthened finger - and his old, pre-injury way.

Before the surgery, Andy was basically a straight-hitter who held the club neutrally (with neither hand more in control than the other) and let the club rotate and release during his swing. He spent all his formative golfing years practising and perfecting this method. It was in his subconscious. Now, his conscious mind was fighting the subconscious because his new method of swinging involved aiming right and pulling the ball to the target. This allowed him to use his right hand to grip the club more strongly.

There were too many thoughts going on in Andy's head to make sense of a golf swing that, at its best, is a natural, free-flowing motion. Despite feeling pain in the whole of the left side of his body, Andy did what all quality pros do: he ground out the best possible score. He mitigated his six over start with an eagle, shot a few steady pars and finished with a 4 over round of 75 that left him still in the hunt for a place in the top 20 and a trip to Final Stage. In round four, Andy hit some early birdies, stayed patient and concentrated like a veteran. He shot a 67 (beaten on the day only by the School's eventual winner, Roope Kakko of Finland) and finished tied for 15th place, one shot inside the mark.

"I figured anything under par would be good enough and I knew I had lots of experience. I got off to a good start and then it's just about being patient. It was a good day," he says. After an hour of watching his rivals complete their rounds, Andy jumped in his car and headed south to Final Stage of Q School.

The weather was awful in San Roque for the last six rounds of Q School 2006; it caused two days of delays. However, this worked in Andy's favour by enabling him to rest the strained left side of his body.

Andy had played in seven previous Q Schools and knew the value of staying calm, especially in poor conditions. After two rounds, Andy was stuck in the middle of the pack following a 73 and a 74 that left him 3 over par. It was not disastrous, but he needed to make a move during the next two days. Instead, he shot two more inconclusive rounds and was lucky to sneak through for the last 36 holes right on the cut mark, tied 69th.

The next two days were career defining. A day five score of 1 under par moved

Andy to 45th place and into contention for a top-30 spot and Tour Card. As day six began, Andy reckoned he needed to reach 2 under par for the tournament for a Card. He was currently 2 over and not many players shoot 4 under on the last day of Q School in windy conditions, yet that was his goal.

However, he did have some luck: day six of Q School is always a two-tee start and Andy was drawn to be one of the early starters at the 10th hole. It meant he would play in the best of the deteriorating weather. The more the wind blew later in the day at the San Roque New Course, the more it would help Andy.

The gods would smile a second time on Andy. As the afternoon wore on, the driving rain was making the course unplayable and tension was growing throughout the field. There was a question over whether the tournament would actually finish that night. As Andy reached his 18th hole, he was on 3 under for the day, 1 under for the tournament and, because of the horrid conditions, there was a good chance that this score would be good enough for a Tour Card. But the organisers were threatening to stop play and Andy's worst scenario was walking into the clubhouse with one crucial hole to play. Luckily for him, the hooter sounded to signal a rain delay just after he had hit his final tee shot. Andy and his two partners then had the option of finishing the hole or walking in – naturally, they played on, Andy needing a regulation par.

Andy's tee shot landed in semi-rough leaving him a 4-iron approach shot from a slight downslope. For his pre-injury, straight-hitting swing, this would be a reasonable challenge. But for a man with an injured finger and an aching body who is still insecure about his new golf swing, then it would be an immense task. Plus, there was a lake waiting to the left of the green and Andy's current swing method was to pull the ball right-to-left bringing the water into play. "For 10 years, I'd been fighting the ball going left and there was water down the left for my last approach. I knew a par four would be good enough and, thank God, I hit a good shot, two-putted and everyone else had to sit around and wait."

Andy carded a 3 under par 69, a score that would tie the best of the day. He was in the clubhouse, dry and definitely relieved while his nervous rivals had between one and eight holes to complete. "I was in 27th place when I went in after the round and checked the scoreboard. After seeing where I was, I knew the weather conditions would not make the course any easier and we just left. I knew I had my Card later because my phone went ballistic."

There is a smile of huge satisfaction on Andy's face when he talks of this achievement because there is nothing a golf pro likes more than calling it and then doing it. Andy had secured his Card, despite not having played in a four-round tournament for two years.

"I'm almost surprised, I suppose," he said afterwards. "It's a weird feeling. I can't quite believe it. I'm really proud because I only made one bogey (on the last day). Other people in my life are happier than me in a way because I've been through an awful lot. For me, it is nice to just go back to work. The surgeon said it would be a project and it could take three years or five years or ten years. I just needed to make the finger as strong as it could be. This is just the start of trying to get back to where I was. Now I want to go on and win so that I can prove to people that I wasn't trying to pull a fast one when I tried to get the compensation." The injury is still a highly emotional subject for Andy.

With his Tour Car won, Andy loses no time in playing his first event of the 2007 season, even though the calendar still says December 2006. He travels 13,000 miles to play tournaments in Australia and New Zealand. In Melbourne, Andy misses the cut, but he is in the top five after two rounds in Auckland only to drop over the weekend to a disappointing tied 49th.

He then plays in the final two European Tour tournaments of 2006 in South Africa. His missed cut at the Alfred Dunhill Championship puts his injury in context – a chilly early morning tee time meant his hand "felt like a claw" and he has to hit four provisional shots in the first 11 holes such was his alarming inaccuracy. But a week later at the South African Airways Open Andy's game drops into place and he is tied 4th with one round to go. He is paired with Retief Goosen on the final day.

Andy finishes tied 5th and receives €35,000 which, with €2,000 from New Zealand, adds up to a very good start to his comeback. "The course wasn't one I'd seen before; I just felt better that week and took my chances. It is really encouraging. I didn't play fantastic, but it was solid with lots of good shots. The Tour felt the same, lots of the same faces. "True, he is still learning how to deal with his post-surgery injury, but after years of achingly bad luck, Andy Raitt is being re-born and the 2007 season could actually be a memorable one for all the right reasons.

2 – January 2007

Resolutions and Sabbaticals

"If you think about Q School at the start of the year then you are lost. If you just think about playing the best you can then you don't put any pressure on yourself." – Thomas Levet, Tour winner, Ryder Cup player and six-time Q School attendee.

While a few fortunate golfers left the final green at Q School in November 2006 in a champagne mood, most of the players had little reason to celebrate. It is the nature of the event – the majority leave thoroughly disappointed; but there are some particularly sad faces each year, those whose chances of a Tour Card are denied within sight of the finishing line. For a handful of players, success or failure comes down to the very last green, even the very last shot at the end of a six-round slog. In 2006, Euan Little was one of the handful.

The thoughtful, softly-spoken Scot is no newcomer to Q School; last year was his 11th visit. He won his Card a couple of times (2002 and 2003), but Euan never went on to consolidate his place on Tour each following season. He finished 162nd and 182nd respectively on the money list during those two Tour Card years. Then in September 2006, he finished runner-up at First Stage at The Oxfordshire and got through to San Roque after a brilliant last round of 69 at Second Stage. Once at Final Stage, Euan seemed to be building his score towards another Tour Card as he rose slowly over five rounds to be just inside the prospective mark going into the last 18 holes.

But the wind, rain and delays on that last day took their toll. Euan was holding on grimly when he came to the treacherous 18th hole on the San Roque New Course. He needed a par to sneak in for one of the last Cards available.

On a normal day, this would be relatively easy, but not on the last afternoon of Q School and with a 3-club wind gusting right into your face. A bold drive and Euan now needed all his power to blast a long-iron approach to a green with water on the right and a nasty gully on the left. Euan knew that left was better than right; his second shot landed almost pin-high in the gully leaving him with a tricky up and down for the par he so desperately needed.

Euan stalked the chip shot and faced the classic dilemma – get too fancy and he would stay in the gully; thin it and a lake waited to drown his ball. His nerve held as he flipped a delicate shot to within 8ft. His job as a pro golfer for the next 12 months depended on holing a sliding left-to-right putt. Again he stalked the shot, taking a little longer than was normal for one of pro golf's quicker players. He set himself and tapped it forward; the putt lipped out. With that one fateful shot Euan's hopes vanished. Ashen-faced, he walked to the scorer's tent with a last hole bogey and no Tour Card. Nothing could be said; he'd missed a Q School Tour Card on his very final shot. It is a heavy price to pay.

The disappointment cut deep because this is a man who took up golf at age 5 and was tipped to climb to the very top of the sport. Young Euan had a cut-off club in his hand before he was old enough for school and followed in the footsteps of both his parents who were golfers at their local Portpatrick club in south west Scotland. As a young boy, he was a passionate Celtic fan and played plenty of football, but his parents particularly enjoyed supporting their son's golfing ambitions.

At first, Euan's older brother was a better prospect, but by age 13, it was the younger Little who was playing in the Scottish Boys Matchplay and winning through two rounds despite being the youngest competitor. There would be no working on the family farm for this youngster. His mild manner belied his competitive spirit and he was down to scratch at 15 and already under the wing of a famous coach, Bob Torrance, father of Ryder Cup hero Sam.

Bob knows a good prospect when he sees one and Euan was an unpolished gem. Early on, Bob told Euan's parents that the young boy would one day be a golfing millionaire and those words proved both a blessing and a curse. From that moment, Euan had the necessary confidence that he would succeed, but he also developed something else – a belief that he might not have to work so hard because greatness was guaranteed. The full meaning of Bob's early words would take many years for Euan to understand.

So, by aged 20 and still only a reasonably successful amateur, Euan tried Q School for the first time. He missed the Final Stage four round cut, but decided to turn professional anyway. This was 1996 and a few years of grinding up the learning curve followed. Over the next six seasons, Euan would play a fair amount of Challenge Tour (he would eventually win there twice) and then try Q School at the end of each year, but the door to the Tour kept slamming shut.

"When you miss out at the Q School you live for next year; you gear up for 12 months time. Everything you do always has the School in the back of your mind."

Although he succeeded at the 2002 and 2003 Q Schools, Euan failed to retain his Card each time. In 2004 he was unlucky to be hit by salmonella food poisoning at the School (he was lying tied 7th after two rounds of Final Stage). The young Scot reached a career crossroads during 2005. The effects of the food poisoning took a long time to clear up and Euan might easily have lost faith in himself altogether. It was his golfing father-figure Bob Torrance who put Euan back on track by showing faith in him.

There was no way that the coach was ready for the player to give up. "Even today we're still working on his swing," says Bob, "And when he gets that right, he'll be on the Tour no problem."

The Bob Torrance philosophy is that no matter how well you think you have hit the last shot, you can always hit the next one better. For Bob, striving for perfection is like breathing and Euan finally realised that by adopting the same philosophy in total and not just in half measures then improvement would follow. "Golf is the most difficult game man ever invented. Ben Hogan was 32 before he won his first tournament. Euan is a natural player and I've got great hope for him. I say to him that he just has to put his nose to the grindstone," says Bob.

Euan believes that 2005 was a time when he fell out of love with golf. "After I got sick at Q School, I didn't even want to be on a golf course. For a while it felt golf was a job, like I had to be there rather than wanted to be there. But now the feeling is totally different, I do want to be playing. Turning it around was as simple as waking up one day and wanting to do this. It happened after Bob said to me that his greatest fear for me was that I'd be 45 and watching the Tour on TV with my kids and them not believing that I once played in those tournaments. It really hit home. It was a case of telling myself I was good enough; I need to play without fear."

So with 2005 season having been such a disappointing one, Euan put a great deal of store in 2006; he felt ready to not only pass the Q School test, but also to move permanently into golf's upper echelon. He had just turned 30 and – with Bob's help – he had resolved to swap the fun and games of the tour pro's life for a more dedicated outlook. The 2006 campaign was one full of hope, so when the last hole Q School nightmare happened, it hit Euan hard. "I can't describe the feeling I had. I went back to my room and I lay on the bed, called my parents to let them know and basically broke down."

By January 2007, Euan is still coming to terms with the disappointment that occurred a couple of months ago. He is resolved to putting extra effort into his golf and he needs some early evidence that the philosophy of hardship is working.

The proof comes during Euan's regular winter trip to South Africa. He manages to gain entry into two early season Tour events because many top players are still resting and he makes the most of his good fortune. A tied 25th in the Alfred Dunhill Championship before Christmas and a tied 19th in the Joburg Open this month win him over €20,000 and provide one of his brightest starts ever to a pro season.

With each new chunk of prize money in his bank account, the lipped-out putt at San Roque fades further into history and his determination to be a European Tour regular is re-affirmed. Euan is more convinced than ever that 2007 could be his break-through year; it is time for something special to happen.

Martyn Thompson did not suffer the same level of drama at the 2006 Q School as Euan Little, but his quest for a Tour Card is just as real. Martyn represents the thousands of golf club professionals who have never been a full-time tournament pro. These men are excellent players, their lives revolve around golf just like any tour pros.

Some club pros have the ability and not the desire for the Tour; others really want a European Tour career, but are never going to be good enough. Martyn falls into another category: he has always had the desire, but simply never had the chance to prove his ability. For inspiration, Martyn sees men like Ian Poulter (a struggling young assistant pro before making a Q School breakthrough) or Robert Rock (who was working at the delightfully named Swingers Golf Centre in Lichfield just before he made it full-time on Tour). Now, at 37 (although a little older than the likes of Poulter and Rock) with his life and family in tact, it is Martyn-time. This is the year to find out if he is a Tour pro in the making.

Martyn enjoys a lucrative PGA professional's job at Parkstone GC in Dorset; his wife Sally and three children enjoy their home on the delightful south coast of England; and life is generally good for a man respected by his members and fellow club pros in the Southern Region. But sometimes 'good' feels a little underwhelming. Like some kind of early mid-life crisis, Martyn is prepared to risk his comfortable existence for a chance of glory this year.

In 2006, Martyn entered Q School as an experiment; he wanted to see if he could still compete with the new young guns aiming for the Tour. It was only his third Q School attempt and his first in well over a decade, but he reached Second Stage relatively easily and felt he should have gone further. The failure fuelled his desire, something that had lain dormant for far too long. "I was driving the ball past lads 15 years younger than me and didn't play with anyone who I thought was better. With more preparation and a different mental attitude, I could've walked it to San Roque." He also got a real sense that the clock was ticking on his potential Tour career; he now knows there will not be many more attempts at

Q School, so he resolved to make the biggest of efforts for 2007.

This is a man with a naturally rhythmic golf swing whose game has one flaw and it took an old friend of his, Carl Watts, to prompt him into doing something about it. "Carl told me I was a crap putter when he first knew me 15 years ago and I was still a crap putter. Then he asked me what I was going to do about it." That challenge was enough to change Martyn's mind about how far he could take his newly-reawakened tournament ambitions.

For many amateur golfers, the challenge of working on a weakness is ever-present yet rarely acknowledged; we know our faults, but do little to eradicate them. And the pros? Well, it all depends. Most Tour pros are found almost every day – tournament or no tournament – on the practice range or on a golf course looking for a refinement: a higher ball flight from their mid-irons, trying to eliminate a kink in their back swing or whatever. They chip and putt almost endlessly so that their technique will hold up under the severest of pressures; they need their muscle memory to take over when their minds become mush from the stress of winning or even making a cut.

Club pros usually have less time to practice and also, crucially, less need to. Sure, they want to perform well when playing with or against members and they might take part in regular regional PGA tournaments or Pro-Ams, but most of their days are spent teaching or operating their shop; these more mundane matters are what pay the bills, not the occasional prize money cheque.

Martyn has been a full-time PGA pro for 15 years. At age 22, he faced the kind of dilemma that millions of young sportsmen and women will understand – do I follow my dream or should I play it safe? He already had a ready-made family to look after because his then partner (who would eventually become his wife) had two children by a previous marriage, so why would he put this future at risk? Martyn chose safety; he studied hard for his PGA final exams and took the job as a club pro. It was a no-brainer. In fact, it would be a no-brainer for 99% of people in the same situation.

But life was now about to turn full circle. In the years since Martyn's decision to put family first, he had never lost the confidence in his ability as a golfer to play with the best. As a youngster, he had found all sports – particularly golf – very easy. In fact, he has never had a golf lesson and used to get frustrated in his early days as a pro when teaching club members – why did they make a simple game so hard?

"For golf, you turn one way, you turn the other way and you smack the ball in the middle – it's always come naturally to me. It's like walking and talking. I achieved at every level, I played well without putting any effort in. The Q School 2006 was really the first time I'd failed at golf. I won at boys level, county and national level and because I've never had to put any effort in to get better, the work ethic isn't there. Now I've finally got to a point where I would need to put that work in. I'm not lazy, but because golf has come easy, the idea of practising is foreign to me."

So while Martyn had been creating his own glass ceiling, his contemporaries – players like Lee Westwood and Andrew Coltart who came up through the ranks with him - marched onto the Tour and international success, winning huge tournaments and playing in Ryder Cups.

Martyn might be the archetypal club pro at the moment, but he wants to become the European Tour pro that he once dreamed of becoming years ago. In 2007, he wants that Tour Card and the determination comes from one single bad shot at the end of a decent round of golf at Second Stage of Q School in Catalunya last November.

Martyn had arrived early in Spain for two days of practice rounds, but while others were pounding the driving range or tied to the putting green, the man from Dorset was relaxing. One hour's chipping and a quick putting session, these were all the extra fine-tuning that Martyn would undertake for one of the most important tournaments in his life because that is his normal routine.

In his first round, he was cautious yet confident. He played 17 holes to near perfection; he had hit all but one green in regulation and was lying 3 under par, a score that would eventually be beaten by only a handful of players in the 82-man field that day. But on the 18th, Martyn missed a 4ft putt and dropped to 2 under. He felt a huge surge of disappointment that his game's most obvious flaw had come back to haunt him once more. He should have been sitting in one of the 20 qualifying places, but instead he was back in the pack. At this level of golf, one shot per round is the often the difference between a pay cheque and an early trip home.

The next day Martyn felt "jittery" for no reason and seemed rushed throughout his round. A bogey on his first hole and two more on his 5th and 6th left him a self-confessed "jibbering wreck". A 77 was the end result; his lack of top tournament play was letting him down. It seemed he lacked the necessary level of intensity. Martyn's chances of reaching Final Stage fizzled out after that second round.

Over those four rounds at Catalunya, Martyn would hit 60 out of 72 greens in regulation, the kind of ball striking that should have guaranteed qualification to Final Stage for the first time. It was putting that let him down. It was a short time later that Carl Watts made the "your putting is crap" comment and this time Martyn was listening. "It was just what I needed because I had proved to myself I could compete. I told Carl I'd done nothing to improve my putting in 15 years and he said 'Well, you got what you deserved'. And I knew he was absolutely right."

So after that, a 2007 New Year's resolution was put in place to practice more (especially putting), to get fitter and commit to all-round better preparation.

Martyn pledged himself to Q School preparations on a scale approaching that of the full-time Tour pros and certainly above anything he had previously attempted. "I called Carl and said I wanted to work with him. I'm someone who's never had a coach or a manager or a psychologist before. I've been self-taught, never practised, but got by just on raw talent. People say you only get out of golf what you put in, but I've got 20 times more out of it than I've put in because I've never actually put much in."

Martyn's epiphany had been a mental one, he had finally realised that his so-called effort to be a Tour pro had been totally undermined by his attitude – if he didn't really try then how could he really fail? Any self-respecting golfing mind guru would see the error of such an attitude.

So this year, Martyn resolves to really try, not just pretend to. He admits that a Tour Card is of vital importance to his final career audit, to his self-respect, to himself as a pro. In doing so, he is prepared to put other things at risk and realise that deep down inside him, not ever getting through Q School would be devastating. "It's like I've had an excuse already lined up before I even started Q School."

In 2007, there would be no more excuses and the change would go beyond working on Martyn's putting stroke. Carl reckons it was the circumstances of Martyn's everyday life – family, mortgage, money issues and the like – that blocked his way. These issues needed to be tackled first. Martyn remembers: "Carl came down and spent the day with me and it was all about sorting the rest of my life out rather than my golf: how I run my business, the people around me, my diary. When he told me what I needed to do, I thought 'Christ, he's right'. We sorted out all the things that were blocking my mind from playing. Then at the very end of the day, we walked onto the putting green and he watched me hit a few putts."

Martyn's preparation for Q School 2007 would start immediately so that he could be fully prepared and expect to qualify. "Previously, I'd gone there (Q School) just to learn, just hoping. Being a Tour pro is something in me that is trying to get out. Other people – even my wife – probably don't understand it. But I've got more enthusiasm for it now than I did 10 years ago. Maybe it's because time is running out. This is me trying to turn my life around. Perhaps I can still fulfil my life-long dream."

Martyn's new-found resolve has as much to do with his non-golf life as his golf one. "I've had financial problems in the past with my pro shop and some local rental properties as well as a building project. Even when I was at Second Stage in November last year, just before one of the practice rounds, I was on the phone to my solicitor sorting out something, so I was hardly focused on what I was doing. But after talking to Carl, I've scaled everything back and sold some of the rentals. I'm spending money on my golf instead. I'm building a 16ft x 12ft putting green in my shop so that I can close the door at the end of the day and have an hour's practice. In the past, I've not used my free time for me. Before, I'd've gone to the bar for an hour and had a drink with the members."

This is a man who has seen the very best at close quarters. Martyn beat David Duval during his amateur days; he caddied for his friend Lee James – then the British Amateur champion - when he played in The Masters with Tiger Woods in 1995. That same year Martyn qualified for the Open Championship at St Andrews and in 1999, he qualified again - this time at Carnoustie - and played a practice round with Colin Montgomerie. He came back with a cheque after making the cut.

But although those memories are from a different decade, there is still hope for Martyn. "Golf is not about age. I hit the ball as long and as straight as any of the young kids coming through now. Look at Tom Lehman who came back into tournament golf late and then won an Open Championship at 38. And there are endless number of stories like this, players who win big on the Seniors Tour because they've been journeyman pros or club pros for years. It's not a 100-metre sprint race. You can win on Tour in your 40s and I've just been too stubborn with my golf in the past. There is a part of my game – putting – that has let me down, but now I realise I have to change it. I need to change my whole technique and if in a year's time it hasn't made a difference then I probably will say that it's not meant to be. For me at my age, I need to find out."

So, for some Q School pros, the new year brings a new resolution, but for others there is still a feeling of numbness. It's not like Phil Golding had never experienced disappointment at the School before, but he did not expect it in 2006. This is a player who had reached dizzying heights as recently as 2003 with a remarkable first ever Tour win in the French Open. There was talk of Phil finally fulfilling his talent and even making the Ryder Cup team. But three seasons later in November last year he was back at San Roque and, after just four of the six rounds, he was staring at the tournament scoreboard in utter disbelief – he was out of the Q School again. He had played poorly, just as he had during the entire 2006 season, and maybe his career on Tour was over. Falling down golf's ladder can be fast and brutal.

In the November 2006 Q School Final Stage, Phil had started off a little tentatively with a 76 in the worst conditions, but brought all his experience into play so by the crucial fourth round he needed a 2 under par 70 to make the cut. He got to 3 under for his round by the 12th, but his pushed drive on the 13th hit a cart path and flew out of bounds; he eventually dropped three shots at the hole and never recovered.

So now, in the first month of 2007, Phil has no real idea what lies ahead for the year. His tournament ranking is so low that he can expect entry into only a tiny number of Tour events plus an invitation or two, definitely one to the French Open as a past winner. But this is a difficult time for Phil. The 2006 Q School was his 16th visit (only one other player, Jesus Maria Arruti of Spain, has been more often) and 11 have been unsuccessful, but none were as bad as this. Phil's expectations are so much higher this time. Now at 44-years-old, Phil is thinking that his days on Tour could be over. Or maybe he has one last chance to resurrect his dream. Could he make a quick return to the Tour at Q School in 2007?

His troubles last year really began when his long-time coach Nick Bradley emigrated to America to work more closely with young English star Justin Rose. Phil looked for a replacement, and also tried different caddies; he even visited a putting guru; but he was still missing cuts. Eventually, he found Jason Banting to coach him, but the damage to Phil's season had already been done. "I missed the cut by a couple of shots all year. I wasn't going to go to Q School at first, but my wife said 'What else are you going to do?'".

More than two months after his San Roque disappointment – Phil finds it hard to speak about his future. "It's a bit of a shock, to be honest. I was a bit numb when I came back from the School. A couple of mates said that they didn't know what to say and were treading on eggshells with me."

Uncertain what his management company or some of his sponsors will do to help him, Phil is facing an enforced sabbatical, a year out of action, that is unless something remarkable happens and he wins a bundle of money on one of his few Tour outings. But that seems unlikely; he could simply be twiddling his thumbs until Q School 2007 almost 11 months away. For a man so used to the life of a tournament pro, it will take some getting used to being at home, practicing alone, a few pro-ams maybe, some corporate work or even yet more trips to the gym.

This state of the unknown is exactly what tournament pros hate; they thrive on the rigours of a playing schedule mapped out in advance. One of the huge advantages of a Tour Card is the ability for the players to plot their 25 or so tournaments for the year, avoiding courses they do not like and allocating time for rest before the bigger events. As he sits in his home in Hertfordshire in January 2007, Phil knows that this season's Tour events are already taking place without him. "I don't quite know what I'm going to do. I haven't been in this position for a while. Maybe I'll do some company days, but these aren't what I want to do. I want to play (in tournaments) again badly."

Invitations to Tour events may well come to Phil, but that causes another problem – they can be last-minute and the player is less prepared, plus he is under extra pressure to perform because his opportunities are so limited. And Phil is already missing the fellowship of the Tour, the feeling of glamour and excitement of a tournament, the applause from the large galleries of fans.

A player of Phil's experience also has a lot of pride at stake; he is the former French Open champion and had enjoyed an elevated status, teeing off in the middle of the day with the featured players during the TV coverage. He has served his time with the also-rans either starting at the crack of dawn or finishing as dusk falls. Right now Phil is almost embarrassed not to have his Card; this tumble down the rankings is not in his plans.

However, whatever his status, Phil Golding continues to be the epitome of a modern golf pro: he is strikingly handsome, with a mop of fine, blonde hair; he is chatty with his fellow pros and also the press; he is respected for his persistence and his French Open triumph which was greeted with cheers from his contemporaries; he has the air of confidence that the best Tour pros exude. Also, his story of persistence gives hope to so many other golfers; any European Tour golfer who wins after so many Q School visits gets mega-respect.

There are so many more youngsters coming through each year, Phil could be forgiven for resting on his laurels. But the desire for another Tour Card is too strong; somewhere inside him Phil knows he is good enough to win again on Tour. He will be returning to Q School in November if he has to; as a recent Tour champion he will go straight to Final Stage. It could be a huge advantage. So he will play when he can, earn money on some corporate days and work with his new coach. With each passing week, his desire for a Tour future becomes stronger. For Phil, it is time to believe that wisdom – not the scrapyard – comes with age; this is simply a sabbatical year and his career can be re-born.

3 – February 2007

The Long Wait

"Q School is gut-wrenching. It's not a nice week and once you're through it, you want to make sure it's the last time you see it. If you get into your mind what (Q School) means then you'd never make a backswing." – Sandy Lyle, double major champion and Q School winner.

For most tournament pro golfers, the winter lasts far too long. The few who are fully eligible on the European Tour can play all year round these days, but the majority of players contest tournaments on mini tours that operate mostly in the summer months. Many pros travel abroad during the winter just to find a few odd days of sunshine and reasonable weather in which to play and practise, but that option is not open to everyone. The pros at the lower end of the tournament ladder are more likely to put on an extra sweater and head for the covered section of the driving range. If this is the best you can do, then you have to do it, there is only so much indoor putting any man can endure.

However, it is never too early to start planning for Q School. By February, First Stage 2007 is only just over six months away and the mini tour golf pro must be ready to burst onto the new season and hit his best form as fas as he can. Planning ahead is better than looking back. However, human nature means that both past and future slip into players' minds when time is on their hands.

For someone like James Conteh, the past shapes him as a person. Mention the name 'Conteh' to any sports fan who lived through the 1970s and it's John

Conteh - James's father - who comes straight to mind. For James, it is his father's past that follows him around; it gives him strength, but it also fuels extra expectations, actually more from those around him than from himself.

John Conteh won the World Light Heavyweight Boxing Championship as a 23-year-old back in 1974. Born in Liverpool to an Irish mother and Sierra Leonean father, John took more than his fair share of hard knocks and promised himself that his children would be given a more protected childhood.

James was not born when his father was enjoying his glory days and, instead of the tough backstreets of Merseyside, the son was brought up in the refined English Home Counties. Although he grew to be a taller (6ft 4½ins) imitation of his father's light heavyweight frame, James was never going to box. A few trips to the boxing gym at aged 6 were enough to turn the boy away from the ring; being hit with boxing gloves was not his idea of fun. John was happy with this outcome because he knows that the best boxers are from poor backgrounds and James was going to be educated and given a decent start in life. So, golf became the son's game at an early age and throughout his teenage years. By his early 20s, James was showing considerable promise, he was a member of the winning squad in the English Club Team Championship and later became an assistant pro at the prestigious Moor Park Golf Club in Hertfordshire. But for James there had to be more; John had his world title, so it is no surprise that James wanted to reach the top of his chosen sport, play on the European Tour and win there.

But a famous father from another sport is only of limited help. John knows how hard it is to get to the top of a sport and he might have some wealthy friends willing to sponsor his son, but he sees only slight similarities between the ring and the links. John the boxer was using anger to fight someone else, whereas James is using controlled calm and is – according to his father - like every other golfer, fighting himself. It is James alone who must hit the shots that will either make him a great golfer or leave him stuck in the ranks of the journeymen. John, who took up golf later in life and plays off a competitive 12 handicap, finds it difficult to even walk the fairways with his son; he feels helpless even in such close proximity to James. The father's best advice is often to just put the disappointments into perspective, maybe with a touch of Scouse humour.

"I feel emotional for James, I feel compassion for him and sorry when things don't work out, but he's just got to do his best; golf's the same as boxing when it comes to doing your best," says John.

So James plies his pro golf trade on the mini tours; he is a regular on the third level EuroPro Tour and has even enjoyed a few outings on the two-year-old, Jamega Tour which operates low-key, two-round events in the UK. He loves golf, it is his profession, but James lives in that twilight world between making a living out of his career and having to continually supplement your income with whatever paying work he can get.

Winters are particularly long for pro golfers like James. He no longer works as an assistant pro, so when Q School and the mini tours end each autumn, there is little tournament golf until the spring. James will practice as much as he can in chilly England, but he does not have the financial resources to fly to warmer climes for more than the occasional few days. Instead, he will work training barmen (a company operated by an aunt) or join up with a friend who is a tiler; he needs the cash.

"It's hard work as a golf pro and pretty stressful, but I still want to reach the European Tour a lot more than I want to quit." Of course, 'it' is the kind of golfing success that ranks at least somewhere close to his father's achievements in boxing. James looks and sounds the part, he has some innate understanding of what it might take, but he's not there yet. James will turn 30 in August this year and he has still to have a significant professional tournament victory and has not even been close to the European Tour; a target for 2007 is to progress for the first time to the Final Stage of Q School.

Last autumn, James progressed through First Stage at The Oxfordshire with a solid, but unspectacular performance. Q School is the one of the few or even the only time of the year a player of James's ranking will play four consecutive rounds of golf, so he is at an immediate disadvantage. Nevertheless, Q School is James's annual focus and this is how he tests his progress as a pro golfer each year; it means a lot to play well

On that first morning last November, James's surname is not the only one of note in his threeball; one of his partners is a Ballesteros, Raul the nephew of Seve. The third player is a young pro from Lancashire, Steve Parry, a man with no famous relatives to talk about. Whereas huge crowds would have flocked to see John Conteh train in the gym in his heyday or Seve Ballesteros just practice his chipping, there are absolutely no fans watching the latest sporting Conteh and Ballesteros at The Oxfordshire.

James is not surprised to be playing far from public recognition. He and his fellow First Stage players understand that they are golf's equivalent of lower League teams that play near the base of football's professional pyramid. If Monty, Sergio and Padraig are Man Utd, Arsenal and Chelsea then players on EuroPro Tour players are Rochdale, Wrexham and Accrington Stanley.

To continue the football analogy, the opening Q School events are like the FA Cup 1st Round; it is a breakout opportunity for pros like James who are still on a low-ish rung of the ladder. Lower league football teams sometimes reach the later stages of the FA Cup and the golfing parallel is that a handful of players from the six First Stage events will progress all the way through to win a Tour Card. Why should it not be James?

The fact is that James is a super golfer by most people's standards. Neither he nor any of his counterparts at First Stage Q School are bad players. They hit the ball with precision and control. Just like the superstars of golf, they can (and do) pull off amazing chip shots or near-impossible approaches with long irons and they smash drives over 300 yards. It's just that there is something missing from their game. Maybe they are still learning to fully understand their swing or they might be comparatively poor putters or their ability to scramble pars is not fully honed.

In the final analysis, the difference between a journeyman player and a pro champion is more mental than physical; James has still to prove to himself that he can make the big time. He is searching for the answer, hoping for the breakthrough, dreaming of soaring to the highest level.

There is little evidence of glamour around James's career and there certainly was none at last year's Q School. At First Stage, there were no entourages, maybe the odd WAG, a couple of agents plus an occasional kind sponsor, a local inquisitive club member or two, no autograph hunters, no groupies. However, James Conteh did have his mum.

Veronica Conteh is a caddie, a driver and a supporter at Q School. "I come when I'm allowed," she says. "I do love to watch him play." She watches him with a mixture of thrill, amazement and nerves. Her husband – now a regular on the after dinner circuit – thinks James should have a professional caddie, but that is an expensive option. "In boxing, you wouldn't want to come back to the corner at the end of the round and have a mate give you advice; you'd want a professional in your corner," says John. Like many other fathers of golfers, John is too tense to be much help on the course, so his encouragement comes before or after a round. That system works for James as well because the son obviously wants to make his father proud, but both of them recognise that their relationship needs space. "They get on really well," Veronica says. "John just complains that he doesn't get any golf lessons from James."

On the golf course, James does not speak much to Mum - Veronica plays only a little and would never think to offer advice – but the fact she is there in support means a lot to him. If fact, the support of a loved one - there are a few other mums, dads, sons, daughters, uncles, friends and even girlfriends either performing caddie duties or simply acting as an very interested spectator – is a common theme during Q School's early rounds.

The four days at The Oxfordshire ended successfully for James in November 2006; he finished right on the mark at 2 under. Five weeks later at Second Stage in Emporda, Spain, the heat is turned up both in terms of temperature and opposing talent; however, in between stages James does not play in a single pro event.

In the Spanish sun, James fails to break par on any of his four rounds, he was 1 over in each of the first 54 holes while the leading scores were already well under par. "I hit the ball as well as anyone out there tee to green. But my putting was no good." There was a glimmer of light at the end of round two; he was 2 under after 17 holes (one under for the tournament), but proceeded to triple bogey the last hole. His chances after that disappeared. Playing in EuroPro or Jamega Tour events just does not make a player sharp enough over four rounds.

It is not that James deliberately avoided tournaments in 2006; he is competitive like his father and always wanted to be a tournament professional rather than settle for the life as a club pro. It is just that James's career is driven by cash and sometimes he simply cannot afford to play in a tournament. He is prepared to do almost anything to bring in some money to feed his golfing obsession and if he has to give up practice or tournaments sometimes in order to guarantee a wage, then so be it. However, it is a lifestyle that undermines his chances of making the Tour. Money is a continual problem when he is planning his annual schedule – how much can he earn determines how many tournaments he plays. In 2006 the cash did not match his aspirations and he played in just five proper pro events. By Second Stage, this absence of tournament practice caught up with him. James had done well to progress from First Stage, but the next step up is huge and almost impossible without either massive talent, heaps of preparation or bald-faced luck.

James is convinced his desire is "100% in there" and nothing will stop another Q School attempt this November. In some ways, he is happy with his progress in 2006 after such limited tournament play – this was the first time in all his four Q School attempts that he had even made Second Stage. Yet the gap between him and the eventual qualifiers is wide and he needs to bridge it.

So in December James made his most comprehensive plan ever of how the following 12 months would pan out including extra practice during the three months of winter inactivity. The hunt also began for a sponsor with a friend putting a professional CV and sponsorship proposal together for him for the first time. He has plenty of time on his hands over winter, so why not use them wisely.

As each year goes by, James's goal to one day join the game's top professionals on the European Tour does not alter. "I changed my coach two years ago and that really turned my game around, both my swing and my long game. It has made big improvements. But I could only practice in the lead-up to Q School. That's not enough. I know I'm capable of enough birdies, so now I need to cut out the bad play."

A pro like James has spent too much time waiting and not enough in the heat of tournament battle. This year, more than ever, he is ready to play.

Another young man with an equal level of determination to succeed is Guy Woodman. For a journeyman golfer usually playing on the EuroPro Tour, Guy is remarkably famous. It's all thanks to an unexpected TV appearance. It was the kind of recognition that Guy had hoped for when he left behind thoughts of being a rugby player as a young boy growing up in Berkshire. At aged just 9, his parents persuaded him to swap his rugby boots for golf shoes. Within three years, he was totally hooked and now admits that his dream to be a top golf pro is a compulsion – it costs him money, a normal 9-to-5 job, long-term plans with various girlfriends and it even threatens his relationship with his parents. Wouldn't it be easier just to give up?

"A lot of people would give up. But from the age of 12, I knew that golf is what I wanted to do and it's always been that way. You get doubts about yourself, you ask yourself "Do other things mean more to me?" And you get into a relationship and meet a woman and it's fantastic and after a while you wonder what you're going to do about it. But I've always aspired to be a golfer."

Guy's introduction to golf came by chance when a game of rugby was cancelled. His parents were about to have a golf lesson and persuaded him to join them rather than sit at home doing nothing.

"I said to them at first: "No, it's an old farts' sport, it's boring." But they said what else was I going to do, so I went along and I loved it, from the first time I picked up a club almost. I couldn't believe that I could actually not hit the ball when it wasn't moving. I thought I could just stand there and whack it. I immediately wanted to improve. I fell in love with the game and, anyway, I stopped growing enough for rugby so weekends turned into golf."

After some junior success and leaving the amateur ranks at 22, Guy turned pro, trying his hand on various tours including the Sunshine Tour in South Africa. But he stayed under most golf fans' radar until a chance encounter with the makers of a new television programme on America's Golf Channel in 2005 called Big Break. The show had become a hit in the States, matching journeymen pros against each other in skills playoffs until one player walked away with invites to real tour events. Big Break had become golf's favourite reality-style TV show with each golfer interviewed extensively about his performance, about his opponents and about life in general. There were insights into the minds of these men who all aspired to join golf's gravy train. The fourth series of the show – Big Break IV – centred on an ingenious idea to bring in young European players for the first time and pit them against Americans in a kind of Ryder Cup-style event. Again, one golfer would eventually prevail and win a number of tour appearances. Ironically, the show was not originally Guy Woodman's idea of a good time.

"Big Break is massive in America. But over here, not a lot of people have got The Golf Channel or at least not then. I'd seen it and it looked like a bunch of hackers playing for a big prize. I saw the ad at the end of series three that said they were doing auditions for series four, Europe vs America. I never thought anything about it. Then I get to my first EuroPro Tour event and there are posters up saying the Big Break crew are here doing auditions. A roommate said he wanted to be on the programme and he couldn't wait. I said it was just some tuppenny-halfpenny show and I didn't want to be on it. But he said I should come with him. Next morning, I thought it was going to be just filling in a form, but once I did that some woman said I needed to go down to the practice ground to hit some balls; I hadn't even done any stretching. A guy on the range told me to hit all kinds of shots – a low one, a high one – then to get my driver out and stuff. It was all being filmed. Then they interviewed me on camera. I thought that went well because I made them laugh, but my mind was on the tournament and this was just a bit of fun. I never thought I'd get on. Two months later I got a phone call to say I'd been short-listed and was I available. By that time, I liked the idea and said I'd love to do it."

The show would be filmed during two weeks in June in Scotland, but Guy was only told to be on a plane to Edinburgh on a certain day. "It was like being a secret agent; we weren't supposed to say anything to anyone, but word had got out that there would be three Englishmen and Warren Bladon (a former English amateur champion) would be one of them with me. There was a lot of apprehension: what was I getting into, what are the other guys going to be like, am I going to look like an idiot? In the end we couldn't have been treated better. I got to Edinburgh and Warren had been waiting about four hours before the next person turned up which was me. Then we were all put in our team bus and it was great. We all got on pretty well straight away. We were told it was a Ryder Cup format and we met the Americans the next day. They were a bit of a crazy bunch to say the least. They blanked us all at first because they wanted some antipathy between us all, but it didn't happen. They were actually great guys."

Big Break IV was a big success and Guy was one of its stars. It gave him a taste of the high life, but also of the pressure of being the centre of attention on a totally different level. The programme was filmed at Carnoustie (scene of the following year's Open Championship) with no less than 35 cameras and a 70-man crew. He would eventually finish runner-up in the competition; it was the biggest moment of Guy's career.

"It taught me a lot. My first shot on the show was a three-iron off a tight lie straight into the wind. There were cameras around me, the crew and all your peers who haven't seen you hit a shot yet; you don't know how good they are or what they're thinking – I was absolutely crapping myself. It was alternate shot and my partner had just hit; I had the approach into the green. It wasn't a great shot; I was just glad to make contact. But you learn how to deal with pressure, especially the longer you go on in the show. I remember it was about my breathing and being in that moment. OK, there were three or four really good players there and you could say the standard wasn't great, but unless you've done it, you have no clue."

For Guy, it was an amazing experience. "The contacts I made were great. My girlfriend and I went on holiday to America afterwards, we wanted to visit The

Golf Channel headquarters. Big Break is a huge show over there, I was signing autographs at the airport, it was great. They said I was going to be famous and I thought I'd go over there and see what was happening. I wanted to see what tournaments I could get into. I met a commentator on the Nationwide Tour who said his son was my No 1 fan and invited us to stay with his family for the rest of the trip, to make ourselves at home. Winning it, you do quite well, but coming second, you don't get a lot out of it." However, Guy is now trying to take all that experience and use it to good effect in Q School.

Guy is one of hundreds of young pros for whom Q School is the central point of their season; it's the way forward, the pathway to the glory that they have sought since first swinging a club. Pushing 30, though, it is getting to the point of now-or-never for him to make the European Tour. Nevertheless, he is buoyed every year by stories of players just like him making the grade despite their age or experience. Almost every Q School produces a couple of surprise players, those who come right through from First Stage simply on an unstoppable wave of good form. Last year, Guy failed at Second Stage of Q School despite his freshly-minted Big Break mentality helping him along; it made him want to succeed even more.

Guy is still waiting for his season to start, but he is already visualising his possible future – if he can keep improving with each tournament and peak at Q School then the dream will be realised. Why could it not by Guy Woodman's year?

In the past, Sion Bebb had been one of the tournament pros who sat around during the cold English winter waiting for action. But that is not his life now on the Main Tour; in fact, the winter is perhaps the most important part of his season because if he can get off to a good start, retaining his Tour Card will be much easier.

However, Sion's opening two tournaments in South Africa in December last year ended in missed cuts. It took him until tournament No 3 (the Joburg Open just a few weeks ago) before the first cheque was in the bank. It might only have been tied 73rd and €1,447, but it was another landmark. In addition, Sion had started to adapt to the new conditions he encountered: in December's tournaments, it was the heat; in Johannesburg it was the altitude; he was getting 30 yards extra flight and it took all his three days of practice rounds to acclimatise, but he found a way to overcome the altitude and that sort of determination will define his season.

"A 68 at the South African Open in December was more like me even though I missed the cut. So then it was progress to get some money on the board in Joburg. If you start missing too many cuts then you start concentrating just on that and not on winning or getting a better position. I got that monkey off my back and needed to press on. I haven't played so well since I got my Card; I've played indifferent, really. You don't get many starts at the beginning of the year and the tournaments are in places where I've never played before. I was still on cloud nine for the first couple of tournaments after San Roque and I had really wanted to rest until the spring; but I do like South Africa and wanted to go there. The main problem in the winter is it's one week playing, but then it's three weeks off; really, you want just to keep on playing to get in a rhythm. You have a month of hitting balls in the freezing cold at the driving range and then you turn up somewhere where its 100 degrees, 100% humidity and playing against guys who know the courses and understand the heat."

The underlying fact is that Sion's so-so form early in the season has come after a small change to his grip. His left hand grip was becoming too strong; normally a player should be able to see just two knuckles on his left hand on the grip, but Sion was seeing four. Amateur golfers often think it is only their games that need such fundamental tweakings, but it is not the case. There are plenty of small, technical changes being tried out on every pro driving range at every tournament, so Sion is far from alone in his quest for an answer to the golfing puzzle. But the changes can sometimes take weeks to bed down and it is far from ideal to attempt them during a season like this one, but Sion has no option; he needs to start earning some decent money and, anyway, it seems to have worked.

Yet although that first cheque was gratefully accepted, Sion's lack of overall form has been highlighted by Ariel Canete of Argentina who could not even gain his Card at San Roque last November, yet he shot four rounds in the 60s in Joburg last month and won by two shots.

Canete was only able to play in the tournament because some of these co-sanctioned events early in the season allow larger fields of up to 200 players rather than the normal 156 (the European Tour has been joining forces with the Asian Tour, Australasian Tour and the Sunshine Tour since 1999 to stage events in the northern hemisphere winter). The Argentine had been on holiday, but decided to travel to South Africa for want of nothing better to do. He expected nothing, yet Canete walked away a winner.

By the time of the Indonesia Open this month, Sion has forgotten about Canete's good fortune and is trying to uncover some of his own. However, there are extra difficulties to contend with. On the course, Sion has to adjust to very grainy greens that are typical of this part of the world, but not in Europe. Notwithstanding the greens, the trip to Indonesia - a mind-numbing and buttock-numbing 29-hour flight via Dubai, Colombo and Singapore – caused an old back problem to reoccur. Then there was the heat.

"I've never felt so hot in all my life. I'm not bad in the heat usually and I knew it was going to be sweaty. I usually wear a larger glove than normal, but I bought an extra large one for Indonesia and even that wouldn't fit me because my hand had swollen so much. When I bent down to pick the ball up, I could feel the heat from the ground; I was seeing stars." Sion was feeling his back pain as well as being totally de-hydrated, so after an opening round of 80, he withdrew and caught an early flight home. "The heat just got to me even though I was drinking a bottle of water every hole, doing everything correct. I had slept to the right time zones and everything, but it was just too hot. You never know, so I can't say it was a waste. With my Card, you can't turn down any starts."

Sion now knows a lot more about what is in store this year and it is not the start he wanted. He has now played four tournaments of the 10 to have taken place so far and made only one cut; he is not fully fit because of his back and conditions have been fiercely against him; plus what luck he has had has all been bad. Just one tournament this month and, as the year unfolds, more of the top 100 players will contest the events and make his life even harder. Sion has been as busy playing tournaments as he has ever been during this time of the year, but he has also spent more cash than ever before with little prize money to offset it. After such a long wait to be a Main Tour regular, Sion almost wishes he had stayed at home.

CHAPTER 4 – March 2007

Near & Far

"I didn't realise what Q School meant because I was playing well at the time. You can't think about the future (at Q School), that's what separates the journeymen from the good players." – Lee Westwood, former European No 1 and Q School graduate in 2003.

By early spring, the PGA European Tour has already staged 13 tournaments and visited a total of 10 different countries including China, Australia, South Africa, Dubai, Malaysia and the USA. This is a remarkable change from the European Tour of even a decade ago.

The so-called 2007 season actually started in November 2006. It is a quirk of the European golfing calendar that dates back to before the 2000 season when sponsors Johnnie Walker wanted to stage a warm weather event during the northern hemisphere winter. The European Tour agreed to the Johnnie Walker Classic being staged in Taiwan in November 1999 with the event counting for the 2000 season. It was judged a success, even though the next tournament on the schedule at that time took place two months later. A new trend had begun and the period between November and February has slowly filled up with tournaments as more warm weather venues secured more events.

So whereas springtime once saw the dawning of the European golf season, nowadays one fifth of the Tour events have already been played. The change is considerable: in 1997, there were no European Tour events pre-January and only six before the first day of March; in the 2007 season, six pre-January tournaments have already taken place and another seven have been played up to this point. Overall, the 30 Tour events on the European calendar 10 years ago has grown to the current total of 52.

Some of the winter events are co-sanctioned with other Tours like the Asian, Sunshine and Australasian, so half of the field is full of local players, but the tournaments also provide European Tour players with more opportunities to earn more money.

Like most new Q School graduates, Andy Raitt has been clocking up plenty of air miles. He was one of the few Q Schoolers to visit Australia, New Zealand and South Africa before the 2007 year dawned.

Generally, Andy can handle the travel, but his troublesome finger injury is almost impossible to ignore; the uncomfortable feelings from his left little finger, hand, arm and shoulder are an ever-present problem. During the first three months of this year, Andy visits South Africa (again), Indonesia, China, Spain and Portugal, but does not make a single cut in any of the five tournaments. By the end of this month, the 5th place finish in December that seemed to give him a perfect start to the season is a lifetime ago. "It's a nightmare right now. I've never missed five cuts in a row in my life; maybe two, but never five. It's weird. I'm in a transitional period, I suppose, trying to open the club up and actually hold my width on the back swing, but I didn't expect this. Plus there's a mental side to it, I just don't know where my bad shots are coming from. It's incredibly frustrating." Lack of form accentuates the journeyman golfer's anxieties: Andy is missing his home life more than ever, he wants to see more of his daughter and have some cash in his pocket.

Despite the signs of trouble ahead, however, Andy's personality is one of continually looking on the bright side and that is what he decides to do. He knows the Tour is a grind and he must keep working on the technical side of his swing to find the key to overcome the necessary changes brought on by the injury. "I've got to be patient and get physically stronger. I need to stabilise my left shoulder and balance my body. It still feels good to be back on Tour because, if you have one bad week, then at least you know you can have a better one soon."

The difference, though, between Andy in the past and now is stark. When he first made the Tour in 1999, Andy made 15 cuts out of 24 events and he proved himself to be a consistent, if not hugely successful, performer from then until 2004 when he decided to have the finger surgery. After missing two seasons, he is now almost back to square one in terms of developing his swing and with his recovering injury as a further disadvantage. "You don't have to do much to miss the cut on the European Tour because they're all good players." So more hard work is now required, not something that Andy has been afraid of.

Andy was introduced to the game by his Scottish father and showed enough talent to get a scholarship at Nevada University in the US for four years. He returned home a better golfer and also with a degree in communications. Living life abroad was good for Andy and after his American experience, where he learned to work on strength and consistency, he believed life as a tournament pro was his destiny. Initially, Andy was a hot prospect, but he never reckoned on a freak injury and, although he is working as hard as ever on the range, the pain of his body is not the only thing undermining him. His mind continually reverts back to his financial problems.

"I still owe £43,000 to the dog owner who took a portion of my former house; the rest of the profit went to my ex-wife. Now I've got a legal aid bill just come in for £26,500. I'm writing a few letters saying I'll give them whatever so they'll go away and leave me alone. It would be easy just to go bankrupt. Unfortunately, my earnings are public knowledge which doesn't help. I might earn a big cheque one week and nothing for ages. I've just had to give up worrying about money. The rest of life has got to get easier."

Andy's fragile confidence needs a boost and he is entering a crucial part of his season. But if the missed cuts continue much longer then his Tour Card win will be for nothing and even his whole career could be in jeopardy.

Sion Bebb is trying to make the most of every opportunity in this breakthrough season. He has managed to start about half of the 'winter' tournaments, but missed out in the lucrative Middle East swing just over a month ago where more top players joined the fields chasing the biggest prize money of the season so far. Q School grads like Sion know that most of the 20 or so starts they will enjoy this year will be in the lower prize fund tournaments; it is just another barrier for them to jump to maintain their top-level status.

The Tour calendar is something that players like Sion study almost from the moment that their Card is secured. There are new places and courses to visit, a whole different Tour rhythm to understand. It all sounds incredibly exciting, but reality sets in pretty quickly.

The fact is that Sion's ranking as the 14th best player at Q School only gives him a Category 11b playing status, which does not allow him to pick and choose every event. There are a large number of far more eligible players on the Tour with better playing categories who get to pick first. For example, the winners of major championships or the other most prestigious tournaments are Category 1; Tour champions from the last two seasons are Category 3; the top 115 from the previous season are Category 7; and even the top 40 career earners over the history of the Tour, the top 20 finishers on the Challenge Tour plus local qualifiers and invitees get first stab at entering each event before Q Schoolers. The full list of eligible golfers is easily greater than the 156 players who compete at each tournament and the Q Schooler is a poor relation, often waiting patiently on the entry list for last-minute drop-outs. But there is little sympathy for Q Schoolers, they just need to work harder, grab the chances when they come and try to improve their category maybe with a win.

So, although the 21st century European pro has more opportunities than ever to scoop his share of the millions of euros in prize money, there are two obvious downsides: firstly, the amount of travel it required and, secondly, the extra time away from the family. No one can avoid the air miles, but for a relatively new father like Sion, the second downside is considerable because while the superstars can afford to bring their families along to tournaments at the drop of a hat, the journeymen are almost always alone.

The irony is that success in San Roque last November has definitely changed Sion's life, but not always for the right reasons. "It changed my life because I've got less money now," he jokes after his first winter of playing on the Tour. Sion has put in the extra work but has yet to gain extra reward – he is spending considerably more money than he is winning.

Every start has become crucial and Sion is on the reserve list for Singapore this month as the Monday morning of the tournament week dawns. Then he gets 'The Call' – he is in the tournament starting line-up. But this only underlines the dilemma of the journeyman player – do you make the costly, last-minute effort to play on a course you have never seen before and arrive there barely in time to either practice or acclimatise? Or do you stay home and wait for a better opportunity?

For Sion, there is no question: with so few opportunities, he rushes from south Wales via the motorway to Heathrow for a 15-hour flight. By the time he arrives, it is 8pm on Tuesday evening which leaves only one day to loosen up and practice. Now if this tournament was being played on just one course, then Sion would be almost on a level playing field with the other players, but the Singapore Masters is a two-course event at the Laguna Golf and Country Club. Again, fate is being unkind to the Welshman.

In his first round, on the one course he has been able to practice on, Sion shoots a one under par 71, but playing the tighter, second course blind the next day leads to too many missed fairways. His 76 means another missed cut and it is a very long flight home with nothing to show for it.

Sion's stop-start season is giving him little chance to build confidence and sharpness, but there are two events in Europe at the end of this month. It is just what he needs – no long haul flights, no time differences, no extreme heat.

In Madeira, however, it is the wind that causes problems. Shooting an opening 76 means Sion is chasing again and his 4 over total for two rounds is well short of the cut. There is further bad news because the tournament is won by a fellow 2007 Q School Card holder, Daniel Vancsik. The Argentinian has achieved what all Q Schoolers dream about: he has left his Category 11b behind and is now ranked in Category 3 as a Tour winner. The win means no last-minute call-ups and no worrying about his schedule because only the majors and the World Golf Championship events are not automatically on his list of tournaments to play in.

In Portugal a week later, there is still lots of wind and Sion is not holing any putts; he misses this cut by two. "You can't let yourself get too worried. You try to do everything cheaply, flights and hotel and stuff. But once you're out there, you can't let that bother you or there's no point you going out; you have to concentrate on the golf. It's only once you've failed that you look back and think 'Oh, God what have I done.' One of the other downsides is not being with Rita and the girls and when I go away it's very easy to think of the family back home, but you just have to put it out of your mind."

It is, of course, true that new players on Tour can struggle before bursting into form. Justin Rose is often quoted at such times; the Englishman missed his first 17 cuts on the European Tour, but is now regarded as a golfing superstar. Although there is solace in that story for all Tour pros, Rose was just a teenager when he turned pro and was the exception, not the rule. For Sion, it is now four months on Tour, seven tournaments played, one cut made and just €1,447 in prize money. Sitting next to Roger '007' Moore in a departure lounge in Dubai was not the kind of highlight Sion had hoped for by this stage of the season.

Although his spirits are relatively high, he knows he has already slipped behind many fellow Q School graduates. He has put aside some savings to fund the early part of his year, but how many costly trips and missed cuts can he afford? He hopes that this is a question he will not have to ask either himself or his wife Rita. By now, the Welshman knew that 2007 was not going to be an easy season.

For lots of reasons, James Conteh would love to have the problems of Sion Bebb and Andy Raitt. James is trying to make preparations for his season, but instead of travelling the world and testing himself as an international tournament golfer, the young Englishman has been stuck in Hertfordshire struggling to even practice in the dull, damp weather.

James's playing plans revolve around the EuroPro and Jamega Tours which stage events almost exclusively in the UK. It means relatively short car journeys and staying either with other golf pro friends in one house or in a cheap motel, but it also means no events until April. Friends from his Moor Park club help with money to give James a chance to plan his own schedule, albeit that it bears no comparison to the jet-setting done by those on the Main Tour.

The life of the mini tour pro has some similarities, though, with those in the higher echelons. James and his contemporaries will sit around and talk about the game, its anguishes and its triumphs. There is a camaraderie that is part of the joy of being a tournament pro and, right now, it is what James is looking forward to.

"The game is a big puzzle really, it's just so difficult, so we do tend to help each other on the tours; I might ask someone to look at my putting stroke and it's not a faux pas to do that, you might even see something in your own technique when you're helping another player. It's feedback we all need and it's kind of strange in a way, I suppose, but some of us share the same coach and we know what we're working on. It's good to have friends at these events. However, in an ideal world in any tournament, I want to finish first and all my mates to finish second, third and fourth. But if it's them who have the great scores then I'm really pleased for them."

In addition, whether it is mini tour or Main Tour, the pros are forever working on the mental side of their game. Pro golfers seem able to remember almost every shot of every round they have ever played, especially the significant ones. For James, he sees his off-season job as recalling those good rounds, the best memories – like his course record at Stoke Park - and filing away nightmares like the triple bogey on the 18th at Emporda last November in his opening round at Second Stage. He is also thinking about how he would spend a few extra pounds.

"I think the more you play in competition, the better you become, but I seem to have a longer off-season than on-season and I've never had a full winter of golf. Ideally, if I had some money, I'd go down to the Sunshine Tour in Southern Africa. It's harder to motivate yourself on a cold English day, but if the option is doing nothing, then you still go out and practice. I work on technical aspects of my swing rather than just playing. The problem would be that if I started playing really well, then there is no tournament to take part in."

When practice is postponed by weather, there is always some cash to be earned such as working with his friend the tiler. James admits that doing other work helps take his mind off his golfing dreams and makes him hungrier to return to the sport. After all, this is only his fourth year as a pro, so he still has plenty to learn about himself and how to survive even on the third level of pro tournaments.

"Mentally, it is better for me to work than just hang around waiting for a tournament. I don't get pressure from my girlfriend or my parents or at least they never express it to me. How long do I give myself, being a golf pro like this? I don't think about it that often, but I want to do it for as long as I think my goals are achievable and I know the guys around me – even those I played against at Second Stage - are no better than me. So I know I can be on Main Tour. I'm getting mentally stronger, I'm a bit more focused during a round and my technique is improving. I just need to play more."

So until there is a tournament to play in, James will have to wait to prove his theories are true.

Euan Little's theory of how to put his 2006 Q School disappointment behind him is to ply his trade thousands of miles from home on the Sunshine Tour. Euan knows South Africa very well; he has summered down there for the past five years and even had an Afrikaans girlfriend for a while. Yet until this year, he had never committed to a long run on the Sunshine Tour. It is a mistake that he was only now beginning to realise.

"I am staying in Cape Town with friends as I have done for the last six summers. It was laziness really (not playing Sunshine Tour before). For me it's like a re-dedication or maybe a dedication for the first time." Words of encouragement from Euan's coach Bob Torrance have hit home, but there was also a moment closer to home that helped spark the change. It happened in July last year and was not one of Euan's proudest moments.

"I can remember the day it happened. I was at the lowest ebb I've ever been because I had a terrible falling out with my mother. I was going to leave for a tournament that day but got in late the night before. I had slept in and, probably because I'd been misbehaving, I had a row with her; she ended up in tears and I ended up in tears and I jumped into the car and drove straight to the tournament. I felt like it was probably the lowest point in my life; I thought, how am I going to see through this?"

The Littles are a close-knit group and Euan is particularly close to his mother. This is a Scottish farming family dating back several generations with many traditional values and morals. Being a young, single man in such an atmosphere is bound to cause tensions.

"I had had a late night, a lot of alcohol, but when I saw my mother crying because of the hurt that I'd caused her, I realised I had to give myself a shake. I stayed away for two weeks and hardly spoke to her. The only way I was going to get myself out of trouble with her was to raise my golf game and that's what happened. I finished second and then second the following week as well. Then I thought this is the mindset and mentality that I have to have every week and that was the turnaround in my career. I now believe that I have to keep that feeling and there's nothing that I can't achieve."

The family row had finally shaken a player who thought golf would make his fortune before he was 30. But now he was 30 and there was no fortune, just a lot of heartache. Finally, he was taking responsibility.

"I've always been a mother's boy, going to her when things go wrong. I was feeling sorry for myself, ashamed of the hurt I caused when I got to that first tournament. I've never tried as hard in all my life. I had to prove something to myself and to her. I had got into a rut. Now I really believe that good things can come out of bad things."

Euan's reluctance to commit himself to the game of golf had its roots when he was 13 and visited the noted coach Bob Torrance for the first time for a lesson. "I will always remember a statement Bob made to my parents. I was playing with ladies clubs and he wanted me to go to Ben Sayers in North Berwick to sort out some proper golf clubs. My parents picked me up that day and, as we drove off, I told them I had to get these new clubs. Bob was going to speak to the boss and sort it out. My mother told my father to stop the car and turn back; she didn't believe it. By the time we got back, Bob was in the bar and he said: 'Don't worry about your son, he'll be a millionaire by the time he's 30.' There was I, a young boy all wide-eyed, and I thought that life was going to come very easy. Here I am now talking about failing at Q School at 30-years-old and I'm still not a millionaire. But I've never forgotten what Bob said."

The truth is that those words probably ended up doing more harm than good. The Euan of today admits that for many years after that incident he never worked hard enough on his golf game. And, while Euan indulged in the good life rather than the rigours of the driving range, thousands of young pros following behind him entered the sport with a more dedicated attitude and stole a march on him.

"Golf hasn't come easy like I thought it was going to. But when I turned pro in 1996, it was a different ball game altogether, the guys were still partying at nights and I fitted right in there. Now I think about winning tournaments, but I've never felt like that before. Ten years ago I'd be going to Madrid for a tournament, for example, and thinking that it's a big party. This is how I started when I turned pro; it was a totally different lifestyle and mindset at tournaments back then. So much had been expected of me and it was coming easy. It's a terrible attitude to have and it's why I'm in the situation I am now. I'm 30-years-old and done very little with my career. Now I see that it's a privilege not a job. Now kids are coming to the gym after a round. If you'd've said to someone in 1996 that you were going to the gym after a round they'd have looked at you like you were crazy. It was the bar then. Now it's even me who's going to the gym. I hate the phrase, but 'last chance saloon' slips into my mind. It's about finding desire and this is the first time I've had it; I'm going to bust my arse to get where I want to be."

The proof of this particular pudding is in the bare facts – Euan is making cuts and making money in South Africa with ease. The two co-sanctioned events with the European Tour and Sunshine Tour landed him €20,000 by the end of January and since then he has maintained good form. In the subsequent weeks, he had two top five finishes in other Sunshine Tour events and has found himself in contention for titles. Now he is back Scotland for more coaching from Torrance; Euan is itching for another chance on the Main Tour. His chance comes at Madeira this month, the European Tour's first event of the year on 'home' soil.

A cautious opening 73 by Euan provides no proof of his early season form, but he follows that with a 66 to put him in tied 8th position. This is Euan at his best and a third round 69 brings him up to tied 4th place on 8 under. The only problem is that this is the tournament where Argentinian Daniel Vancsik is playing like a god. Euan is fighting for the minor placings and at least wants a top 10 finish to guarantee another start the following week. His last day is relatively uneventful, but he does hang on to 4th and earns another €29,000.

"I was a little bit tight on the greens, there was no freedom in my putting stroke. But you have to find out why and learn from it; it could be because I haven't been in that position enough. I had two birdies and only one bogey; my game was good."

Euan has another impressive finish in Portugal seven days later; he finishes tied 25th for another €11,000. Astonishingly, he has made so much from his early season travels that he has achieved his highest ever world ranking (407th) while the money he has made will take the pressure off the rest of his season even though more opportunities on the Main Tour will be scarce.

"What I do know is that since the run-in with my mother, I've tried my hardest on the golf course. I'm now playing to the best of my ability and if it's not enough each week, then that's it. I think the penny's finally dropped for me."

For some golfers, the hundreds of rounds, the thousands of golf swings and the millions of air miles are not enough to change their minds; instead, just one row with a loved one nearer to home will do the trick.

Martyn Thompson understands the importance of a happy family. While the vast majority of his future Q School rivals will be travelling near and far for competition, the club pro from Parkstone is staying close to home. As a club pro, his normal week includes playing the occasional round with a member, giving lots of lessons, managing the pro shop and simply being around the place as much as possible because a sociable pro is an asset to any club.

Martyn's 'office' is a delicious parkland golf course with groups of tall fir trees and gently rolling hills. He is a pro golfer who tries to be a pro father; he provides a good life for his family with his club job, but also dabbles in a few seaside apartment deals. His wife, Sally, works four days a week in the health care industry, his two eldest children have flown the nest and his eight-year-old daughter provides joy in the home. Who would ever want to leave all this for the suitcase-style life of a top-line tournament pro? But this is Martyn's annual question.

His happiness at home is actually part of the career conundrum that Martyn is still working out in his head; sometimes it seems he would rather be fixing up a beach hut or worrying about the next family holiday than practicing his much-maligned putting to get on Tour. He has committed to a stronger golfing work ethic - probably the key to his Tour dream – yet it is spring and there is little sign of his renewed effort. Funnily, Martyn is the first to admit his failing. "Rather than putting in the work I'm doing other things, it's like I'm afraid of failure, so I have an excuse already there for when I don't make it."

Martyn's dream is buried under a mountain of stuff that most of us simply call 'life'. One of his problems is that he is the consummate club pro - he is trained to help others play the game better rather than himself. So that is what he does – he says 'Yes' to others rather than to himself. Martyn puts on a brave face, but something inside him is screaming: "I want to follow my dream to play on the Tour!" He is not practicing his putting every evening as he promised himself or thinking any more about Q School now than he ever has.

So despite the money he spent on a new indoor putting green, right now Martyn is undermining his New Year's resolution to bring his golf game up to Tour standards. When he is away from Q School, he cannot focus on how much the tournament means to him; his Tour Card ideal is just too far in the distance sometimes. Yet Martyn represents so many club pros when he leaves behind the every day worries and thinks of what might be. Catch him in that mood and it is clear that Q School is still a mountain he wants to climb. The question is the same as for many club pros: what will it take for Q School to come to the very top of his list of life priorities? It is not a very complex psychological question, but if Martyn Thompson, club pro, is ever to become Martyn Thompson, European Tour golfer, then it is a question that he needs to address immediately.

– April 2007

A Question of Cash

"I remember being absolutely devastated (when I failed at Q School) because it's your year's work done. A few of the guys get drunk, a few cry and then, after a few days, you have to think 'Well, how am I going to pay the mortgage?'. You have to re-group. It's our living after all." – Barry Lane, multiple Tour winner and Q School graduate four out of seven attempts.

Like most major sports around the globe, golf is now a multi-billion dollar business. There are two significant reasons behind the spectacular growth in television audiences, prize money and sponsorship. Firstly, there has been fierce competition for TV rights since the early 1990s because of the emergence of more digital television channels covering nothing but sports; secondly, Tiger Woods burst into golf's world and captivated not only a whole new generation of golfers but also intrigued a wider audience of non-golf fans.

So for the last decade and a half, more TV coverage of golf (including lots of Tiger) has brought in larger audiences which has prompted more sponsorship which has delivered bigger prize money which has led to television executives wanting more golf (especially Tiger) and so the virtuous circle has continued.

Bidding wars between broadcasters now take place over the major championships and the Ryder Cup and the money is staggering. In 2001 when the BBC was due to renew its £10 million, five-year deal to screen the Open Championship, the new price was rumoured to have tripled. Around the same time, the US PGA signed a deal with American broadcasters worth $900 million.

The change for the players has been just as stark. In 1985, for instance, Scotland's Sandy Lyle won the PGA European Tour Order of Merit with what seemed then like a very large amount of money – almost £140,000. Yet five years later in 1990, Ian Woosnam was top of the money list with £574,166 – more than four times Sandy's amount. Another five years (1995) and Colin Montgomerie was European No 1 with £835,051.

Then golf's global pay TV negotiations added another vital element – Tiger Woods. The man who could become the greatest ever golfer helped take prize money into another stratosphere. By 2000, Lee Westwood's Order of Merit total was over £2 million (€3.1 million) and the European No. 1's earnings peaked at almost £2.75 million (€4 million) won by Ernie Els four years later. In 2006, Sandy Lyle's 1985 earnings would only just be enough to creep into the top 115 on the money list.

For the very best players there is also tens of thousands of pounds or dollars in appearance money. And, if not an appearance fee, then what about a sponsorship. Tiger signed a deal with Gatorade to brand a product with his name and press reports suggest it could pay him $100 million over five years.

Obviously, Tiger is streets ahead of any other golfer on the planet when it comes to earnings: in 2006 he earned nearly $12m in prize money and a further $87m in endorsements according to figures from Golf Digest magazine. The cash has certainly filtered down at least to those regulars on the European Tour and US PGA Tour. Even the 100th best player in Europe is earning over £125,000 (€200,000) a season nowadays in prize money and, although he might well spend £50,000 on travel, accommodation, caddie fees and other costs of the job, there are also plenty of extras.

The tournament organisers have to stand out from the crowd; especially in America, they accomplish this with a range of gifts for the players and even their wives. There might be watches or electrical gifts and gadgets like iPods and GameBoys; perhaps designer clothing, expensive luggage or luxury spa treatments. The countless freebies make golfers feel a little bit like film stars and the very best players then spend their fortunes in ever more lavish ways – a string of magnificent houses (second and third homes in tax havens like Monaco, Switzerland and Dubai are common nowadays), high performance sports cars or vintage automobiles (Miguel Angel Jimenez and Darren Clarke have many), top class racehorses (Gary Player breeds his own thoroughbreds), fabulous paintings (Luke Donald is a collector) and spectacular vineyards (the Nick Faldo Shiraz 2001 is particularly fine or you can visit Ernie Els's huge winery in South Africa).

It is worth saying, though, that such levels of cash and prizes are for the few and the gifts are a little less brash in Europe, but everything given is accepted with alacrity.

So with all this glamour, it is not surprising that the number of players vying for the top prize money has grown almost as fast as the cash on offer. But the money does not trickle down very far. Talk to the journeyman pro and he will tell you that only those inside the top 150 of the European Tour money list are making a good living. For every tournament pro with a fat wallet, a garage full of flashy cars and no mortgage repayments on his three uniquely-designed homes, there are hundreds of others who are taking second jobs during the off-season and worrying about their next credit card bill.

Phil Golding is one of the luckier ones. He has won on Tour, he has earned well over £1 million (€1.5 million) over a 17-year tournament career and he has invested sensibly. But his earnings are certainly not in the superstar stratosphere and his near-record number of returns to Q School shows there have been plenty of fallow years. In fact, without his wife's income, Phil would have spent years really struggling. Now, with no Tour Card, the Hertfordshire pro must wonder if his chances of returning to life at the top of the golfing world are over.

Last year Phil's season was a financial disaster as he finished 185th on the Order of Merit. He played a staggering 29 events - definitely at the upper end of the Tour pro's normal number - and his €51,000 in winnings (the Tour uses the Euro as its main prize money indicator) was a paltry return; no one played as many tournaments in 2006 for so little prize money. The point is that the more he played, the more he spent; for the struggling pro, such a scenario is like throwing good money after bad. Phil's golden year of 2003 (when he won the French Open and pocketed almost €650,000 for the season) had allowed him to believe that struggling on Tour would be a thing of the past. The next two seasons after that had been reasonable, including 2005 when he finished 77th in the money list with €300,000. So 2006 was a major shock as well as a disappointment.

"I bought a new car after I won in France, although it took me two years to pay for it, but I remember my accountant saying we should buy property. At that time we didn't actually do that although we did make some reasonable investments like long-term savings plans," he says. But Phil's sudden dip in fortunes have led to him liquidating some of those investments, cutting down on expenses at tournaments and watching his diminishing cash flow with alarm.

"Don't get me wrong, I'm not pleading poverty and liquidating the savings plans is OK because, I suppose that's what rainy days are for. But now I'm much more aware of the money. Before, I'd spend a couple of thousand pounds a tournament and not be conscious of it. Now I am."

It is easy for a Tour pro to spend £2,000 (€3,000) every time he tees it up for an event. There are flights and airport transfers; accommodation for at least five nights (providing you make the cut) and a professional Tour caddie who will charge as much as £850 for the week plus a percentage of any winnings. Add in money to your golf coach, perhaps your mind coach and a little cash for spending and there you have it.

The other problem for a player in Phil's 2007 situation is that he will play the events with the smaller purses; these are tournaments that the top players usually stay away from because the rewards are so low. Plus, the low-ranked player will definitely miss his share of cuts and so the pressure to make more money becomes obvious. Phil has already played in two such low prize money tournaments – in Indonesia and Portugal and missed both cuts; it is too early to panic, but he is already half thinking that he will earn less in prize money than he spends this year

"For 25 events a year, that can mean £40-50,000 a year in expenses. You hear about some players almost going bankrupt, some re-mortgaging their homes just to keep going. I know a couple of players who have had to sell their houses and downsize. It's dangerous ground to do that. Fortunately, I don't have a mortgage and I've my Taylor Made/adidas sponsorship this year of about £8,000. They've been loyal to me this season which is good. But I'm deliberately keeping down my outgoings; I'm trying not to spend very much."

Even though Phil is not among the worst off, there is an inevitable strain on the player and his family. "My wife Sally has been very supportive, but not all players get that; any wife could easily say 'OK, pack up; go and get a normal job'. This year has been like being made redundant. Luckily, Sally understands. She had a good job with EMI and reluctantly left with a pay-off. She'd been all go-go in a busy world, but now it's the best thing that's ever happened to her. She's said she'd go back to work if necessary, but I hope that doesn't have to happen. She has her own nest egg from the redundancy and if she didn't have that then we would really be struggling."

Many tournament pros on the European Tour have been winners for much of their career – as amateurs or in regional pro events and on mini-tours - and to hit a level of golf where the chance of winning disappears is mentally tough. For Phil, finding the words to explain his lack of performance on the golf course leaves him slightly tongue-tied. The modern tournament golfer has been taught to find the positives even from the most negative situation. But although this might work easily within the sport itself, it is a different matter to the outside world.

"I kept meeting this guy at my son's tennis academy on weekends and he'd say 'So you missed the cut again?'. I began to resent him saying that and even the word 'cut' was difficult for me to hear. When I'm not playing well, the way I speak about myself is subconsciously positive. I have to make myself speak this way. I've seen Tiger (Woods) interviewed after a bad round and he says: "Well, actually, I'm hitting the ball quite good." Yet I've just seen him knock it all over the place. It's also important not being around other negative players and sometimes you have to disassociate yourself from them."

Much of the uncomfortable feelings for Phil relate back to a bruised pride. The missed cuts, the subsequent lack of money, the need to explain himself – the tournament pro in the doldrums is not a happy person to be around.

"You do bottle your emotions a lot on Tour. Sally used to say how she'd be treading on eggshells with me when I came home after missing a cut in case she upset me for the next week. I wasn't easy to live with. Since my son Lucas came along, I'm much better than I was. Before him, I was miserable and sulky and Sally would say I shouldn't get so low because I need to get back up for the next tournament. Also, pros can be selfish and self-absorbed. I might go practising or to the gym to do what I have to do for my golf; maybe I'd say I'd go out for an hour and four hours later I'd still be hitting balls. I'd come back late and get bollocked for that. Tour pros need a very understanding partner."

Phil actually dreams of returning to the Tour for two reasons other than money and bruised pride. Firstly, he has a need to be the provider for his family. For most of his pro career, his wife Sally brought home the steady salary and he pursued his golfing ambitions come what may, but more recently Phil has taken over the role as the major breadwinner and it is a role he is happy to play.

"We all like nice things – cars, holidays and stuff – but it's not about the money now. There are players who have to make a career decision forced on them - either your family or the Tour. You either stay home or your marriage is finished – that happens. But, for me, everyone knows that Sally had a very good job and she played the mortgage for years while I kept on playing. When she packed up, I wanted to be the provider. It's pride for me. It's my turn now and I did it in 03, 04 and 05. Last year was a blip. It's taken a year to find the coach that I wanted and now I need to compete again."

The second reason for Phil's desire continuing to burn is his son. "What is keeping me going is to do it for Lucas. It's a vision for me to win again and have Lucas come out on the green like Ian Poulter's daughter Amy did when he won a couple of years ago. It's not about the money. Lucas is the drive for me; I want him to be there when I win again. The other day he said to someone "Do you know my dad's a professional golfer?" He's so aware of things now. It's so sweet; you can't buy that sort of stuff."

There are many tournament pros who have never reached the heights of Phil Golding's career and are living each year from hand to mouth, taking jobs in the winter or asking parents, partners and local sponsors to help tide them over until they make the grade.

Guy Woodman is such a case. The golf bug bit him from around the age of 12, it was then that he started wanting to emulate his heroes, the likes of Nick Faldo, Greg Norman and Bernhard Langer who he saw on TV. But it wasn't going to be easy. He had some talent, but there was no brilliant amateur career to alert sponsors and no rich parents to pay his way. With only a little help from family and friends, Guy has been funding his own dream for over a decade.

"I've always had extra jobs since I left school, just so I could keep playing, both as an amateur and a pro. The deal with my parents after I left school was that if I wanted to play full-time amateur golf and pursue a career in it, I had to get a job. I started in Little Chefs and Harvesters washing up in the evenings, anything I could do; I was 17. I'd play all summer as an amateur and work all winter. And that's pretty much been the case ever since. I've done all sorts – landscape gardening, security guard, stacked boxes in warehouses, whatever's needed to save some money and play a little. I might go out once a month or once every other week if I'm lucky and if I do go out I don't drink. I can't afford to do it; it's as simple as that; anything to keep the costs down. Basically every penny I earn now goes into my golf."

And Guy's costs are not just a bit of travel, accommodation and equipment. "I have to see my chiropractor - £50 a pop - once a month; there's a masseuse once every other week - that's £50 as well; and I regularly drive up to Middlesbrough to see my coach Andrew Nicholson. I've been working with him for two years and he's a fantastic coach for me."

In 2005 to help kick start his career, Guy offered 300 £1,000 shares in himself to friends, business contacts and members of Stoke Park GC where he works. It is a fairly common alternative to normal sponsorship and Guy sold 10 shares in year one, six in year two and another 10 at the start of this year. But this is not money to live on; it simply feeds the dream.

"You aspire to be in the Rolls Royce class, but you start off as a Skoda. Each EuroPro Tour event costs £275 to enter and then another couple of hundred in add-on costs, so it's effectively £500 each time you peg it up. Even then, you still need to get off to a good start and earn some prize money or then you have to ask your parents or someone for some help. People think all golf pros travel the world and have a great lifestyle, but it's not like that at all for lots of us. The public don't know the amount of hard work it takes to get there. People only see the top guys and that's what they presume you are. When they know a bit more, they say "Well, you're not a professional then, you're like a semi-pro." And I tell them I *am* a pro and I'm working my nuts off to get to the top."

Like many sportspeople – especially those in solo sports like tennis or athletics – there is often a certain selfishness that golfers show as part of their characters; they push others aside, they defer alternative lifestyles or a quiet, 9-to-5 life; they want their dream and they want it fulfilled on their own terms. The selfishness is not malicious or mean, but a product of the depth of their desire.

For Guy it means a wife and family are not even on his radar. "Before you get involved in any relationship, you have to tell the woman that golf is your thing. And they start off saying they're fine with it. They have this idea you're going to be a rich guy in a couple of years time. Then after a while it hasn't happened and the relationship goes tits up. At the end of last year, my relationship was going awry. We lived two years together and we moved back in with my parents and that's where it all went wrong. My closest friends and family know my dream to play on the European Tour and understand it, but there does come a time when they ask what's going on.

"I know I'm one of the luckiest guys alive following my dream, not a lot of people can say that. They might have more money, wife, a family, but they might not be the happiest at work. I'm doing something that I really love. To me it's not a sacrifice giving all that stuff up, but there comes a time when I have to make a living."

Having understanding parents is a must, but the strain of little money coming in is often just below the surface. "My parents only have to say a question in the wrong tone and it upsets me. You're on edge a lot of the time. I know I can be quite grumpy. If I get frustrated, I don't want to talk about it and we have our fall-outs but we know now when's the right time to say something. I shout and scream a bit and in past years we've had moments when my mom's picked every trophy up and thrown them in the bin; she's taken my clothes and thrown them out of the front door and told me not to come back. But a few days go by and everything gets talked over and you make up, so there are the times when you look back and wonder if it's worth it. Some people go through their lives and don't have the same kind of trouble, but these things make us stronger in the long run."

Guy's competitive life revolves around the EuroPro Tour, the third level tour for pros in Europe and, although it is healthy, three-round competition and the winner will take home £10,000, the rest of the prize money does not reflect the effort of the players. "I am a PGA member, so I can play some pro-ams and I would aim to do half-and-half perhaps with the EuroPro this year. But it's a tough tour – 150 guys playing each week for first place. The winning cheque is good and fourth place can get £1,200, but it's costing £500 a week just to enter let alone all the other costs. You play your heart out, finish top 10 and even then you are probably playing for a loss. That's brutal."

Guy will room with a bunch of his pro friends at EuroPro events to keep the costs down and he has almost no social life. He is also trying to become a fully qualified PGA professional, so when not practising or playing a tournament, he is studying or even spending many hours in the club shop at Stoke Park earning extra cash. He lives this strange, spartan existence because his dream of playing on the Main Tour burns so bright.

"I wouldn't give up my dream even if someone gave me money to stop. No chance. The dream is worth a lot. I wouldn't take a million to give up the dream. I'd rather earn it. I know if I was playing good golf then I'd earn that anyway. Not everyone is the same. A lot of guys are doing it just to feel fine. They're out there dreaming but they don't want to put the hard work in. They want to say that they're a tournament professional trying to get on Tour and if someone dangled a carrot of some money then they'd give up. And there are some who have loads of talent and don't have to work too hard. I'd rather earn through my dream, through my passion. Life would be a bit empty if I just had a million pounds from nothing."

This month, the EuroPro season starts and Guy has high hopes. He sees former EuroPro players like Marc Warren and Ross Fisher both winning on the Main Tour and earning the kind of money he seeks. His early season form is nothing to write home about, but if nothing else, Guy enjoys the tournament atmosphere.

"On EuroPro events I room with a bunch of guys and there's lots of camaraderie, it's good craic. We all talk about golf. We're friends, but we're in it for ourselves ultimately. If you see one of your mates in the hunt then you want them to do well and encourage them. We want a positive atmosphere and we can feed off one another. If it's not yourself then you want one of your buddies to win and make money. If you're up against that person, you have to put friendship aside; we all know that. When it comes to the battle you never wish bad on any of your friends. You want to win with good golf, you want to test yourself and if you're better on the day then so be it, you move on. If you're not good enough then you congratulate them."

Guy is hoping that the battles ahead this year will be significant enough for those words to have real meaning.

If Martyn Thompson ever rises to the heights of a regular spot on the European Tour then his accountant would be the first to notice. As a club pro in Dorset, Martyn is paid a very decent retainer by his club, makes good money from lessons given to members and, thanks to his PGA training and pleasant manner, also makes a living from the profits of sales of equipment, clothing and a host of other golfing items in his pro shop. He may not quite be in the six-figure income bracket, but he is certainly financially comfortable.

Every club pro will receive a retainer from the club itself (maybe around £25,000 or more) as well as income from lessons (he will charge probably £15-25 a time) and profits from sales of equipment, clothing and the rest of his stock in the shop. However, if the club pro were to succeed at Q School and acquire a Tour Card then he would have to give up his pro job and all its benefits and risk going into debt. However, it is a risk Martyn is prepared to take.

The reason is that 11 years ago, when Martyn went to Q School for the first time, he found out that he was good enough to live with the top players who chase the millions of pounds in prize money rather than just be the man working in the pro shop for eight hours a day. That year (1996), he qualified for Final Stage and was actually joint leader after two rounds. "I psyched myself out of it; I'd studied the Q School for years and seen all these great players come through, but then got there and wondered why I was in the lead. I thought to myself I should be learning about the event, not winning it. I put myself back down where I thought I belonged at the time that was the middle of the pack. I think I missed a Tour Card by about four shots in the end."

He was even invited back to the Final Stage the following year via his high position in the PGA British Order of Merit for club pros, but decided he could not jeopardise his final club pro exams that took place the following week.

"I now realise such an invitation could be worth a fortune; I'd give my right arm for that invitation now. But I had an offer of a pro's job, so I could see me failing at Q School and not doing the preparation for the exams and failing that too. I could've been left with nothing. The right option for me at the time was not to go to Q School."

Martyn does not regret that decision, but it took another 10 years before he felt the financial safety net was in place so that his Tour Card dream could re-emerge. "I have probably got more enthusiasm for the idea now than I had when I went to Q School in 1996."

But although the rewards are bigger, so are the expenses and potential losses. Martyn believes a Tour Card would generate local sponsors to cover his costs and news of his friends and contemporaries on the Tour provides further incentive. "Now when I see players on Tour doing well who are no better than me, it frustrates the hell out of me. They aren't more talented, they have just used their time better."

But as the club pro approaches his busiest time of the year, Martyn's thoughts of the Tour are becoming fleeting. His good intentions are falling apart, he is still not devoting enough time to practice and First Stage is just five months away. Those around him wonder if Martyn will actually be there at Q School in September and, even if he is, perhaps the more relevant question is whether or not he will be ready.

6 – May 2007

CHAPTER

The Big Challenge

"I think Q School is a tougher test (than Challenge Tour), but if you've given it five or six attempts and still not getting your Card, then you might want to go and do something else." – Jamie Spence, Tour winner and six-time Q School attendee.

May is a big month for golf's small Tours. In years past, golf in Europe only really began in the spring: April would provide a gentle start and then May was when the season would hit its stride; by early October, the season was over. Nowadays the Main Tour has expanded into a worldwide travelling circus so that it spans almost every week of the year, however, the mini tours have generally maintained the shorter seasons.

The Challenge Tour (these days growing into a mature shadow tour for the Main Tour) is something of an exception within Europe as it pushes its events onto different continents searching for suitable golfing weather. Meanwhile the EuroPro Tour, the Tartan Tour in Scotland, the Alps Tour across central Europe, the various other national tours in countries such as Spain and the regional events in Britain all get busy about now and will not be active much past September.

For some pros, these smaller tours are their regular hunting ground, while for others they are starting points, stepping stones to the higher levels of golf. In this level of pro golf, there is a particularly rich mixture of young players cutting their competitive teeth and older pros licking their wounds before trying to climb the back up the golfing ladder.

The standard on the Challenge Tour in particular is very high; it now has a reputation for delivering some of the best European pros of all time. Thomas Bjorn, Henrik Stenson and Trevor Immelman are among many world class players who graduated through the Challenge Tour. The fields of players are multi-national, the courses are usually of a high quality and to win here requires four highly polished rounds of golf. Nowadays the top 20 ranking players after the end-of-season Challenge Tour championship receive full eligibility on the Main Tour. Their initial 11a Category is even one higher than those players who succeed at Q School. The Tour bigwigs want the Challenge Tour to be the No 1 pathway to the Main Tour.

The EuroPro Tour – supported by the Professional Golfers Association and recognised as the 3rd level of tours in Europe – stages tournaments mostly in the UK and attracts plenty of pros with Main Tour experience for its three-round events. Finish top of this pile and you win eligibility on the Challenge Tour.

There is plenty of high class competition in these tours, but the main gripe among players below the Main Tour is the prize money. Apart from the top couple of dozen players at the top of the Challenge Tour, tournament pros outside the Main Tour do not make much of a living from their winnings alone. Although a Challenge Tour tournament winner receives €20,000 and a EuroPro champion will pocket about €15,000, the minor prizes can be miniscule. Fifteenth at a Challenge event is worth just under €1,500 while the same slot on EuroPro pays out only about €750. By contrast, on the Main Tour, 15th – even on some of the smaller events – is worth 10 times as much as on Challenge Tour, in the larger tournaments 20 or 30 times more.

For most players with some Main Tour experience, it is often hard to find motivation on the Challenge Tour. Euan Little is certainly one player who does not relish it. He played two Challenge events this month – he finished 63rd place in Belgium for the Telenet Trophy (earning him the grand total of €377) and missed the cut in Manchester where he was suffering from a heavy cold.

"The Challenge Tour does not motivate me in the same way as the Main Tour. I know I'm going to an inferior golf course 95% of the times and it is not set up as tough as a Main Tour course. The Challenge Tour standard is good and I am prepared to play there, but over the past 11 years, it has put me into financial problems. You need to finish 15th to break even for the week and I'm not prepared to put myself at that kind of risk. In the Main Tour, there are better monetary rewards. You see guys on Challenge Tour doing well and there are young kids who relish the opportunity, but I've been in that position; this will be my swansong on Challenge. It'll be Main Tour or another Tour for me from now on, but not Challenge, unless the prize funds increase, but more especially if the courses get tougher. At 31, I'm not prepared to stump up £750 to win a thousand."

For Euan, his Challenge Tour events are in danger of undermining the progress he has made with his renewed dedication. Just before his two disappointing results in Belgium and England, he missed the cut in Andalucia in a Main Tour event by a single shot. His season still looks relatively healthy considering his few opportunities to play, but the chances of avoiding Q School (he is eligible to go straight to Second Stage) look almost non-existent. And, although his on-course attitude on Challenge Tour disappoints him, he is at least aware of it. Euan has also learned that Challenge Tour events were the scenes of some less-than-professional moments off the course.

"In the past, on the Challenge Tour, we partied at the wrong time; we'd party on a Friday nights sometimes. But now I'd rather focus on my golf during a tournament and wait for a week off. Partying is definitely still part of the culture of all the Tours, but it's getting less and less."

The Main Tour during the 70s and 80s boasted far more good-time-Charlies than Euan ever saw when he started out in 1996. It was all manner of players who joined in the fun, from the journeyman pros to the champion golfers and the Ryder Cup stars, and the drinking culture that existed back then was legendary. Twenty or 30 years ago was a time when Tuesday was "the big night out" as the players often got together for a pre-tournament celebration and if you missed the cut on a Friday night then drowning your sorrows alone was not an option.

The quantity and quality of the drinking at that time meant that Wednesdays (the normal pro-am day, 24 hours before the official start of the tournament) were a blur to a regular gang of party animals. In addition, these confident, young sportsmen travelling the world, living the lonely lifestyle of hotel after hotel for much of the year, were not without attraction to the ladies. True, the music and film businesses probably boast more groupies, but men's sport – yes, even golf – is not without its band of happy female followers and a couple of decades ago there was no media spotlight or kiss-and-tell consequences to worry about when it came to the off-course activities of the players.

This is not to say that every Tour player of that era was straight to the hotel bar after every round, but the preference for the company of fitness coaches and mind gurus or appointments at the gym were things of the future. The European Tour in particular has always been a place where players have socialised more openly; it is one of the most pleasant aspects of the Tour itself, but at times it went too far. Now the party culture is fading into history.

Nevertheless, European Tour pros have never all retreated to their hotel rooms to order room service (a claim made more often about the US Tour) and will at least dine together in groups. It is a convention that is often given as the reason Europe's Ryder Cup team bonds so well – the players actually meet up away from the course. Nevertheless, the young professionals of the 21st century have their eyes fixed on the potential massive cash rewards and are far less likely to risk their on-course focus for short-term benefits of an off-course late-night party or two.

"It is very difficult not to party sometimes, especially because at some tournaments, there is a social event every night for us," says Euan. "There are some guys who still like to socialise and I have seen lots of players – grown up on Tour with them – who enjoy a drink. Now, though, the younger guys don't generally consume any alcohol at all; golf rules their lives." And golf is ruling the life of Euan; there are many like him who have needed to re-dedicate themselves.

Simon Dyson is such an example; he is one of the modern-day stars who has reformed after a previous reputation for a little too much of the high life. Nowadays, he knuckles down to practice his golf in an evening of a tournament rather than take a trip to the hotel bar.

Simon is contrite when he talks about his good time image. This year he even boasts of off-season fitness plans aimed at helping him get off to a flying start. "The drinking has been calmed down a hell of a lot. Last year I gave pretty much everything up; I was in the gym five or six times a week. I've felt the reward for that. When I let it slip for a couple of weeks, I start to feel it. I don't smoke much unless I go out on the lash and I don't have time for that. I've taken everything into moderation. I know how it felt now when I gave everything up and felt fit; I felt really good about myself."

The proof of Simon's new regime will come later this year at the US PGA in Tulsa where final day temperatures reach 110° Fahrenheit. Simon will shoot a best-of-the-day 64 to finish tied 6th and best European. For him, progress is now a question of fitness. He knows Tiger Woods is the fittest player on any Tour and that is one huge reason why the world's No 1 can handle the end-of-tournament pressure.

Simon Dyson has risen from Q School failure to successful pro via the Asian Tour and finally near-superstar status in Europe. He certainly has no thoughts of returning to lower level tours or even the Q School any time soon, but that is the challenge of the very top tournament pro: the number of players keeping their Tour Card after each season remains constant, yet the competition for those places intensifies annually. There are increasing numbers of top class players feeling unsafe about their status on Tour at the start of each season and if it means push-ups rather than parties then the choice is obvious.

Both Phil Golding and Sion Bebb have played plenty of Challenge Tour events and won on that tour, but they agree that once you have dined at the high table, it is not easy to return to a place below the salt. Sion began his pro tournament career with regional PGA events and moved on to the old MasterCard Tour; he gained his place on the Challenge Tour from there, but it was not much of a living. He could only continue to play there because he had saved up some seed money and got some sponsorship. He spent five years trying to make the next leap forward to the full Tour.

"It was all about trying to fulfil my dream. My first year on Challenge Tour (2002), I made a loss and in the second year I just about made a profit. It was always tough financially and my wife and I would go through each year and see how the finances were. It's risk and reward. I had a bit of sponsorship from the Ryder Cup of Wales; it's difficult to live without it."

In those days only the top 15 finishers on Challenge Tour money list at the end of the season earned a Tour Card for the following year, so when Sion finished very close in 2003 (he managed 18th place and won just over €50,000), it kept him going for another couple of years. "[My performance that year] showed me I was capable of making the Main Tour. I had a 2nd and a 3rd everything bar a win, but I didn't make any money. We gave up holidays, we were still in the same house, still with no conservatory and we were driving the same old cars. Rita was fantastic with me being away and money being short. We had no kids at first, but then Alys turned up in 2001 and that was extra responsibility; it makes you want to play well for her sake, you're trying to win money to look after her. Rita could quite easily have said 'No more, I want you home'. Many wives would have. I've got a lot to thank her for."

Challenge Tour was teaching Sion how to be a top tournament pro, but after the 2005 season, he was not making enough progress or enough cash; it was almost time to think again. "I'd given it four or five years, but there were difficulties with our financial situation and Rita was pregnant again. I couldn't keep leaving home with £800 and coming back with £500 even though I was doing relatively well. We made the decision that if things didn't turn around quickly then I wouldn't play the tours."

Sion started looking at alternative jobs during the winter of 2005 and 2006 even though in his heart of hearts he wanted one more year as a touring pro. "I wasn't looking forward to another type of job, but I had to do it and that was that. I went for an interview as a limousine driver one time; I would've done anything to get a few hundred quid to keep me going." As the 2006 season was about to start, Sion went for an interview for a job in a south Wales factory as a car parts fitter, but the lure of the golf tours was too much; he and Rita decided that with his first tournament about to start, life on the shop floor could wait.

So during early 2006, Sion was on the edge of retiring from both the Challenge Tour in particular and tournament golf in general. Then he made his fateful decision to play in the North Wales Ryder Cup Challenge at North Wales during the week of the arrival of his second child. That win was the confidence boost he needed. Now Sion has no wish to return to Challenge Tour.

Phil Golding is in very much the same situation. He will play a little Challenge

Tour this year just to have four-round practice and, although the competition tests him, the atmosphere – lots of slim-hipped, hair-gelled twentysomethings – is not conducive for as man in his mid-40s. Phil tees it up at the Oceânico Developments Pro-Am in Manchester at the end of this month and, although he plays fairly solidly for level par after two rounds, he misses another cut. The fact is that Challenge Tour events do not mean enough to him: finish 10th here and it counts for very little either financially or in terms of prestige; a similar finish on the Main Tour is worth real gold and automatically provides the player with entry to the next event.

"All the young kids hit it miles and there are good players here, but I don't know hardly anyone on Challenge Tour these days. I've been there and done it, but I suppose it's all about belonging and I wonder why I'm there nowadays." As a recent Main Tour winner, Phil is exempt from both First and Second Stages of Q School, so there is little incentive at the occasional Challenge Tour event; even a win on that tour would not change his Main Tour category for the season. "Yes, I want to win and play good golf, it's just that most of the older ones among us, we don't believe we should be there." However, there are other fortysomethings who choose to think differently about Challenge Tour.

Peter Baker was a star of Europe's 1993 Ryder Cup team, the same year as he reached No 7 in the money list. But instead of his career taking flight, Baker slipped inexorably down the rankings. He had three wins on the Main Tour by the early 90s, but nothing afterwards. By the new millennium, Baker was finishing outside the top 115 who keep their Tour privileges and he was relying on the career money list rankings (being in the Tour career top 40 gives a player Category 9 for tournament entry compared to Category 11 for successful Q Schoolers). However, after the 2006 season, Peter slipped down the career money list and faced the School. His preparation consisted mostly of being an assistant to his good friend Ian Woosnam in the successful European Ryder Cup team in Ireland. But being a part of the Ryder Cup win was not enough to inspire Peter to win his Tour Card last November. However, his Q School failure prompted the Midlander to revitalise his career on the Challenge Tour despite those who saw this decision as a fall from grace.

"I had a grandstand seat at the Ryder Cup and I was jubilant at winning and it was very inspiring, but then I had to get on with my own career. Sometimes, you just burn out and that had happened to me. When I failed Q School, it wasn't a difficult decision to try the Challenge Tour."

It took the 39-year-old from Wolverhampton a while to settle down, but by May this year he had adapted to the Challenge Tour rhythm and finished 6th in the Telenet Trophy in Belgium.

"I enjoy Challenge Tour," he says. "I like the fact that you have to do everything yourself. You realise how spoiled you are on Main Tour with free food and courtesy cars and everything. Challenge Tour is similar to how Main Tour was 20 years ago; you even carry your own bag instead of having a caddie. It helped me prove I can compete again."

In June, Baker would go on to win his first Challenge Tour title and then repeat the feat in October to secure his Tour Card by finishing 12th on the Challenge Tour money list. But is Peter viewed as a fallen hero by his fellow pros? Euan Little does not think so. When talking of Peter's determination to succeed on a lower level Tour despite having once reached the immense heights of a Ryder Cup spot, Euan provides a telling quote about how the pros understand the ups and downs of their chosen career. "Well, at least he's played in the Ryder Cup. Who wouldn't want to have done that just once?"

But there are not too many stories like Peter Baker's. Many pros who slip off the Main Tour for a few years are not going to return. However, golfers love competition and they often need to test themselves. There are many different tours around the world and they are graded by prize money. Outside of the PGA European Tour and its equivalent in America - the US PGA Tour – the prize money drops from the staggering levels of near-excess through to the plain ordinary. The Nationwide Tour – America's equivalent of the Challenge Tour – is the only possible exception. It boasts top money earners who can bank almost $500,000 in a year. By contrast, a Challenge Tour season champion might earn half that amount.

The Asian Tour, Japan Tour, Australasian Tour and Sunshine Tour are independently-run second tier tours and, although they do not provide the mega-money events of their more prestigious rivals, there is a reasonable living to be made here for a select number of pros.

Below these four are third tier mini tours including the Canadian Tour, the Tour de las Americas (South America), the EPD (European Professional Development) Tour based in Germany; the Alps Tour (sanctioned by countries including France, Switzerland, Italy and Austria) and the EuroPro. Although not all stage four-round events and none of them are big money tours, they often provide the real first multi-national test for pros who want to make a living out of tournament play. Some are almost a throwback to the earliest days of professional golf when pro tournaments were simply a case of all the participants throwing some money into a pot and the winner takes all.

Before even reaching the third-tier level, a British pro will probably have started in PGA-organised tournaments and Pro-Ams at clubs in his region where a few hundred pounds may go to the winner. The regional strokeplay events obviously allow the aspiring pro to experience the level of opposition near his home base – for example, in the North Region he would play with contemporaries drawn from an area stretching south to Cheshire and as far north as Northumberland – before national PGA events bringing in the rest of the UK and Northern Ireland.

In fact, golf history states how it was the PGA and the leading tournament players who set up the PGA European Tour (separately operated from the PGA itself) in October 1971 in order to elevate the standards of competition. So while the PGA looks after club pros, trains them and operates national and regional tournaments for them, the PGA European Tour has grown to represent the highest level of international tournament players.

Nevertheless, the lower rungs of the pro golfing ladder are vital in order to feed the European Tour with endless talent. Thankfully for the good of the pro tour system, the EuroPro – with its increasingly cosmopolitan field of players contesting two dozen events staged over 54-holes from April to October – is well established.

Guy Woodman is one player who is still taking his chances on the EuroPro Tour. May is, in fact, the month when the first full EuroPro tournament takes place. However, his opening 82 at the Wensum Valley International Open in Norfolk is not the start to the season he had planned throughout a long winter lay-off. The pressures of golf at this level are no less than those of better players on better tours; in fact, they are probably more acute in some ways, mostly because 'The Dream' seems so far away and Q School is the solitary escape route.

"Playing on the EuroPro, you're going to be on edge all the time, it's the normal thing. If you've got the finance behind you or if you've got support or if you're born into money, then it takes a bit of burden off you. But I didn't have those things. My father was a policeman and now works as a warden at Windsor Castle and my mother is a secretary. My dad has a decent pension, but my parents could not support my golf. It was my job to find the cash. Most of my career, all my eggs have been in one basket: progressing via the tournaments I play in is how I've survived and that's why I'm tense so much of the time."

There are four EuroPro events this month and Guy can play in only two; he misses the cut in both. Despite the setbacks, he is thinking ahead to the Q School and each EuroPro tournament is practice for the challenge ahead.

"You know Q School is coming up in a few months and you try to peak [for it]. You can miss every cut all year and peak at the time of Q School and that would be great. But if you're missing cuts on the EuroPro, your confidence suffers. I make sure I don't play too many events; I work with my coach instead and make sure I'm physically fit. I periodise my practice. There's a lot of golf to play in a year, so you make sure you're prepared in every way you can."

Preparation for players on tours like the EuroPro is no less intense than those at the higher levels; everyone is practicing hard and looking for consistency over several weeks or even months not just the occasional one or two rounds. It is consistency that will lead to progress up the ladder. For instance, a top five finish on the EuroPro Tour at the end of the season guarantees a year's exemption on the next season's Challenge Tour and also means direct progress to Second Stage of the Q School.

"We do everything the very top players are doing just to get that edge. That's where I'm aiming – the very top. But things off the course are different for us." It is the lifestyle of many EuroPro players that is in stark contrast to the superstars of the game.

"I still live with my parents," says Guy, "and that's difficult. They've been incredibly supportive, but they're on at you if things don't go well. They'll say: 'If you don't get through, what are you going to do then? What are you going to do next year? You can't keep living here.' And then there's the relationships off the course, like with your girlfriend. If there's very little money coming in, it puts a strain on a lot of areas of your life. You've got a lot of pressure on yourself."

The third-tier tournament professional basically has a low-paid job with high-cost expenses; it is a classic formula for disaster as the players often are blinded by the prospect of potential rewards one day in the far distance on the Main Tour. Many thousands of aspiring EuroPro players over the years will never taste the full PGA European Tour, but there are always exceptions. In 2006, Englishman Matthew Richardson topped the EuroPro money list and then went on to win his Tour Card at Final Stage of Q School. Guy knows that this year it could be him.

However, Guy needs to stop worrying about the practical problems involved in his tournament life, especially the money. A EuroPro tournament costs £275 to enter (by comparison, no one pays to enter European and Challenge Tours events because there is so much sponsorship and TV money) and, if travel and accommodation is added, then the costs can take some finding on a regular basis at this level where a few hundred pounds feels like ten thousand. "The big money in golf doesn't leak down to us; it's just like football. On EuroPro, you've got to finish top 15 to win any prize money at all and every week there's 156 guys and they can all play a bit. You might be able to dismiss a third of the field; to be fair, they're wasting their time, but all the rest could win."

By contrast, if a player simply makes the cut on the European Tour then he can still pocket decent money; at a prestigious event like the BMW Championship played at the glamorous Wentworth Club in Surrey this month, 70th place picked up almost €8,000.

Players at the EuroPro level cannot look too often at events like the BMW or it might crush their hard-won self-belief. Their major concern has to be winning the next tournament within their current ability range and they can only worry about the next level when they arrive there.

The EuroPro player has the same single-mindedness as any top tournament pro and he is prepared for sacrifices, but sometimes he also needs an alternative option for his life, a safety net. Guy denies himself many things, but is also smart enough to now be training to become a fully qualified PGA professional. This might lead him to become a club pro one day if his tour dream ends.

Both for money and for experience as a club pro, Guy works regularly at Stoke

Park Golf Club; any golf practice time for tournaments is on top of his many hours in the pro shop. "It's not the ideal option. I'm attached to Stoke Park, I pay a membership fee and they're very supportive to me. Members have been good, especially with sponsorships, but they want to see results."

Guy works about 30 hours a week in the pro shop – usually all day Sunday and Monday and then a few shifts that need covering during weekdays – and also has to find time for studying for the PGA course. He understands intellectually that committing to a fallback situation as a club pro is a slight undermining of his dream, but it is a pragmatic step.

"I want to play on the Main Tour so much that, subconsciously, you can go into the tournaments carrying this big burden. Maybe training to be a PGA pro means I've dropped some of the burden, but I still have to sacrifice a lot, I still can't make plans. All I know is that I could be a pro in three years earning a club pro's salary. I'm fed up of being broke basically."

Just avoiding being broke is a lot different from gathering in the riches on offer on the European Tour, but everyone has to start somewhere.

CHAPTER 7 – June 2007

Persistence & Pain

"Q School is a frightening experience, like a bright light panic. It's the kind of place where you want your mummy, but you can make some decent money if you get through and have five good years on Tour." – Richard Boxall, Tour winner and two-time Q School attendee.

By June each year, the European Tour has taken root again in its home continent; journeys to Asia, Africa and Australia are things of the past. This first month of summer marks the start of a huge run of big-money tournaments all in Europe and with the world's foremost golfers now all well into their schedules. These top dogs will be turning up at most of these summer events and expect to run off with most of the prize money. Meanwhile, at the journeyman end of the scale, this extra level of competition is another huge test. This is the height of the season when a player will either raise his game and fill his bank account or be pushed aside by the stiffer competition and fall down the money list. It's crunch time for the Tour's strugglers

The first June potential pay day for Main Tour golfers comes at the Wales Open at Celtic Manor near Newport, the venue of the Ryder Cup in 2010. While the actual Ryder Cup course itself is not quite ready for this year's event, a quality field turns up to play on one of the original 18 hole set-ups and almost all the current crop of top Welsh players are in the line-up. Sion Bebb is among the home hopefuls and by now his season is coming to a crossroads. Last month in Andalucia, he banked only his second cheque of the season after he scrambled into the weekend right on the bubble and finished tied 44th to land just over €5,000.

There was also another painful reminder of how cruel the European Tour can be. In Madrid at the end of April heavy rain caused huge delays. Sion started his first round a day late on Friday, finished at 3pm and had to be back on the tee for his second round 20 minutes later. His head was spinning after an opening 77, but he grabbed the early chance at redemption and by the 14th was four under for the round. Then darkness closed in and play was halted for the day. He knew he needed one more birdie to make the cut, but he had a whole night of wishing and wondering before a crack-of-dawn start. That single, desperate birdie never came despite good approach shots on the four remaining holes. However, there was still an outside chance that the field would under-perform and the cut would drift upwards. Sion waited the whole rest of the day for the other 155 players to finish round two; it was a cold and windy day, so his chances increased by the moment. In the end, it came down to the final group and if one of the three shot bogey on the last hole then Sion was in. Unfortunately for the Welshman, the bogey was avoided and he was on his way to the airport once more without any prize money. The casual golf fan is often not aware of such small-scale dramas, but they are the heartbreaking facts of life for a player in Sion's position.

The Welshman has missed eight cuts in his ten scheduled tournaments and lost more momentum because a re-ranking of the Q School and Challenge Tour graduates has now taken place. At the start of the season, Challenge Tour graduates are given Category 11a status with Q Schoolers at 11b. Halfway through the season the two groups of players are lumped into a single, new Category 11 based on their earnings since last November. For Sion, the complicated system has actually left him precisely in the same position as before – he was 14th in 11b Category behind 15 Challenge Tour players and now he is 29th in the newly aligned Category – but the point is that some players took the chance to move up the rankings and he did not.

Nevertheless, Sion is finding positives wherever he can and it is no time to give up on his first full season on Tour. The Wales Open had always been circled in his calendar as a chance to shine; after all, he knows the Celtic Manor course as well as anyone. Add in some local support from family and friends and this could be his turning point. That is certainly how his story begins.

In fact, on day one it seems like all the Welsh players are inspired, but none more so than Sion who is among the early starters. Being followed by a small but appreciative crowd, Sion is playing with authority. The hilly course is at his mercy and there is no prouder fan than his cousin Huw who takes a photo of the scoreboard after 12 holes because Sion is leading the tournament on 4 under. After several weeks at home practicing for this most crucial of weeks, the home field advantage seems to be working.

However, Sion duffs his tee shot on 13, hits a reasonable recovery only to find it plugged in a greenside bunker; a double bogey 6 knocks the wind out of his sails. Until then this was a very good round of golf, but an unlucky break so often happens to a golfer struggling for good form.

There is more scrappy play towards the end of the round as heavy rain starts to fall. A one under par score of 69 - one of Sion's best rounds of the year - is still a disappointment. Sion says he lost a little concentration and did not account for the slowness of the greens after some heavy rain. Afterwards there are TV, radio and print interviews to do and, with little Alys on his arm as the press circle him, Sion still looks confident.

But the next day, he needs to improve on his 69 because the whole field is enjoying a birdie-fest in Wales. Today he is among the later starters, so he will have a good idea of the cut mark. He begins with some solid pars, but his putter is stone cold; it seems the harder he tries, the less likely the putts are going to drop. Despite all the expectations, he shoots another 69 and finishes one shot off the cut mark. It is one of the most disappointing moments of Sion's recent career, especially as his season is now well past halfway and his chances of playing in the bigger tournaments are few and far between. He looks on disconsolately as other Welsh journeyman players like Kyron Sullivan and Liam Bond are interviewed by reporters because they did make the cut.

There is a small shaft of light when he travels to Austria the following week and plays all four rounds, finishing tied 33rd and earning over €10,000. But the cool facts of this small success cannot disguise that Sion is a long way off retaining his Card. After Austria he is 230th in the money list with just €16,852 from 12 events, this is close to disastrous on his finances because he has spent over double that amount in travel, accommodation and other tournament-related expenses.

Another small success in France the next week is also of little comfort. Sion ties for 26th place, his best finish of the year, but it is in the wrong tournament. The Open de St Omer takes place in Europe at the exact same time that the US Open is staged in America. The prize fund in France is comparatively tiny and a week of effort brings in only €4,600 for Sion and not even that much for the winner, Carl Suneson (€83,000) especially when in Oakmont, Pennsylvania, Angel Cabrera of Argentina pockets a cheque for €943,000 for first prize and even last place is worth over €12,000.

"When you get into a rut of not making cuts, you are not surprised when you miss them. You can't turn up at tournaments just thinking about not missing the cut, it is a bad mindset. I've felt I've hit the ball well but not been able to putt. During a 20-tournament season there are usually a couple of times when it all gels together, but that hasn't happened yet. Of course, it's a bit worrying," says Sion who is trying desperately not to think about another Q School. At the moment, he has to simply believe in his talent and persist until his entire game comes together for one profitable week.

At least he has been relatively injury-free so far. Sion is currently in rude health although earlier in the year he had a slight back injury brought on from wearing six-year-old orthotics that were supposed to be solving a case of flat feet. After a trip to an osteopath and a new set of orthotics, all is well. Strangely, if injury was behind the lack of form then Sion's situation might be easier to swallow. Right now, however, he has no excuses.

Injury is one of the tournament pro's greatest enemies, especially at this time of year with so much money to be won. It is to be expected that almost everyone is suffering from a twinge or two because the pro golf season is long and hard: playing, practicing, travelling and constant tension. But anything more than an occasional ache is not on anyone's agenda.

Guy Woodman is one young pro constantly aware of how injury can wreck his plans, as it did five years ago.

During a winter in South Africa on the Sunshine Tour 2002/03 he was playing some impressive golf. One top ten finish won him an unexpected place in the prestigious South African Open at Erinvale and he also teed it up at the Dimension Data at Sun City and the Tour Championship. Life was good and he returned to the UK full of confidence "I shot a course record in the first stage of the EuroPro Tour qualifying event in the spring and won it; I even finished sixth in my first tournament that year. The next week I flew to Portugal and that was when my back went."

Just like so many pros, Guy's back is his weak point. The golf swing is a very unnatural, repetitive motion; the turning causes stress and the back takes plenty of the strain. Although he had never suffered a serious injury before, Guy had a real problem.

"We were playing practice rounds in Portugal and I felt a little niggle. Tiger Woods was on the golf scene by now and I was doing some heavy weights to bulk myself up because that's what he was doing. I just wasn't working on my flexibility. The weather was cold and it was raining. I felt a twinge in my back and took some Nurofen. By the end of my round I didn't know if I could play the next day. I rested well, but I got up in the morning and it was still really hurting. So I took lots of painkillers and played the first three holes and suddenly I could hardly walk. I thought I'd be alright in a week, but it was never the case."

Guy's decision to turn to tablets to regain his sense of invincibility rather than seek immediate advice would prove a long-term and costly mistake.

"I had treatment for nine months seeing all these different people saying different things. One guy said I had to have my jaw broken and re-set. I had MRI scans that said I had two pro-lapsed discs. Someone put me in touch with a specialist in Harley Street who worked with lots of the players like Justin Rose and Retief Goosen. He was the first person to know what was going on. He gave me exercises. The way my pelvis was aligned with my vertebrae, they were opposing one another and putting pressure on my discs. So it was a lot of re-hab, re-alignment and icing to get rid of the swelling."

Guy's first attempt to return from the back problem failed and, in all, he missed two full summers of golf. In all that time, he earned no prize money, yet the cost of being a tournament pro was still evident in all the medical bills.

Guy is by no means alone with his injury woes. Most serious injuries do not completely disappear from the bodies of sportsmen and women who will do almost anything to prevent the problem flaring up again: bandages, body supports, warm-ups and warm-downs, gym work and, of course, painkilling drugs. Injury stories on Tour are as common as golfers on the driving range. The question is: will an injury end Guy's dream?

Now in his 40s, Phil Golding knows that an injury is probably his biggest potential problem as he tries to extend his career on Tour. This is the age when no player can afford a season of recovery from a something like a knee or shoulder surgery. Phil's relatively injury-free career has been a major factor in allowing his dogged persistence to keep returning him to the Tour via Q School so many times. This season's break from the Main Tour is about bad form not a bad back and Phil's past seven months have actually been more relaxing on his body than for many years. Although he is conscious of the stress of not earning any money on tour, he has still been able to enjoy an extended home life with his six-year-old son Lucas and wife Sally while staying healthy and fit at the same time.

"Nowadays, I always eat well and I do plenty of gym work; I'll work out four or five times a week. I make sure my diet is good, I do a lot of stretching; even on holiday I'll go for a run for half an hour. I'm the same weight as I've been for years – about 180lbs (82 kilogrammes). It's about making an effort. I've even been to see a biomechanics expert who gave me a routine just for myself. When you look at what the body does to hit a golf ball and the amount of balls you hit, then you will get problems with wrists and shoulders. The problem is being forced to play to try to keep making the money. You have to sometimes limit the practice or at least do less dynamic work, more on your short game."

Phil's recent fitness improvements came after years of good luck avoiding injuries. "I get a bad back now and again, but I've learned how to stretch it out. I had tennis elbow a few years ago and had to take a bit of time off. It was hard not being able to play and I even tried playing with a strapped arm. I feel I played too much golf a few seasons ago; it happens, though, especially when you're chasing results. The top players only play 20-25 times a year."

One reason injury has probably stayed out of Phil's life is that he came from a sporting family and was an accomplished multi-sportsman in his teens. He originally wanted to be a cricketer, but golf got in the way. He became a top Middlesex golfing amateur before turning pro in 1981 and qualified as a full PGA

Professional three years later. But £15 a week as an assistant pro selling chocolate bars and giving lessons to members was not Phil's dream; he wanted a life on the European Tour and went to Q School for the first time in 1983.

"People make a big deal out of me going to Q School so many times, but the first four or five years I should never have gone. I was an assistant pro and I wasn't good enough, but club members paid for me to go, so I kept trying. There were 50 Tour Cards available in those days and I was one of the youngest players there." It would be 1993 on his 10th Q School visit before Phil finally secured at Tour Card.

The prize funds on Tour at this time were still relatively modest by today's standards (the staggering upward spiral would only begin after a certain Mr T Woods came on the scene a couple of years later), but Phil was always driven by money. He still remembers searching for golf balls to play with as a youngster and, as an assistant pro, he would clean the toilets or wash cars to earn extra cash and then spend it playing tournaments.

"I was conscious of money then (1993), not having any to spend. Now every tour golfer has plenty of golf balls and shoes and the like. You get blazé about it after a while, spending £1,500-£2,000 a week on Tour."

Even when money was tight and there were crises of confidence, Phil kept aiming for the top. "I could've give up the game many times, but it's an addiction, it's a drug. Even when I got married, I was dedicated to my golf. Sally believed in me all the way through, but if she had not supported me then I would've chosen golf. Nowadays, I think what else would I do? I'm qualified to do a club professional's job and I'd never say never and getting a club job is not a bad life – teaching, a bit of playing, corporate stuff – but I wouldn't want to do it. I still have the drive to be a tournament pro."

Despite being close to the seniors end of the pro game, Phil will play on the Main Tour for as long as he can or is injury-free. The desire still burns. "Deep down, I'm pretty tough. You have to be in this game. The older pros say how they wish they'd carried on playing. But sometimes it's also a money issue – can you afford *not* to keep playing?"

Having a cut-back schedule this year – Phil will probably only play a dozen tournaments before Q School – actually makes him appreciate each limited chance. But it is also draining him mentally. He made his first European Tour cut in Spain in May finishing tied 40th and this month had back-to-back four round tournaments in France and Germany, but his best showing was tied 33rd. In eight events, he has won only €24,000 and is 220th on the money list. He has high hopes for his French Open invitation next month (as a former champion, the tournament organiser rolls out the red carpet), but it might be his last chance in 2007. Q School is looming large already.

At this point in the season, the continuing story of Andy Raitt and his injury is the personification of pain and persistence. To put things into perspective: try to imagine a concert pianist who attempts to play the hardest concertos in the uncomfortable knowledge that his little finger might, at any moment, hit a wrong note seemingly of its own volition.

Andy's problems were summed up by then the great Ben Hogan many decades ago when he wrote this: "You can't make the (golf ball) move unless you have the proper hold on the club. It's like steering an automobile. You don't steer to the right all the time, you also steer to the left. That ability has to come from the grip, which is the transformer through which the juice flows." Gripping the club is central to Andy's injury woes and Hogan's words are the kind of testimony he needed a couple of years ago to win his court case.

By the time of the BMW International in Germany at the end of this month, Andy has made only four cuts in 17 tournaments and is a lamentable 184th in the money list. Although he is putting a brave face on his season, his damaged finger is behind an almost total lack of form and there seems no light at the end of the tunnel.

The life of the golf pro can be a demoralising place – waiting around at airports, late night practice on the putting green, waking up alone in another hotel room in yet another country. There is often too much time for reflection, especially if you are missing cuts and flying home early every week. This is all true for Andy, but his torrid recent life delivers yet more potential problems. There is a threat of bankruptcy; his ex-mother-in-law still chases him for money; and his limited access to his young daughter is depressing him. If all this was not enough, Andy's life revolves around a physical solution to an injury that just will not go away. He will sit at a dinner table talking of how stabilising his hand, his wrist and his shoulder will help his golf swing while all the time unconsciously clenching and unclenching his fist almost as if hoping that the pain will suddenly disappear.

Andy's chances on Tour this year are being undermined by forces he cannot seem to control. Perhaps not surprisingly, there are now some dark thoughts floating around in the head of a man who is much more used to smiling.

"It's been the worst stretch of my career ever. No matter how bad I've played, I've never missed cuts like this. I knew it would be a tough year because I set out to go back to trying to release the club like I used to instead of playing steady crap. So my wild shots are really wild and I'm losing balls on a fairly regular basis. My good shots are better, though, and I'm getting more fun out of it even though I'm missing cuts." Andy's dilemma is that he can still play almost-decent golf by taking into account his injury, but he is determined to find a better way, a path to the golfer he believed he would become. It is not helping him that the Tour has moved on since his brief heyday.

"The competition is brutal. When I first got on the tour I made 16 or 17 cuts and a top 10 early on, but now it's difficult. It used to be the top 70 players who made the cut, but now it's only 65 and ties; I'm spending too much time just thinking about if I can make it to the weekend. You don't have to do much wrong to miss the cut now because they're all good players"

However, if he wants inspiration about what can be achieved despite injury, then there are plenty of stories littered throughout the golf world, even some from Q School. A classic is about English pro Jeremy Robinson who was diagnosed with arthritis at the base of his back in 1998, yet tried to play Q School that year.

"It was OK for the first couple of rounds," he remembers, "but then it flared up again towards the end. I had a feeling it was going to be a problem that I would struggle with just by playing four rounds, so six was obviously too much. It stiffened up."

Indeed, it did. However, Q School is a place where the extraordinary is possible and Jeremy was not going to let a whole year's work disappear without a fight. "If it had been an ordinary tournament then I'd've pulled out. It just happened that I kept having reasonable rounds and giving myself a chance to get my Card, so I kept coming back the next day. I was only able to hit about five shots on the practice range each morning to loosen up a bit and was going to the physio for a massage each day. I was also on plenty of painkillers. The main problem was not tee shots, they were fine; it was when I had a shot from a bad lie or out of the rough and had to go after it a bit, that was the worst. The pain was so bad that I even yelled out a couple of times. It was painful all the way around on the last day. I ended up using a 3-iron as a walking stick to ease some of the pressure off my back plus my caddie was picking the ball out of the hole."

Things got so bad that part of Jeremy's mind was telling him to shoot a bad round just so he could go home and stop the pain. "Each night I could hardly walk because my back stiffened up so badly. My memory of the whole week is just being in pain."

Still well in contention on day six of the Final Stage, Jeremy played the San Roque New Course starting at the 10th. He had been in one of the earlier groups, so coming to the last hole he had no real idea where he stood with regard to his Card. Jeremy thought a four was probably the minimum requirement, especially as he had just bogeyed the 8th. The strange thing was that he had been playing steadier golf than normal because of his injury. Jeremy knew his body was unable to allow him to force any shots, so he ended up hitting conservatively short tee shots and the vast majority were straight, so at least he was always hitting his second shots from the fairway. He knew that any shot out of the rough was placing his chances further at risk.

On his last hole, Jeremy was in no condition to reach the green in two and his 3rd shot was a short pitch to the green. After almost six rounds of pain and with the winning post in sight, he duffed the chip. However, luck was on his side and the ball settled 20ft from the hole, leaving him with a reasonable chance of par.

"By that stage, I'd had enough; I was really just thinking about getting finished and heading for home. Being bent over every putt was one of the more painful positions for me, so it was not easy to concentrate. I just tried to make sure I wasn't short of the hole."

Despite all that had happened, somehow Jeremy holed the putt and won his Tour Card; it would be the last one awarded that year. "I could literally hardly walk for days when I arrived home the next day after the flight. Of course, because I got my Card, I can look back now and say it was the right decision."

Jeremy did no permanent damage to his back at that Q School, but by 2002, four years later, his tournament career was over. Nowadays, he runs both a corporate golf events management company and his own driving range near Worcester in the Midlands. He fought through pain at Q School because of what a Tour Card meant to him. Right now, Andy is putting up the same kind of fight to maintain his career.

"The only way I've learned to cope with it is not to give a shit," Andy says. "Otherwise, a lot of the time I look at my hand, my career and my financial situation and I think that if I got hit by a bus then it wouldn't be the end of the world. Seriously, I walk around the golf course thinking about it a lot. Yes, it's dark, but it's a pretty hard thing to live with. You spend all your life trying to get better at this game, but you get worse and worse; then you're going to get some compensation for it, but you end up losing everything you have."

Has he changed? "I think the injury has affected me more than anything else. I'm trying to become more positive, but it's really hard. I got divorced a month after the court case was over. I was probably a difficult bloke to live with because I was in constant pain. We'd had problems and huge financial difficulties and I'd been out for nine months with shoulder surgery. The idea was that we survive until the court case was over. We thought we'd walk out with a load of money - the amount was academic - but it didn't pan out that way. Then my wife said enough's enough. As it turned out it helped losing the court case because if we'd walked out with four million quid then I can't imagine how difficult the divorce would've been. In fact, I walked out with a quarter of a million pound debt and it was still difficult to get rid of her."

So despite the flashes of darkness, Andy wants nothing more than to prove himself worthy of his place on Tour. At least these days he is surrounded by people who want to help - his girlfriend, Lindsay; a sponsor for the first time assisting him financially; and a good friend-cum-coach working on his swing. Andy has fought back so hard and with such determination that any independent observer would want him to succeed this year. But as summer reaches its height, Andy's place among the elite is starting to slip away.

CHAPTER 8 – July 2007

Winning and Worrying

"Winning is easier (than succeeding at Q School). If you're in with a chance to win then you know you're playing well, so you can let the pressure go a little. But if you're playing a six round tournament you can't afford to have a couple of bad days, so I'd say Q School was more stressful when you come down the stretch than winning a tournament." – Miles Tunnicliff, two-time Tour winner and 12-time Q School attendee.

American comedian Jerry Seinfeld once quipped that the New York Marathon was a pointless event to take part in. "It's a race with one winner and 30,000 losers!" Well, you could argue that many sporting events are the same, especially in individual sports like golf. Most pro tournaments gather a field of 156 players and only one wins; this is not good odds, yet every single player will hit that first tee shot either believing or hoping that it is their turn. That's because they know that winning changes everything.

The win can be a fleeting moment, a single peak in a career or a sign of long-term progress, a regular occurrence, a significant move up the golfing ladder. And, of course, the pro win may never happen at all. The majority of tournament professionals, of course, are winners on some level; early in their careers (even as amateurs), there will be club titles, county championships, regional trophies. There are likely to be strokeplay and matchplay victories, fourball events and even foursomes where they will rise to the top of the field. But at each new level of golf, winning becomes harder; this is particularly true once they gravitate to a tour.

To win on the two-round Jamega Tour in the UK or the Alps tour on continental Europe can help launch a career, but the biggest prize of all is a place on the full European Tour where the best of the best fight it out for millions of euros almost every week of the year. It is on the tour that a victory means the most.

Winning on the European Tour offers many things: a large trophy, heaps of prize money, lucrative endorsement deals, the admiration of your peers and an automatic ticket to lots more chances to win again at the highest level. Only about 2% of European Tour golfers actually win at this level, but there is still plenty of riches for those who are miss out on the titles. Take Roger Chapman of England. In over 500 tournaments on the Main Tour between 1982 and 2006, he won only once (in Brazil in 2000, beating Padraig Harrington in a playoff) yet he is still in the top 80 all-time career earners with over €3.3 million in prize money. A win on the full European Tour also provides a guaranteed Tour Card for the next two seasons and a Tour Card is a highly-prized possession.

One win as a pro - at whatever level - may be enough to clear a few doubts and guarantee a year or more in golf's worry-free zone. But the sport is cruel sometimes, even to those who succeed and one win may not be the whole answer. That is the perversity of golf – you win once, but the immediate requirement is to win again either to confirm your arrival at the new level of the pro pyramid or just to show yourself it was no fluke. Winning removes one pressure, but replaces it with another.

Guy Woodman left the amateur ranks seven years ago and started this season still waiting for a first win as a professional. It is not that he lacks talent, it is just that winning as a pro is not easy. Guy was regarded as a gifted junior and won trophies as a teenage amateur, however, becoming a golf pro was all that he ever wanted to do. The pressure would be enormous: the need for constant practice, the evening jobs to fund his tournaments, the stress from parents and girlfriends, the unrelenting talent and competition of his peers. For many young players, this lifestyle of living for tournaments is frustrating. For Guy, it was as necessary as breathing.

But chances for a first pro win have been rare. Guy's opening few EuroPro results this year have been mixed – a few missed cuts, a few pounds in the bank. Then in the fifth EuroPro tour event of the season at Collingtree Park in the Northamptonshire countryside of the English East Midlands, Guy makes a change to his normal tournament routine.

He took a friend to caddie for him at Collingtree. Brian Keely had gone to the Wales Open, but couldn't get a bag and Guy asked him to work for him instead. "I said I'd pay for his digs and 10% of my winnings. I thought the most I'd give away was a couple of hundred pounds. I'd missed the first two cuts by a shot this year and I wasn't in the best of form mentally. Brian knows a bit about the mental side of the game, so it was good. I thought just to make the cut and a top 15 would be progress."

After two rounds, Guy is in the mix, but so are at least a dozen other players. He will need something special to lift himself from the pack for the final round.

On the front 9 of the final 18 holes, Guy hits every green in regulation but two-putts each time; he feels that he has failed to make a significant putt all week. He turns to Brian for some advice. "I knew I was being over-analytical, but it was the same every week. I couldn't seem to make any putts. Brian told me to see the ball tracking into the hole, bring my eyes back to the ball and - still imagining it tracking in - hit the ball and see what happens." Guy tries the new technique with a 20ft putt up the hill – the ball goes straight in for a birdie. The next hole, a 30-footer also falls into the cup; and it happens again on the16th, he holes a 25ft putt.

By now, Guy is within a shot of the leader. But he bogeys 17 and takes a peak at the leaderboard. He thinks his chance has gone – one more hole and two behind. But the par 5 18th at Collingtree is a fabulous finishing hole and offers a death-or-glory opportunity. Seeing the scoreboard loosens Guy up and he decides to risk everything by going for the green in two shots.

"I was very nervous; tough par five – water down the left, trees down the right and an island green. But Brian again got hold of me and said: 'This is what you practice for, this is what we want. Let's do this.'"

Guy rips his drive down the middle of the fairway and uses a rescue club (a cross between a wood and an iron) for his tricky approach; it is 230 yards to the pin. "Deep down I didn't know if I had that shot in me. I'd looked up at the leaderboard and the leader had gone to 10 under; there was a logjam of people on 8 under with me. I thought I would go home with nothing if I didn't make it." In the end, the ball stops 25 feet from the pin and he rolls in the putt.

The two leading players in the last group – Russell Claydon and Adam Frayne – match Guy's 10 under mark, so there is to be a three-way playoff. Both Claydon and Frayne are more experienced (in fact, the roly-poly figure of Claydon was a regular on the European Tour a decade ago and even finished 20th in the 1997 Order of Merit), so Guy is not favourite and his feelings at being in the playoff are surprising. He had felt pure joy on the final green having pulled off such difficult shots under pressure. Moments later, however, it is a different story.

"On that 18th, I felt incredible elation, but then - and this is me all over - I was scared. I'd never won and when Adam and Russell were still out there also on 10 under, I was hoping one of them would either birdie the 18th or they'd both bogey it. I thought that if I got in the playoff I'd embarrass myself."

So, on the verge of his dream victory, the mind of a young pro plays the kind of tricks that happens to tens of thousands of amateurs. Luckily, this week Guy has some counsel. "If I'd been on my own, I'd've been a wreck. Brian and I went to the range and tried to play the playoff hole out, driver and then rescue club, picturing the shots each time."

The three men return to the 18th for sudden death and Guy gets lucky again; he draws the No 1 tee position, so he can focus fully on his own shot. Winning a playoff is not about how many shots, but about shooting one fewer than your opponents.

"It was only after getting the No 1 driving position that I got the feeling of Big Break; the people and the TV cameras, I felt at ease. I thought I'd got nothing to lose and hit driver." The TV programme had been Guy's first real exposure to high profile glory; he finished second in the series and during one round drained a 45ft putt to win a car for a year. Although there were no fans around to cheer him on, the thought of a TV audience of many millions was enough to infuse the whole event with a special kind of tension. Guy's understanding of that tension is now paying off.

The Big Break runner-up hits his driver straight and long; Adam and Russell take 3-woods and are 20 yards behind him. Adam is undecided about his second shot; he changes clubs to a 4-iron and this proves fatal to his chances as his ball falls short and into water. Russell makes the green in two, as does Guy, and they both score birdies. Adam's brave par after a penalty drop is not enough; Guy's chances of his first pro win just doubled.

Back to the 18th tee and Guy's drive finds the semi-rough; Russell, however, pulls his drive into the water hazard on the left. The door for a professional tour win is now wide open for Guy, but he must hit another perfect rescue club approach.

"I had a slightly smelly lie in the semi, so I still had to hit a good shot. I knew if I got on the green in two I would win. I stuck to the process, the same routine and made the swing."

Claydon failed to get even a par and Guy's victory was assured. Strangely, though, there would be no massive celebrations on the green.

"It was mixed emotions, actually. I had a one foot putt to tap in for the trophy; I knew then I was going to win and as I went to mark my ball I felt all these emotions welling up inside me; I thought I was going to cry. It suddenly hits you you're going to win because of all this hard work you've put in over the years. And I know it's only the EuroPro Tour, but any level now you have to play well to win and it was my first professional win. And when I knocked the ball in, it was weird; it was a huge relief to know that I could do it and beat some good players in a playoff. Now everyone could see that maybe I have got what it takes to move up to the next level. But, at the very end, it was like 'Is that it?'. I felt numb there was nothing there."

Guy shakes his head when he remembers the feelings. All that worrying about winning for the first time and he knows that one win is not enough. "That night I had to go to a wedding reception. I drove back home and my parents were in tears. Seven years just to win at this level – it's crazy really."

Despite the trophy and £10,000 in prize money, Guy is still heading for Q School this year. If he can finish in the top five of the EuroPro order of merit then he will go straight to Final Stage for the first time and also receive exemption status to play on the Challenge Tour next season; that is his new goal, but his mixed feelings after the win do not auger well for the rest of the season.

Some professionals do not have such a long wait for their first professional win. Ross McGowan is a case in point. Seven years? Try seven months.

Ross was still a very promising amateur when he faded out of Q School's Final Stage last November. He put the disappointment behind him, signed with Andrew 'Chubby' Chandler's ISM agency and was promptly sent off to the Sunshine Tour in Southern Africa for experience.

And it was good experience. Ross made cuts and made money; he began to learn the ropes of the constant travelling, new courses and week-to-week pressures of professional golf. He even got to the top of the leaderboard a couple of times. Back in the UK by February, the 25-year-old had a run of tournaments on the Challenge Tour lined up, definitely a step-up in class.

Again, Ross looked the part of a pro tournament player and, by the spring, he faced another test – two full European Tour events.

The prize purses at the Madeira and Estoril Opens are among the smallest on the European Tour, so the field was not exactly full of major champions. In Madeira, Ross shot an opening round 77 and went on to easily miss the cut, but the following week was a different story.

Two opening 68s caught the attention of his fellow pros and the media – he was leading and players with far more professional pedigree including Nick Dougherty were chasing him.

Gale force winds are notorious on the Quinta da Marinha course on Portugal's Atlantic coast. They blew even more fiercely in the third round than in the previous two and Ross suffered through a horrid front 9 of 40 shots. From there, he slowly slipped out of contention and finished the tournament tied 17th. However, this result actually gave Ross encouragement on returning to the Challenge Tour. His season's goal now was to finish in the top 20 Challenge Tour rankings at the end of the season to gain his Tour Card rather than attempt to achieve it via the Q School. To do so, he would need to win.

When Ross turned up in Manchester for the Oceânico Developments Pro-Am Challenge - a strange format where amateurs play alongside the pros in the final two rounds of the tournament – he was buzzing. During his second round, he had a stunning final 11 holes – six consecutive birdies giving him an astonishing 63.

Ross said that the birdie burst was down to patience, and every pro knows that a hot putter is often the key to winning. For Ross, the putts kept dropping and only a 64 by fellow Englishman Stuart Davis prevented him from leading going into the last round. On the final day, though, Ross held his nerve and again the putter was working well. Two 10ft birdie putts in his first two holes reduced Davis's three-shot lead and only Michael Lorenzo-Vera hung around the top of the leaderboard. Ross eventually beat the Frenchman in a playoff.

Ross felt relief to have proved to himself, his family and friends that winning the English Amateur title 12 months earlier was not his absolute career highpoint. In fact, one month later, Ross had a second Challenge Tour victory, it came on the same course as his near-miss on the Main Tour, Quinta da Marinha. This time Ross kept his form for all four rounds and won, almost at a canter, by three shots. Not relief this time, but a feeling of reassurance that he was now an accomplished young pro with a very bright future. Two victories had put him on top of the Challenge Tour rankings and Ross was already a shoe-in for a Tour Card. Winning does indeed change everything.

Yes, winning is great, but when is the next title coming? Phil Golding wishes he knew the answer to that question. By June 2003, Phil had been around the circuit long enough to know that golf can be a cruel game. He had just passed his 40th birthday and was playing in his 201st European Tour event, plus he had already survived 16 trips to the Q School. Then something magical happened. He won.

Phil had won as a professional before - on the Challenge Tour in the earlier part of his career – but this was different. The French Open is one of the larger events on the European Tour with 1st place prize money of around £300,000. It attracts a very strong field each year and former winners include Colin Montgomerie, Nick Faldo, Retief Goosen, Seve Ballesteros, Greg Norman and Jose Maria Olazabal.

Many thousands of pros never win on the Big Tour and Phil taking the French Open trophy was as welcome as it was unexpected; just a year earlier he had lost his Tour Card, finishing outside the top 115 at the end of the season. Now he suddenly had a two-year Tour exemption as a champion and Q School was a thing of the past.

However, the French Open win only came about after a brief moment when his persistence to succeed began to waiver at the end of 2002. Phil had to finish in the top 10 at the Italian Open, the last tournament of the season, to get his Card that year. He was out early in the last round, shot 63 and was indeed in the top 10. He was interviewed by Sky and everyone thought he had done enough. Then there was a burst of low-scoring late in the day and Phil ended up 12th. It would be Q School again.

"I was gutted. I wanted to finish right then, give up, but I spoke to a couple of players on the way home and they said that I couldn't not go to the School. I'd just shot a 63 and played well. Sally said I should do it. So I went there alone; carried my clubs in my lightweight, pencil bag; practiced on my own and then met a guy who wanted to caddie but who'd done only one other tournament. I trained him up in a day and we finished third."

From that moment, Phil had the kind of momentum that golfers dream about and the 2003 season was a huge improvement. He led a couple of tournaments over the next few months going into the final rounds and missed only four cuts in 16 events. Consistency is a much sought-after currency and Phil had some. Even so, he had no inkling that the French Open would be the tournament he would cherish for the rest of his life.

"I didn't think it was my week, I was quite tired, I'd been playing five or six weeks in a row, I'd had appalling practice, but found something on the range, something clicked. It was to do with my set up, about holding my right knee on the way back and firing it on the way through. I had fallen into a bad habit, I guess. Anyway, I hit the ball straight and shot 66 on the first day and was leading. All the papers said it wouldn't last. The guy from the Daily Mail wrote some naughty things about me, but I had a nice warm feeling that week. I was hitting the ball better and better. And I putted well and any player who's in contention for a pro tournament will have to putt well."

The first round 66 was one of his best ever on Tour, but by round two Thomas Bjorn and David Howell both came into contention. Phil kept his cool and another classy 68 - including a birdie on the last hole - put him into a one-shot lead with 18 holes to play.

The stories coming out of the pressroom talked of the widespread sense of déjà vu because the 2002 champion, Malcolm McKenzie, had won at the age of 40 after 20 years of trying. Phil's story seemed almost a carbon copy, if only he could hold on and do it.

On the Saturday night Phil slept fitfully but still felt good in the morning. During the final round, his good form held, but Phil was struggling to keep his emotions in check. "It was tough out there. Every time I thought of my family I got a bit emotional on the course. I knew how they would react to every birdie and I had to bring myself back to the present and remind myself to concentrate on every shot. It was the longest day of my life."

Phil kept checking the scoreboard to make sure he did not miss his chance. "I saw David (Howell) had made a birdie on the 18th so I knew I needed four to win." The par 5 18th at Le Golf National in Paris has plenty of frightening water, but Phil would not be denied. He hit the green in two, took his two putts and took the trophy much to the delight of himself and also his fellow pros.

The 20 years of work as a pro and the 16 visits to the Q School were never far away from his thoughts both during and after the battle for the trophy. He quipped after winning that his normal November routine was so well trodden that he might just have to go along to the next Q School to watch.

"After I won, I had to do a drug test; it's not normal on Tour, but French laws state you have to. I was so dehydrated I couldn't pass water for two or three hours and I missed my flight home. I got a later flight and then got picked up by a limo at City Airport and was finally back home at 10.30 at night. My whole family were outside the house banging on pots and pans; that was about the only celebration I had time for."

In fact, the joy of victory is often short-lived for professional golfers because as soon as they achieve one level of success there is another level waiting to be scaled.

"I did feel different the next week. But I actually felt more pressure. I felt like I had to do it again quickly. I put pressure on myself because it came almost out of the blue; you find yourself having to live up to your win."

The newly-discovered pressure destroyed Phil's post-French Open week. He spent the Monday after his victory talking to the press; flew to Dublin on Tuesday for the European Open where he enjoyed the congratulations of his peers; played in the pro-am on Wednesday (not part of his normal schedule because previous to his win, his status on the Tour was one of journeyman); and so, by the time he teed it up on Thursday for the start of the tournament alongside Tour superstars Padraig Harrington and Thomas Bjorn, his head was in a total spin. His first round score was a 7 over par 79.

"All my time was taken up [in the week of the European Open]. I should never have played there, but I had never won on Tour before and I didn't know how important it was to take time out to enjoy the win. I had no time to practice in Ireland and in my first round, I was in the water two or three times. I was really embarrassed."

Other players knew how he felt. Colin Montgomerie tried to soften the embarrassment for Phil by telling him how he shot 80 the first time after winning. Phil recognised his concentration was shocking that first day, but the real reason for his performance was that he did not feel he belonged with the other top players on Tour.

But the taste of victory remains. The pro golfer dreams of these winning moments and there is considerable pleasure to be had in recalling the memories that do not diminish over time. When Phil talks of the experience, he looks into the far distance and the listener senses the pictures in his mind. "You don't eat very much on the last day, you don't sleep very much the night before, but you can remember the whole week from start to finish - the noises, the atmosphere, what people say to you. It's amazing."

This month's French Open is perhaps Phil's best chance of avoiding another trip to Q School. Along with his fond memories, he brings coach Jason Banting with him to Paris and tries hard to play down the possibility of a repeat to all those who ask, even though it is what he wants most of all. He stays in the on-course hotel, is treated well as the past champion and plays the best he can. A 4 over par opening round leaves Phil too much to do, however, and he misses the cut by two shots.

The former French Open champion is downcast; this was his big chance and it blew up in his face. Phil had meant to use this week as a springboard, but Q School is now virtually inevitable. There are bound to be 30 players at Final Stage in better form than Phil, plus – despite his healthy regime – he is approaching the wrong end of his 40s, so the odds are stacking against him. This year's School will be his 18th visit and there has to come a time when enough is enough. It is going to be a long four months until November

At the end of the day, everyone remembers the winners, but in golf there are other ways to acknowledge excellent performances. James Conteh is still without a win in his four-year pro career, but a 7 under finish on a two-round Jamega Tour event this month for tied 6th is followed by an 8 under for tied 3rd a week later. These are his best showings of the year by far and give him some hope for First Stage of Q School that is now just over two months away.

July is also the month of the Open Championship and in 2007 it is staged at Carnoustie, one of the most feared courses on the major roster. James is among hundreds of pros from all over the world playing in the local qualifying rounds for the Open in the week before the tournament begins. Apart from gaining his Tour Card, to play in an Open Championship would be the next best thing for James.

In the two-round qualifier, James actually plays some of his best golf of the year and is never far from the leaders. But his chances are tiny: there were only three spots for the Open in Scotland and 100 players. Eventually, despite some hope on day two, James finishes 10th and misses out.

The casual observer might say that James is fooling himself to think he can make a tournament as prestigious as the Open. However, professional golf is full of young men who are one round away from the greatest achievement in their lives. "The margins are so small," says James, "and it's hard to pinpoint why one player is doing better than another. Most often it's on the greens. You can play almost identical tee-to-green golf with someone and they knock in a couple of putts and you don't. That's all it takes for them to be 2nd and for you to be 40th."

If a pro like James needs any sort of indication that anything is possible, then it comes in tournaments like the Open qualifiers. At a separate venue, another twentysomething English pro shoots 65 on the second day to finish joint top of his field. The young Lancashire lad has surprisingly qualified for Carnousite against far more experienced players.

Steven Parry is the pro in question who achieved one of his life-long dreams; this is the same Steven Parry who played with James in the first two rounds of First Stage of Q School last September at The Oxfordshire. Steven did not even make the three-round cut in that tournament, yet 10 months later he is playing in the Open and James is not.

As it turns out, the toughness of the Scottish links and the atmosphere of a major championship are too much for Steven; he fails to make the cut, finishes tied 138th but takes home nearly €4,000 for his trouble. James and thousands of other mini tour pros wish they could have swapped places with Steven. For James, the fact that a counterpart whom he believes is no more talented than him has played in the Open is another indication that his dream of a Tour Card is not so far-fetched as some people might make out.

CHAPTER 9 – August 2007

Seeing The Future Now

"Q School is horrible. I was very inexperienced in the early ones and had I made my Card in the first stab, it would probably have been a mistake." – Ian Poulter, multiple Tour winner, Ryder Cup player and four-time Q Schooler.

The end of the European Tour season seems to arrive very quickly for some players, especially those journeymen with limited opportunities. The summer boasts lots of high profile tournaments and, by now, the likes of Andy Raitt and Sion Bebb would have planned to be progressing high up the Order of Merit. Between the Wales Open which opened June and the Johnnie Walker Championship at Gleneagles in Scotland that sees off August, both players would have 10 tournaments to play in – a decided luxury after the uncertainty of the early season. The courses or conditions are reassuringly European and if good form is ever to return then it will most likely be in this period of the season.

But the counter to all this positive thinking is that the tournament fields at these height-of-summer events are definitely the most competitive. In addition, all the other journeymen in just the same situation as Andy and Sion will be trying their hearts out as well. And once the summer ends then only a handful of further chances come the way of players at the lower end of the money list.

Of the two men, Andy is the one suffering the most heartache – June was a disaster and two more tournaments in July brought no money. This month he first goes to Sweden and Holland, but still no luck and by the time he comes to Gleneagles, Andy is very despondent. Even though there is a natural cheerfulness about Andy that seems to portray continual hope, there is also an intense, internal exasperation at his situation. His fortunes are still linked inevitably to his finger injury and, despite all his efforts, it still dominates his conversation.

"The other guys on Tour are all bored with it (the injury). I don't like talking about it and I never used to, but when I went to court they said 'Why don't we hear about this injury? You don't you complain about it'. But if I had played well and went on talking about the injury then I'd've sounded like a prat. I guess I played this thing all wrong. It's funny because my ex-mother-in-law sent text messages about being so proud and invited me over for dinner when I got through Q School. The next thing she's threatening to sue me for money.

"I genuinely don't think anyone else would be doing this (playing on Tour) if it had happened to them. If it happened to Monty or Darren (Clarke) or someone like that right now then they'd just quit. Having been as good as they were, they'd never be that good again, ever; so they'd just stop. I don't consider my life like anyone else's on Tour because they're playing their own game and I'm playing whatever game I can salvage. So I'm on a mission now because I want to win a tournament to prove to the people who made it turn out this way that they can't do it to anyone else."

Andy admits he is a work in progress. He is spending the season trying to recover the type of game he played before his injury; it means that his game is much more inconsistent. When he first started playing after the finger healed, he coped by changing his swing, but now he wants his old swing back and although his determination is strong, the good results are slow in coming.

"My hand and shoulder and all the new muscles stiffen up when it gets cold. It is getting better; my arm is stronger and my body's getting better. But it's all about building up those new muscles. You can see that I struggle because I've got completely different calluses than everyone else on the Tour (he has them on the lower third of his left little finger rather than the top of his palm). The hand does function better and I think in six months it will be better still. Before the surgery I could only play the one shot, basically a pull hook. I would aim right and pull it back to target and my misses were smaller than they are now. By trying to get back to how I used to play and have more than one choice of shot, I'm paying the price because my misses are a joke, so far right or left it's hard to comprehend. I used to be so straight and steady."

Thoughts of retiring from tournament golf or even leaving golf altogether are creeping into Andy's mind. "I never get away from my hand; my life is about trying to get my hand and arm and shoulder decent. If it doesn't feel alright at the end of this year then it's time to make a decision about whether I carry on or just quietly go away and do something else, not be a tournament pro. Part of me wants to leave golf alone altogether, but I'm not qualified to do anything else, it's what I do. Maybe I'd be stupid to walk away."

When a Tour player suffers a significant loss of form, his counterparts are never quite sure what to say. No one is ignored on Tour and there is a family feel about the place, especially on practice days when players are in a hail-fellow-well-met kind of mood on the range. There are congratulations for last week's winners or good performers; family or friends to introduce; Tour gossip to mull over; and the press hangs around waiting for interviews. This pleasant buzz of activity does not usually allow for too many dark reflections; out-of-form players are likely to keep their thoughts to themselves. Players have been trained to find positives in every situation; they want to mix with people on Tour who will bring sunny optimism rather than dampening rain to a conversation.

Andy and all those players struggling are never shunned, but everyone is ultimately responsible for his own welfare and there is only so much whining anyone can take. Andy has tried to be as chirpy as possible and is finding new ways to keep his own chin up.

"I've been driving a lot to tournaments. I went to Madrid and to Italy, then I drove home. I drove to Hamburg instead of flying. I stick on some music and get some alone-time, it's trying to get my head around it all. And I enjoy the craic. Last week (at the KLM Open in Holland) I came within an inch of winning a BMW M6 convertible car with a hole in one. We were all saying 'This would be a good one to hole!' and I nearly did; it was on the 17th and I was within an inch. I saw all my debts disappearing in one shot. I wouldn't care if I kept the car or not, it'd just be nice to have some cash."

There is also plenty of support from his family and girlfriend Lindsay. "She has been so fantastic. I don't know how I'd've managed this without her. I used to have a wife who did nothing but take, but now I have a girl who gives me her full support. My parents have been supportive too, even though my mum feels horribly guilty because she told me to take the dog for a walk that day the incident happened. They've been great and I don't think they'd like me to give up. They know I've wallowed a little bit in my head, but I try to make each week better."

At Gleneagles, despite help from his friend, coach and caddie Paul Thornley, Andy misses another cut and becomes resigned to going back to Q School; he will have to start at Second Stage.

"I really thought I was going to play better than this at the start of the season. I thought it would be the first year I'd have a chance to finish top 60 or 70, play steadily better rather than this. Some of it has got better; I've had more days at practice when I can put my hand up and say I'm striking it better, but I'm finding it difficult to take it onto the golf course. I'm more liable to have a good week, but I'm just not giving myself enough of a chance. Considering what I have been through, struggling out here doesn't phase me compared to walking out of a court room a quarter of million pounds in debt for having your finger bitten off."

There is another man who is unhappy this month; it is Sion Bebb. His first season as a regular Main Tour professional is so far, at best, disappointing, or at worst, a disaster. As he tees up at the Johnnie Walker Championship at Gleneagles, Sion has made only six cuts and missed 15; he is 227th on the Order of Merit and has won just under £20,000. He is a worried man because he might be frozen out of tournaments for the rest of the season due to his ranking.

"This (Gleneagles) could be my last tournament because there are shortened fields from now on. I'm 18th reserve for next week (European Masters) whereas normally I'd easily be in the field. I might have to play some Challenge Tour events; it's something I've had to look at. If I don't get in next week, then I'll play in the Welsh Pros which I won the last two years, so who knows. I could have a good week in Cardiff and few good Challenge Tour events and change my season around."

But although Sion speaks with sincerity, there is a lack of complete confidence behind the words. He knows that time is running out for him and that money is now a major issue when it comes to deciding his next step, to such an extent that he has even considered not returning to Q School in November if it should come to it.

"The money has almost run out and I am having serious thoughts about whether to go back to Q School yet again – the cost, the potential disappointment, the upheaval for the family and even if I got through, the fact that this year on the Tour has been frustrating, costly and with very little reward. I could have earned a lot of money just staying at home this year, but you have the opportunity and you have to give it a shot. Some players are not playing on the Main Tour because they are not earning any money. Guys who came through the Q School with me last November like Julian Foret and Matt Richardson are concentrating on Challenge Tour. I could do the same and still maybe get into the top 45 there (which means a direct route to Final Stage). Right now, it looks like I'll got to Second Stage, but I've also looked at not going. It'd cost me three grand to go and we could do with that at home through the winter rather than following the dream. Rita wants me to do it, but if I'm at home next month and we're struggling to get by, then we have to make the serious decision about whether I go through with it. We're dipping into savings; it's something we don't want to do. We have only so much left and when that goes through we don't know what happens next. I don't want Rita to go back to work. With what she was forking out on crèche fees for our first child, it wasn't worth it."

With a 20-event schedule on the Main Tour, a professional can easily get through up to £40,000 and with Sion's earnings being less than half of that, then it is easy to see how the pressure starts to build for players at the wrong end of the money list. The locker rooms are full of the ghosts of players past who had the briefest of lives on tour and lost a fortune in the process; for some it is just not meant to be.

At Gleneagles, Sion has Rita with him and both his daughters. It is the family's first real holiday together of the year and it is doing Sion a power of good. Rita is in charge of the couple's two girls over the practice days, but Sion still finds time to ferry them from the range to their hotel and back. For six-year-old Alys, Daddy already has plenty of trophies at home so she does not seem to mind what is happening to his career; she is just excited to be the centre of attention in the players' lounge and among the caddies. Her mood rubs off on Sion who is noticeably more relaxed although the lack of success this season never goes away. While Sion is hitting golf balls, Rita and the children meet up with other players' families in the lounges and the contrast between those who know their futures and those who don't is almost palpable.

"I should have my Card in my back pocket by now," says Sion. "We're talking with friends here who have done well and it's difficult, they're all excited about where they're playing next year and I've no idea what I'm doing. I might need to get another job to supplement my income again. It's just frustrating. I should be doing better because there's more money out there to win and I'm not playing well."

The search for the change in form never goes away. For Sion – like so many players – it is a matter of lining up all the best parts of his game at the same time. He has been hitting consistent drives and approach shots, but his scrambling around the greens and his putting has been sub-standard. There is much truth in the average pro's claims that a good short game will win the most money.

Sion knows what is required, but seems powerless when it comes to finding the answer. "I've been hitting the ball well all season; last two weeks, I've played poorly and putted well. Normally, there are a couple of weeks when both come together, but this season it hasn't happened. It's been one or the other and it's not all gelled together which is quite worrying. You never know when you're going to play well and when your luck changes; you have to grind it out until that happens. It's a little bit of confidence that you need. I was looking for something in my swing this week that would click and, in the last six holes of practice, I felt it and I birdied 16, 17 and 18. I need a good start and something to hang on to rather than being a few over par in the opening round."

For once, Sion gets the good start he is looking for; perhaps it is a mixture of a course that he enjoys plus his family's close proximity and inspiration. He opens with three birdies in his first seven holes; it is the start of the "good week" that he has been waiting for. He ends day one with a 2 under par 71 and goes on to make the cut easily. A little slip in round three (a 74) is overcome on the final day with another 71 and a 4 under par finish for tied 26th and the biggest cheque of the season and, indeed, his whole professional career – £12,880. It is a shot in the arm and lifts him to 209th in the money list. But the best news comes after the fourth round is over – Sion has actually gained entry into the European Masters in Switzerland the following week. He has suddenly found a bit of form and now his luck has changed in terms of getting another start. Is this the beginning of something?

Four days later – now in early September – Sion gets to Crans Montana with a new confidence and also a new caddie. Gary Marshall is normally the bag man for respected French pro and three-time Tour winner Jean-Francois Remesy, but he has a free week and the Scotsman teams up with Sion for the first time. Gary is an experienced caddie – something Sion has not always been able to afford – and knows the Swiss course very well.

In round one, it seems at first like business as usual for the Welshman; he has a couple of early bogeys. But then he battles back to manage to a level par 71 scoreline; the difference Gary makes is evident from the very beginning. On the opening hole – a par 5 – the ideal landing spot for the tee shot is about 250 metres from the green and Sion normally hits his 3-wood. However, Gary is aware of how a golf ball reacts on a mountain course with 5,000ft elevation and advises a 5-iron instead. The result is a tee shot that lands in position 'A'. "Who knows where I would have ended up with the 3-wood," reports Sion afterwards. For the first time, Sion has a caddie he can rely on. Gary is working out the next shot while Sion is still concentrating on the current one. It sounds so obvious, but Sion is now piloting his game with an excellent navigator beside him.

On day two, the new team gets to work on some early birdies and shoots 3 under so Sion has made the cut by a good margin two weeks running. Not only that, he is handily placed for a change; although the leaders are at 11 under, Sion is teeing off his third round just six groups behind.

Then it happens, what Sion has been hoping for all season. Finally, his whole game – from driving to putting – sparkles. Three birdies on the front 9 are followed by three more plus an eagle on the back – Sion has just shot a bogey-free 8 under par 63, the best round of the week, and has soared into contention on 11 under for the tournament. Today, every fairway seemed enormous and the holes were buckets. It is the first time he has ever made such a mark on a European Tour event; he has broken 70 only seven times in 20 tournaments up to now in 2007.

Sion is playing his kind of game – plotting his way around a difficult course by hitting the middle of fairways and the centres of greens. He is also finally holing his share of putts and goes into the last day with a chance of winning a Main Tour event for the first time, playing in the penultimate threeball with Lee Westwood and Gonzalo Fernandez-Castaño.

Such heady heights can throw many pros, but Sion feels comfortable and grabs the challenge with both hands. His start is a little nervous with two birdies alternating with two bogeys in the opening for holes, but another two birdies have him 2 under for the round at the turn and he is still in contention.

England's Philip Archer and Brett Rumford of Australia are charging and are four shots ahead; Sion needs to match them and hope for some slip-ups. He had shot 5 under on the back 9 just 24 hours before, but as so often happens, today is different; it is a day when pars are a good score. Sion does birdie the par 5 15th to reach 14 under for the week, but Archer and Rumford are too far ahead.

Sion could see what was happening and, with a couple of holes left, he opted for absolute safety and a high finish rather than risk almost impossible birdies. Sion finishes with a 4 under par 68 and the biggest pay cheque of his life. The €100,000 (£67,000) in winnings puts Sion's finances back into the black and a top 10 finish also means an unexpected place in the following week's Tour event at The Belfry. Plus he wins an expensive Omega watch for the best round of the week. But Sion is still a long way from winning a Tour Card; he has moved up to 145 in the money list and will still have to attend Q School Second Stage if he cannot make further progress.

Perhaps most importantly of all, however, Sion has proved to himself that he has the game for the Main Tour and now just needs more opportunities. Nevertheless, Sion's talent for under-stated humour keeps a solitary 4th place in perspective: he claims that he finally has some cash to fix his family's washing machine. Real celebrations will have to wait.

While Sion Bebb is getting last-minute opportunities to turn his season around, Euan Little is left waiting. Since May, he has played only twice on the Main Tour – in Austria (tied 14th and €14,000) and France (the Open de Saint-Omer, a missed cut) plus a Challenge Tour event in Switzerland where he tied 14th and took home €2,000.

Now his opportunities to tune up for Second Stage of Q School are running out fast. He plays in the Russian Open this month, but this tournament has one of the smallest prize funds on Tour and, although he manages another cut and finishes tied 44th, he earns just over €8,000. Then a Challenge Tour event in Scotland is a flop – he misses the cut. Finally, he comes to Gleneagles for the end-of-the-month Johnnie Walker Championship, the same tournament that Sion Bebb and Andy Raitt will play in.

Euan is first reserve with two days to go, so the chances are he will get a spot. He visits the driving range each day where Bob Torrance casts an eye over his swing; he chats to fellow players and caddies; he waits for an official to tell him he is in the tournament. Euan feels good with his game; he likes the Gleneagles course and is primed for a good event. But despite some talk on the range of niggling injuries and the impending birth of fellow pro Sam Little's baby, no one drops out this week and Euan returns to his home in Glasgow disappointed. His tour golf may well be over now for the year.

Strangely, Euan is calm about the lack of play. He has started only 15 tournaments so far this year, but his stroke average for the Main Tour events ranks him in the top 20, a statistic that gives him real hope. He has made six out of eight cuts on the Main Tour and played only one really poor tournament – the 9 over for two rounds at the Open de Saint Omer in June. The limited number of tournaments has the benefit for Euan that he can spend more time with Bob Torrance. He also wants to be hungry at each tournament rather than bored by travelling to endless Challenge Tour events that fail to motivate him. His previous lack of a strong work ethic is well behind him.

"Bob shows great belief in me and I'm starting to believe a little more in myself each week. It's taken a lot longer than I thought it was going to. I was tipped to be quite successful by him and because of that I didn't work hard enough. Nowadays, he's never totally happy with my work rate, but he's definitely more pleased to see that it is increasing."

With so few opportunities ahead, Euan is playing a waiting game. "I've spent over half my life waiting; I'm waiting right now for Q School and maybe a planned schedule and some stability that would come with a Card. It would be great, in an ideal world, to have a wife and kids and be financially sound and playing regularly on Tour, but that will have to wait too. Until then, it's work, work, work on the golf."

Euan has been working towards Q School since March. "I'm going to tournaments and trying to do well, but the School is always my long-term goal. If I don't get my Card, then I'd have to find golf somewhere around the world; there's Canada or America, but the European Tour Card is the one goal, the only thing on my mind. Getting it is the hard part, but the dream is to keep it. It's all about the mental side, but it's taken me a long time to see that. I'm not frightened of Q School because the Main Tour is where I think I should be."

Someone with his mind a long way from the Tour right now is Martyn Thompson. He has spent the summer going about his job as club pro at Parkstone with very little thought of anything else. As recently as six months ago, Martyn made a commitment to make Q School the centre of his world, but that pledge has been shelved most of the time because he feeds his family as club pro not a tournament pro. Nevertheless, he has still found some moments during the year to hone his game for First Stage.

Martyn spent £800 to see one of Europe's most renowned putting coaches, Paul Hurrion, with the hope of solving the mystery of why so many crucial middle distance putts stay above ground. Putting remains Martyn's self-confessed weakness and, although most casual observers would grade him quite high as a putter, his brain does not believe this. He looks at his grip, the ball position, the takeaway of the club and the follow through – he hopes something will provide a breakthrough. He spends a considerable amount of money with Paul, but all he seemed to learn was that his core muscles were not strong enough. Although Martyn could see the sense in that, it was a bit of a disappointment; he really wanted the solution to be something more immediate, something like a change of technique or a simple tip about his hand position or his alignment.

While his club job and his family take up plenty of time, Martyn still has a determination to get that Tour Card; however, he sometimes manages to disguise that determination very well. For instance, Martyn has left the Q School application form on his desk for months without posting it; something is getting in the way, it is the last piece in his mental jigsaw. Martyn needs the full backing of his whole family, most especially his wife, in order to go to First Stage with his mind and conscience clear. He is always aware that success at Q School – however much it would be against the odds – could change his family life immeasurably and even risk their security. At the start of August, Martyn still felt that there was a key conversation to be had with Sally.

"The whole family went off to Majorca for two weeks and I printed off the Q School forms and signed them before we went. I left them ready to go, but wanted to talk to Sally about it while we were on holiday. We were having dinner one night with a couple of friends who said I should go and Sally was hearing all this talk about how good a player I am. She said I should go although I've still got to think about all the other things going on in my life. We sat down afterwards and I said she couldn't stop me going, but I wanted to know that I had her support. Finally, she said 'yes'. So I called the pro shop and told them to send off the forms. At a pro-am after the holiday, I played really well and Sally joined me on the back nine; I made six birdies. She said that seeing me play good golf made her understand why I wanted to go. Sally sees the bigger picture. She knows that I don't really like being away from home these days, but here I am entering a tournament that could take me away from home a lot. She just asks why am I doing it; success would be a double-edged sword. I like playing competitive golf, but I would miss my family, for sure. It's always been my dream to be out on the European Tour and the dream's not out of me yet."

Martyn's journey to Q School is definitely a contorted one. He has spent all year so far placing things in his way, yet somehow he is determined to try. He almost wants to succeed despite his club pro's job, not because of it. At Q School, he will probably have played less competitive golf than any pro pegging it up, yet he believes that fairy tales do happen. Martyn is neither intimidated by the challenge nor in awe of his rivals; he is along for the ride to the Tour and, once he gets there, he will want it to last as long as possible.

– September 2007

First Stage Q School

"It is a war! You have to go into to it thinking that you are in a battle because you have to fight to get the Card" – Benoit Teilleria of France after just four successful visits to 13 Q Schools

The six tournaments that make up the First Stage of Q School are probably among the weirdest in any golfing year; they are spread over two separate weeks in early and mid-September, three at a time. On the face of it, they look like any other golf tournament: fields of over 100 players; professional PGA tournament operation in charge; top quality courses; and a high level of intensity among the players determined to succeed. But if you try to compare Q School First Stage directly with tournaments on the Main Tour then the differences are stark. Q School events involve almost no crowds instead of thousands of fans who watch Monty and friends every week; the Q School prize funds are a few thousand pounds compared to the millions fought for by Padraig et al; and there is an air of nervousness that inhabits almost all Q Schoolers whereas Sergio and his colleagues ooze confidence. But perhaps the biggest difference is the cast of golfing characters that turn up at First Stage – some would shock even the most experienced tournament watcher.

First Stage of Q School is where a few seasoned pros meet the aspiring teenage amateurs; where the fortysomething, long-time underachievers take on the slim-hipped, hair-gelled generation. You almost expect to see golf's equivalent of the old comic strip character Alf Tupper, someone who slept in his car overnight at the golf course, is forced to use borrowed clubs because his were stolen and who goes on to win the tournament with an improbable 80-yard chip-in after six birdies in a row. This is not the Main Tour's weekly circus where the players, caddies, mind gurus, officials, agents and the rest put on another show for fans in another country. This is Q School where the tiny tournament office can be stuck in the old trolley shed; where the players search alone for their stray shots into deep rough; and where golfers of different colours, creeds, hopes and fears meet at an annual crossroads in their careers.

In 2007, the cast list at First Stage included Europe's latest potential superstar golfer, a teenager who might one day be a genuine threat to Tiger Woods; over half the defeated GB and Ireland Walker Cup team; and national and regional champion golfers from more than 40 different countries as exotic and far away from Europe as Paraguay, Algeria, New Zealand, Canada, Kenya and the Bahamas. These golfers might not hold the greatest titles in the world, but they have all been winners at some level of the game and this is their best shot at the big time.

Dig a little deeper and the back stories of some players are more worthy of fiction than fact – a Romany gypsy who was also a former London champion boxer and bare knuckle fighter; the English teaching pro based in Spain who uses the tournament as an excuse to visit his mother in Lancashire; and the club pros who are giving Q School one last chance before they let their dream die. First Stage of Q School is definitely not your conventional golf event.

Perhaps the most obvious example of the craziness at First Stage is the money. Entry to the whole Q School experience is a cool £1,200, an amount that reflects the length and nature of the entire event that spans three stages, 14 rounds and five countries. Of those the near-700 who pay the money at First Stage, only round 200 (under 30%) will progress to Second Stage.

Of the near 500 who fall at First Stage, around half will leave the tournament after just three rounds. This is truly the nightmare scenario – £1,200 for 54 holes of golf. It adds up to a lot of money spent on bad golf, but it is the nature of Q School.

No-one enters Q School to make a profit; it is about the dream. A First Stage winner receives £1,500, second gets £1,000 and third £700 down to £100 for seventh place, not even enough for a round of celebratory drinks. Q School is about the possibility of jam tomorrow, not today.

Mix all the players together in the six tournaments over four different European countries and there are countless stories of derring-do, triumph over adversity, abject failure, car-crash-type collapses and sheer bad luck. And, make no mistake, there will be golf of an incredibly high quality as well because these men are all good players on their day. Plus, a very small handful of First Stage players will succeed and win themselves a Tour Card. But at this stage it is almost impossible to pick them out of the crowd of golfing supplicants.

The Oxfordshire

The one totally outstanding player at the 2007 European Tour Q School is playing at The Oxfordshire less than a week after starring in the Walker Cup. Described as the best player to turn pro in Europe in the last 10 years, Rory McIlroy is the Northern Irish teenage amateur who won the Silver Medal at the 136th Open in July at Carnoustie. The fact that his first round score was better than Tiger Woods' pleased both the headline writers and the public. American Ryder Cup player Scott Verplank's comment was perhaps the most apt: "He's a fine player. He's 18, looks 14 and plays like a 28-year-old."

Rory's talent has been obvious for many years to those following European amateur golf. He is one of several dozen amateur golfers testing themselves at Q School. It is rare but not impossible for an amateur to sail through the three stages and win a Tour Card – Rory's Walker Cup predecessor Oliver Fisher achieved the feat last year and immediately turned professional so he could join the Tour. The difference between the very best amateurs at this year's Q School and the returning professionals is mostly experience. Amateurs feast on lots of matchplay, fourball and foursome events and not just a steady diet of strokeplay that is the week-by-week tournament format of the professional game. Amateurs also rarely play four consecutive strokeplay rounds and so Q School is both an examination of their game in comparison to that of the pros as well as a test of technique and concentration. Whereas a top amateur can go low just like a top professional with a burst of outrageous shot-making or a white-hot putter, the pro will most likely manage his game better and for longer, limiting risk and often using a short game that saves seemingly impossible situations. Over a four round strokeplay tournament, the amateur's occasional inspiration is rarely going to defeat the pro's rock-solid consistency. The difference could be only one or two shots per round, but that is all the difference there sometimes is between a golf champion and a player who misses the cut.

Rory is expected to make the amateur-to-pro transition with ease. His swing is silky smooth and his confidence sky high; top pros like fellow Northern Irishman Darren Clarke have long predicted the brightest of futures for him. Still technically an amateur at this event, Rory's pro career is mapped out because he has agreed to join the likes of Clarke and Lee Westwood at International Sports Management (ISM) and will turn professional next week at the Quinn British Masters at The Belfry, a tournament promoted by ISM which wants to manage the anticipated media hullabaloo for the benefit of the Tour event and its sponsors. In fact, ISM is already lining up Main Tour invitations for Rory over the next few weeks while, at the same time, guiding him through Q School.

Rory attracts the eyes of many of his rivals at First Stage because they know he is a superstar in waiting and is a hot favourite to glide through all three Q School stages. There is another advantage for Rory at this event: he has a Tour-hardened caddie on his bag in Gordon Faulkner, another friend to ISM, whose thoughtful experience balances the 18-year-old's youthful impetuosity.

Rory's idiosyncratic gait as he approaches the first tee reminds you of Padraig Harrington and there are actually a dozen or so pros who leave the practice putting green to watch his opening drive of the tournament – an honour not bestowed on any other player here. Rory is that good. He is also very calm about what lies ahead in Q School and an opening round of 2 under par 70 is perfunctory. "I didn't feel any nerves really, I just kind of cruised. I want to get through, move on and concentrate on my European Tour invite events. I'm not trying to put too much pressure on myself, but it's definitely different than the Walker Cup. It's like playing in a library here."

The library-type atmosphere might not be to Rory's liking, but the weather is. It is roasting hot and The Oxfordshire is also unseasonably calm, the usual high winds that keep low scoring in check are missing. Add in the fact that this course probably has the strongest of the three fields in the first week along with the largest field at 108 players, and par golf will clearly not be good enough this week.

After a 67 in round two Rory – along with friend and fellow Walker Cup star Lloyd Saltman, a tall, chatterbox Scot – is coasting towards a place in the top 29 which means a trip to Second Stage. But Walker Cup golf is no guarantee in the pro ranks, as Llewellyn Matthews, their teammate of a week ago, finds out. In his opening round, the notorious par 3 5th – a 202yd tee shot almost entirely over water – suckers the young Welshman and he takes a horrible 9. Amazingly, he plays the other 17 holes in one under par, but a 77 means his adrenaline is turning to tiredness. He improves to a 73 the next day and after 36 holes Llewellyn finds himself, ironically, nine shots off a place in the top 29.

By contrast, James Conteh has had nothing like a Walker Cup to hone his swing. He travels to The Oxfordshire from his parents' home each morning rather than his own because mum Veronica is both driving him to the tournament and acting as his caddie. Ideally, James would stay in a local hotel and hire a professional caddie, but there are financial considerations; his golf earnings this year consist of a few thousand pounds from EuroPro or Jamega Tour event winnings plus as much again in sponsorship. James is one of many pros at First Stage who have to watch each pound that they spend.

There has been no indication that 2007 will be James's breakthrough year at Q School, but he hopes the heat of battle will unlock his best game. He knows it will happen to someone, so why not him? His opening few holes on the first day will be crucial.

James is understandably a little nervous; he wants to settle into a rhythm and remember the good things about The Oxfordshire from last year when he made it through to Second Stage. On the opening hole, he has a birdie chance, but misses it and then hits a reasonable tee shot on the par 3 second to within 30ft. This should be another regulation par, but James's major worry prior to this week has been his putting; he fails to lag the first putt close enough and the second slides past. A three-putt bogey is careless and a confidence destroyer.

Immediately the thought comes into James's head of how a potential 1 under score has already somehow turned into 1 over after just two holes. James is clearly not tournament-hardened; he has been forced to practice rather than compete for much of the year because of a struggle for cash and it is already telling in his game. He needs to eliminate the negative thinking quickly.

Two pars and then James faces the next par 3 – the 5th, the same hole that fooled Llewellyn Matthews. He avoids the water, but his ball gets stuck in webbing covering some rocks in front of the green; a double bogey 5 is the result. He is 3 over already and immediately in trouble. He searches for memories of 2006 when he began with a few birdies and was much more in control. James takes a few deep breaths and tries to settle himself.

For the next few holes, James manages some much-needed par golf; he is hitting fairways, but the one thing that distinguishes the best pros from the rest – their ability on and around the greens – has totally deserted him. Then at the 10th he loses a ball after his drive and takes another double. There is little that Veronica can say to help and little that her son wants to say in explanation. James plays the final eight holes in level par; a finish that is almost a relief, but 5 over leaves him tied 85th and seven shots off the cut mark. He is massively disappointed; he has been waiting all year for his Q School moment and now this. He is already facing his worst-case scenario – First Stage elimination. It is mostly a product of the lack of competition earlier in the year; to grind out pars is one thing, but the leaders are enjoying a birdie-fest and that is much tougher for a golfer out of touch.

James spends a little time on the putting green before a quiet drive home where he talks to his father. However, although John Conteh was a long-time professional sportsman and has the knowledge of how he overcame hardship and adversity in his boxing career, he cannot provide any real comfort for his son. "I try to put myself in his shoes," says John, "but I can't really. Golf is a whole different kind of pressure than what I had with boxing."

Being the father of a sportsman is never more difficult than this. "You want your kids to be successful, you want the best for them, but I suppose it boils down to how I probably always see him as a kid when he's really a man with his own life. He has to make his own decisions," says John.

In fact, James is a man who solves his own problems; he tends to internalise his emotions and so spends the evening trying to work out his own strategy for the next morning. He has made two very bad mistakes, not made a single birdie and must find immediate improvement.

On day two, James arrives two hours before his round and returns to the practice putting green. Another two-tee start means that James begins at the 10th hole where his plan is to concentrate on making some early pars and hope that the birdies that have so far eluded him will then follow. To pick up shots, he targets the first par five (the 11th) and the short par 4 14th. If he can get a couple under for the round on the front nine then his tournament might just change from a horror story to a fairy story.

The day has dawned just as hot and the wind is still absent, but James begins with no more luck that yesterday. After six holes, he is still dropping shots and not making birdies; his frustration is growing, especially as his two playing partners seem to be holing birdies at will.

James tends to stride ahead of Veronica down the fairways as he searches for some inspiration. It fails to arrive. His second round score is exactly the same, a 5 over 77. He is tied 95th and, with uncommon swiftness, his Q School might be over before it really started.

"This is painful, a huge kick in the teeth. I got through last year, but this year I just can't get the ball in the hole. It feels like a real step backwards. I might not even bother to go back tomorrow."

Such a bad 18 holes of golf makes James feel profoundly tired, he has none of the adrenalin he needs; talking about his disappointment will not help right now, so he keeps his own counsel. He feels bad for his parents who want him to succeed so much; his father can see the pain and helps James to get up off the mat for one last try in the third round. "If it was me, I'd probably throw in the towel," says John. "Golf can drive you mad." But to return to The Oxfordshire is the professional thing to do. James will be on the first tee in the morning.

Martyn Thompson rolled up to the tournament with his usual mixture of renewed determination and self-defeating casualness. Martyn's decision to play at Q School may have been a last-minute one, but once he is here (with son Josh as his caddie) then his competitive instinct takes over and his determination and ambition soar. He even arrives at The Oxfordshire a day earlier than normal and spends three hours of his first evening putting.

Martyn is perfectly relaxed, even though he is far from over-golfed (his competitive preparation has been limited to a pro-am or two). Like James Conteh, his opening few holes could dictate his whole week. The pattern of his round is one that shows a lack of sharpness; he knows that bogeys are likely because Q School will be his first four-round tournament of the year, but every pro is capable of birdies and Martyn needs the two sides to balance. Unfortunately, bogeys outweigh birdies and he finishes day one with a 77.

Strangely, Martyn is calmness personified after the round. In 2006, he opened with a poor round and then improved each day. He believes that he plays his best golf under pressure and is confident that his recovery of last year can be repeated. He decides to spend three hours in the evening on the range to iron out any swing problems – the kind of practice that is anathema to Martyn, but tonight at least it is a mark of how seriously he is taking the challenge.

On day two, he returns to some form; his driving is top class and he picks up two early birdies; he is back to just three over. Martyn's plan seems to be working. However, he trips himself up on two par 3s on the back 9 and eventually just holds on to a level par 72 which means only limited progress up the field – from tied 85th to tied 74th. He is now 5 over, eight shots away from the anticipated score needed to qualify for Second Stage. Martyn is back in the hunt, but only just.

After two rounds, the leaders are on 11 under par while the score to qualify for Second Stage (that is, 29th place and ties) is currently 3 under. By the end of round three the first batch of Q School hopefuls will be checking out of their Travelodges; anyone not within seven shots of 29th place after 54 holes will not play the fourth round. James Conteh will struggle to be among the lucky ones who play all 72 holes; he needs a miracle of biblical proportions – a round in the low 60s at least – to stand any chance at all of making the final day let alone make the top 29. He is currently 10 over par and the anticipated three round cut is probably 3 or 4 under. James's usual smile is replaced by a grim demeanour; he travels up from Hertfordshire alone, he has decided that his chances are so slim that his mother's caddying duties are no longer necessary. James is truly alone as he tees off today; it has been a year of little progress in his golfing career and he has this one last chance to salvage something hugely positive.

Despite his best intentions and best efforts, the inevitable happens quickly: another early double bogey takes away even the slimmest of hopes for James. He trudges around the rest of the holes trying his hardest on each shot, but the game is up. Not surprisingly, he feels a sense of growing disappointment and it is reflected in his final score for the day, a 4 over par 76. He ends the tournament 14 over par and tied 95th.

Pro golfers can usually find something positive even from the worst rounds, but James is finding this is a difficult tale to spin. He is shocked and empty; this is his most disappointing Q School ever. His mood is dark; he turns on his heels and leaves The Oxfordshire as quickly as possible. Another 42 of the original 108 pros will leave with him after round three, but to be one of so many is no consolation.

"It is heartbreaking. The Q School is the focus of my whole year and I didn't even get out of the blocks. I didn't ever get the pace of the greens, it just didn't happen from the very first day. But if I'm to carry on playing professional golf, then I have to sort out what is wrong," he says.

James's latest attempt to move up the golfing ladder has ended in a whimper. There was no drama, no chance almost from the opening few holes that his dream would play out this year; it is probably the most unsatisfactory day of his sporting life. Back home, his mother and father hear the almost inevitable news of his third round failure with sadness. John, in particular, feels powerless and wishes there was more he could do to help his son. "James has to learn through defeat. It's painful to talk about his golf and, yes, thoughts about him giving up [being a tournament pro] come into my head. I think about the fact that if he hasn't made it by now [to the European Tour], will he ever? But I also think 'Why talk about his future? Why go so deep?' I'm not sure if I should even say those things, if it would de-motivate him, but at the same time, you have to see the reality of the situation. It gives me headaches. James is still fighting, he's still on his battleground. I hope he makes it."

It is little consolation that James is not alone in leaving Q School for another year, this is how the tournament ends for hundreds of players; almost before they know it, it is over. Up to now, the Conteh family still only has one member who has reached the top of the sporting world; John is the father with a world title and James is the son with just a dream. Yes, there is still time for James to rise through the golfing ranks to the European Tour, no one wants to deny him the chance to keep improving and hoping. But this latest Q School failure has been a bitter disappointment and he now has to ask himself how many more times he can put himself through the same torture. No one's father can make that decision; it is one for the son alone.

For Martyn Thompson, his third round mission is simply to make it to day four. But on the 1st tee, Martyn experiences the ultimate scare – he feels like he has lost his golf swing. Out of nowhere, he has no clue if the ball is going left or right; the gentle right-to-left draw – his stock shot – seems to have deserted him. For any golf pro, this kind of lack of control is both bemusing and frightening. Martyn is facing the most important round of his year with no feel for his swing at all.

This has happened to Martyn just three or four times in his golfing life, the last time in 2006 at Q School Second Stage. He wonders whether it is linked to pressure, but more likely, it is the change of routine; his time on the driving range has hindered him more than helped.

This experienced campaigner has made a rookie mistake. Martyn decided after day two that, against all his normal regimes, he would spend some hours on the driving range ironing out the wrinkles in his swing. In fact, the solution was probably the exact opposite: less time on the range and reliance on what comes naturally. But Martyn chose to listen to Q School craziness circulating in his brain and hours of hitting ball after ball (something he had not done in years) has now put more questions into his head than answers.

He starts his third round tentatively, he tries to grind out a score and somehow it works. Martyn's score is better than his swing; he ekes out a 2 under par 70 for his best round of the week. It leaves him on 3 over for the tournament and, although he has an anxious wait for a few hours, it is just enough to make day four. Martyn finds out his fate on the practice putting green while playing an impromptu family contest with Josh that lasts six hours until dusk. Martyn has finished 54 holes tied 64th. Tomorrow will be death or glory.

The Oxfordshire Q School field is full of excellent golfers under severe pressure; either their game has deserted them or the standard of competition is too high. Some players carry a worn-down look; their faces capture some of the sadness that the event causes when careers are stalled – or even ended – by failure on an annual basis. It hurts if you are a player who is very good, yet still not good enough.

Among the crowd of regular returnees to Q School is Warren Bladon, a former British amateur champion who has a reputation for a *laissez faire* demeanour, but who is still mightily determined to live up to the promise of his early career.

On the course, Warren maintains the appearance of someone out for a casual stroll in the sunshine; stories about him are legend. The most often told is about a practice round at the 1997 Masters with Jack Nicklaus, a courtesy given to the British amateur champion by the greatest pro player of the era.

Jack had been his usual courteous self for the first nine holes, educating the young man about Augusta and pointing out potential pin positions. All seemed well until the halfway point, when Warren turned to his distinguished partner and told him he was returning to the clubhouse; he was too tired to play any more.

"Nobody can believe I had the best player in the history of the game as my playing partner and I gave up after nine holes. He was gracious, and it's no wonder he had a confused look on his face. But I was tired, "says Warren.

Those that know Warren tell the story with amazement; it sounds like an urban myth, but it is absolutely true. Warren had just turned 30 at the time and his best years of golf were probably just ahead of him. However, that trip to the Masters would actually be the best experience of his golfing life to date.

After his amateur success, Warren turned pro and set about getting a Tour Card at Q School each autumn. Over the years, he has usually made it past First Stage of Q School, but has yet to really get within touching distance of a Card. He has enjoyed an occasional invitation to the Main Tour, qualified for the Open in 2006 and even appeared with Guy Woodman on TV's Big Break, but none of these achievements are the same as being a regular European Tour player.

At The Oxfordshire, Warren is playing the course with a mate as his caddie and a couple of additional friends following him for support. Warren being trailed by a three-man fan club is typical of him and he chats as he walks the fairways seemingly without a care in the world. However, the background to a career like Warren's – one in which early promise has not delivered the expected rewards – is typical of his contemporaries at The Oxfordshire; deep down, they all wanted to be great champions.

Warren is a man of contradictions; he appears to be shy and reticent, yet is also quite intimidating at times, quick to speak his mind. However, his competitive juices have not been flowing too well in 2007; this has been one of Warren's worst seasons, but he would not miss Q School. He is having to work as a framer in his hometown of Coventry to make ends meet and was doubtful about his chances at the start of the week.

"It's difficult working and playing golf. I've only played seven EuroPro events. I have to fund it myself and it's expensive. Sometimes I hate the game and sometimes I don't mind playing. I've been hating it a lot recently. But I never give up on the course, not unless it's mathematically impossible. It might look like it, but I don't. Picture framing doesn't earn me great money, but if I don't work then I don't earn anything. If I play golf and play badly then I don't earn anything there either. It's tough."

Warren begins with a ring rusty 74, but a second round 66 is one of the best of the day and lifts him to 24th. His third round starts well, but his loose shots seem to lead to doubles or even triples rather than single bogeys and he falls to another 74. He is shooting enough birdies, but the good golf cannot overcome the extent of the bad.

"The thing that upsets me is hitting shots without thinking enough; I've done that a few times. That's my weakness, it's what winds me up, it's why I walked off some EuroPro events this year. There are a lot of good players here who play all the time and I don't. That's why it's hard."

Warren is back in the chasing pack after day three, 38th but in sight of the magical top 29 and ties. He will need to shoot well under par for his last 18 holes and emerge from the inevitable cavalry charge of dozens of players in a similar position.

Meanwhile, a young Zimbabwean, Tongo Charamba, leads on an incredible 19 under par; Rory McIlroy and Lloyd Saltman are both in the top 10 and Llewellyn Matthews shot a 66 to end day three on level par. Sixty seven golfers go to bed tonight with their dream – at least to some degree – still in tact; a handful at the head of the field will be fighting for the little cash on offer while most will be happy to finish 29th.

Martyn Thompson's day four starts with a smile. The doubts about his swing have evaporated after his father-and-son putting session. To spend so much time practising might not be in Martyn's nature, but to simply enjoy golf with Josh in the beautiful surroundings of a top class golf course is the kind of relaxation that every father understands. Whatever the outcome of today, Martyn has enjoyed a memorable trip with Josh, both sharing the father's dream; the world does not seem such a bad place.

What Martyn actually wants on the final day is bad weather so that those already within the top 29 will not birdie themselves out of his reach. Instead, it is the hottest and the calmest day of all; nerves might raise the scoring, but these conditions will actually be perfect for going low. Martyn's chances are lengthening, yet he is calm like the weather and chooses not to pound balls on the driving range. Instead he does his normal, short warm-up.

The results of Martyn's return to a normal practice regime are immediate – two birdies in the first three holes. The words 'Hello, I could do something here' go through his mind; his confidence is lifted and he knows it is within his ability to go on a birdie blitz, so why not now? Martyn suddenly has an opportunity to shoot the round of his life.

He remains steady and then misses a real chance on the 9th but recovers by birdieing the 10th. At three under for the round with eight holes to play, he thinks perhaps another three birdies would be enough; there are no scoreboards to tell him what everyone else is shooting, so he must follow his instincts and simply score as low as possible.

On his 12th, Martyn misses a straight 10-footer for another birdie. However, he picks up another shot on the next hole and a fourth birdie on the 16th keeps his unlikely hopes alive. Two final holes and he knows one birdie is needed, if not two. He must now risk everything.

After a solid drive on the tricky par 4 8th (Martyn's 17th), he requires a finessed 9-iron to the green. It is not a difficult shot, but Martyn has to put the ball close to the pin which is tight against the edge of the green; he catches the ball thin and finds water. A double bogey and his week is over. More to the point, his dream is over. One shot with the pressure full on and it proves too much. His 18th hole passes without incident and Martyn walks off the course with a rueful smile. So much effort and the end comes so quickly.

The reaction of one of the handful of club pros at The Oxfordshire is stoical; Martyn had made it through to Second Stage the previous year and that had really been his minimum goal for 2007. But a poor start, the uncertainty of his swing and the acknowledged lack of preparation came back to haunt him. Although tired and deflated immediately afterwards, Martyn is still proud of his achievements.

"I don't feel like a second class citizen or out of place or that I don't belong here.

Having said that, after today I am thinking is it too late, am I kidding myself? At 37, am I good enough, young enough or fit enough? I had good expectations going into this week and I haven't achieved those. The way I feel right now, there's part of me thinking that this is the last go I'll have. I'm not thinking 'Great, I can come back next year'. After all, how many club pros are here? I'm sure my attitude is different because on Saturday morning I can go back to my job and my family."

Right after the tournament is a difficult time for Martyn to properly gather his thoughts. "I still have ambition and this dream, but the more time I've spent here this week, it's put my life in perspective. I don't feel a real hunger and desire this year. It doesn't feel like it really matters. I'm pissed off the way I played and I'm more disappointed that I haven't done what I set out to do, make Second Stage. But already a big part of me is looking forward to going home and that's not a Tour pro mentality. I've enjoyed being at the tournament, I love the banter and being out there and having Josh on the bag. But at the end of the day, getting through Q School just doesn't matter enough to me. I'd love to do it and if somebody said you could have 20 tournaments, I'd go like a shot. But I played badly, my swing let me down under pressure. Maybe the game's trying to tell me something."

The drive back to Dorset with Josh is pleasant in the autumn sunshine and family life plus the daily work for the members at Parkstone will go on. Q School is over for Martyn this year and only he can decide if it is over for good.

Warren Bladon was five shots better off than Martyn Thompson heading into the final round and needed about a 3 under score to sneak into the top 29. However, the pressure of Q School causes mistakes and two crippling triple bogeys relatively early on in the round – both on par 3s – means it is not Warren's day. His 79 is the second worst score of the day. Failure sticks in his craw and he walks away from Q School with little to look forward to. His situation is not uncommon among his fellow pros who ply their trade on the mini tours; at times like this, he does not even feel like a pro golfer.

"I'm not really a pro; I play golf when I'm not working as a framer. Between now and next April, I probably won't play unless there's a EuroPro Tour Championship."

Warren has had a series of jobs to keep the wolf from the door including being a pub manager; he earns enough money to keep his pro golf dream alive and is one of the players who suffers because the game he loves – and at which he has an outstanding talent – does not provide him with a living. He plays his golf in a kind of twilight zone where his hopes of a full-time pro career fade with each passing year. He might say "I'm not that fussed really" but hidden behind that off-the-cuff remark is someone who still believes it is his destiny to be on Tour. It's why he returns to Q School each autumn.

"I played well early in the year, but hit it bad over the last four weeks," he said before leaving The Oxfordshire. "Q School is a big tournament for me and it's a long old haul to get through but I'd rather play and miss out than not play in it at all. It's better than sitting at home wondering if I could've got through. But every day here I've had at least one triple bogey and you can't do that; just stupid shots. Mentally, I wasn't fully focussed on the job in hand."

Warren is one of the mini tour pros who keeps returning to Q School in the hope of catching a wave of good form. He knows such a thing could happen. "I'll never give up, much as I feel like it, even when I'm 50, I'll want to be on a Tour. I'll be back next year."

Warren has a resigned, doleful look about him when he sums up his feelings post-Q School, as he prepares to load up his car and attend a wedding later the same day. There is a huge amount of evident melancholy. At 40, he represents so many fellow pros who adopt the never-give-up-type attitude, continually trying to succeed against the odds. But like thousands of fellow pros, Warren has not succeeded at Q School. Not yet, anyway.

At the other end of the scoreboard, the 25-year-old Charamba wins the £1,500 first prize by a shot from Welshman Alex Smith and two Englishmen Matthew Morris and Paul Waring. Saltman finishes tied 7th and McIlroy eases into tied 13th. Lewis Atkinson from the Wentworth Club is the only man to make Second Stage after an opening round above par; his 78 start was worse than both Martyn's or James's opening 18 holes, yet he finishes with two 67s to progress on exactly on the cut mark of 4 under.

Others are not so lucky. The 2006 US Amateur champion Richie Ramsey of Scotland and Walker Cupper Llewellyn Matthews are out.

Twelve months ago, Ramsey was almost the Scottish version of Rory McIlroy, a young man carrying some of the future hopes of a nation on his shoulders. He was the first Brit in more than 100 years to win the US Amateur, an event open to the best players in the world outside the pro game. The title earned Ramsey invitations to test himself at the 2007 Masters, US Open and Open Championship but only if he remained an amateur, so it was after those three prestigious events that he finally turned pro. He cut his teeth as a pro almost immediately the Open ended; two Challenge Tour events led to top 25 finishes. But it is a shell-shocked Ramsey that stands in the scorer's office after a final round 71 left him three shots short at First Stage Q School.

"I had four similar days. I took 32 putts in an early round and you can't do that. (On the last day) I double bogeyed the fifth and came back with some birdies, but only holed putts that were inside six feet. I actually three putted from five feet once. When you get down to it, putting is half of the game and it doesn't matter about tee to green if you don't have a short game. Of course I'm disappointed, but you've got to take it on the chin."

Llewellyn looks exhausted after his efforts. He looks young for his 23 years, yet perhaps the strain of the Walker Cup was too much for him. "The Walker Cup was exhausting and I did make a couple of tired swings this week and I was tired mentally. Hopefully I'll learn from this, but that 9 will haunt me."

Llewellyn's is one of many wretched stories – a whole year of a golfer's life destroyed by one hole. On that round-busting par 3 5th on day one, he took nine strokes and missed making Second Stage by just two.

Chart Hills

The other UK-based tournament in the first week of First Stage is not too far from The Oxfordshire; it is an hour's drive from London in the Kent countryside. The field at Chart Hills has many similarities to the its English counterpart and the competition is just as fierce.

Although golfers enter every tournament with an underlying desire to winning it, the only real aim at First Stage of Q School is to just qualify rather than be top of the leaderboard. No Tour Cards are handed out in September. Winning is certainly not at the forefront of Guy Woodman's mind playing at Chart Hills. One of his golfing dreams has been realised this season with his first professional win, but his form has fallen away since then and Q School arrives almost four months after the victory, so Guy's momentum is lost.

Guy is a player who can suffer from brittle self-confidence. Nevertheless, he looks the part of the tournament pro (he is one of the best turned-out players on any Tour), talks with expertise and knowledge about his own game and knows both his strengths and weaknesses. But there is a fragility that exists quite near the surface. His mid-season expectations were that the win at Collingtree Park would allow him to push on and finish in the top five of the EuroPro Tour thereby gaining him a Challenge Tour card for 2008. But the win was an isolated good week. He added only just over £1,000 in prize money to the £10,000 winner's cheque and only made four cuts out of 10 events all season. Q School is a daunting place for anyone to arrive at with little or no form.

The rustiness shows in Guy's opening round of 76; 4 over and tied 70th is close to being a tournament-ender. It is a consequence of a summer trying to make money working in the pro shop at Stoke Park GC and not having enough essential time for practice. "I've played most EuroPro events this year, but I'm either in the shop when I'm not playing or I'm at a tournament, so I'm actually not getting time to work on my swing."

After round one, Guy spends almost six hours either on the practice range or the putting green. It is dark when he retires for supper.

"The pattern for me this year has been a bad first round, but backing it up with a good second. I need to just keep it in play and make a few putts. I had a good chat with my coach last night because I was pretty down. I'm quite tough on myself because I thought I'd pretty much blown it, but I looked at the scores and realised level par was still in the cut range." So that is his plan on day two – shoot four under to counter four over on day one.

Next day, however, there is nothing but panic on the driving range. Thirty minutes before his tee time and Guy is unhappy, he isn't feeling any power at the top of his backswing. He tries all his normal solutions, but nothing works. Finally, he throws down a few last-minute practice balls away from the other players and comes up with an answer. "It's not too technical. It's just a case of getting more onto my right side going back and then feeling like I'm hitting to a firm left side on the follow through." Finally, he is ready.

The opening par 5 at Chart Hills is the perfect chance for a fast start and Guy takes it; a booming drive, 3-wood to 25 yards short of the green, a pitch to a foot and a tap in birdie.

Guy's new-found swing feeling starts to pay dividends and he is striding with noticeably more assurance. He makes the turn at two under.

It is a birdie, bogey, birdie start to the back 9, but Guy's long-time friend and caddie Louis says it is wrong club choices rather than a swing glitch that cause his dropped shots. Three more pars and onto the last three holes.

Guy's best chance to achieve his plan is to birdie the par 5 16th and then par the last two holes. He is 3 under and needs just one more birdie to return to level for the tournament. The par 5 16th is duly birdied and the near-island green 17th is found with a 9-iron right over the flag; two simple putts for a par from 25ft. And so to the last, a 449yd par 4 with the pin sadistically placed near the front and on a devilish slope.

As Guy walks to the 18th tee, he tells Louis that one more birdie would really round things off. Now, the experienced pro would know that golf gives, but it also takes away and level par needs to be protected rather than risked. Guy is getting just a touch greedy. Any mistake on the 18th and there will be no chance of redress until tomorrow.

His drive is straight and true once more and his approach stops just 10ft from the hole – surely he is right and a final birdie awaits. But the golfing gods are not easily tricked and Guy's first putt is a viciously-breaking downhiller; it slides just over 2ft past. Then his slippery-left-to-right par putt lips out. Bogey. Instead of walking off the final green in triumph, Guy looks like he has been hit on the head with a 4-iron. He is not that far from tears. All that work undone by golfing hubris.

"I didn't trust the par putt and closed the blade on it. I normally miss putts like that on the left side and it's sod's law that I missed this on the other side." That single shot is the difference between being just on the edge of success tied 29th after two rounds and being back in the chasing pack tied 35th.

That mistake proves to be the turning point for Guy's week and in a positive way. He scores solidly in round three for another 69 to put him on 2 under for the tournament, tied 20th. The usual Q School nerves mean scoring on the final day at Chart Hills is modest and few players burst through the field. Guy shoots a 2 under par 70 round on day four and that is easily enough; he finishes tied 14th and makes Second Stage with ease. Even better, he looks the part of a pro on a mission. To put his performance into perspective, only one other player comes back to qualify after a first round worse than Guy's opening four over par.

But spare a thought for those who miss out. Sam Osborne is a 26-year-old Surrey pro once tipped for the big time. While his counterparts at Wentworth GC like Ross Fisher are contesting for titles on the Main Tour this year, Sam is still struggling mostly with pro starts on the EuroPro and occasionally the Challenge Tour.

Sam starts well at Chart Hills; he opens with a level par round and consolidates each day; he is looking good for Second Stage. With one of the world's most experienced caddies Pete Coleman (former clients including Bernhard Langer and Seve Ballesteros) on his bag, the final round progresses as planned. Sam is 2 under for the tournament with one hole to play, just inside the cut mark. Then, Q School craziness strikes – despite a perfect drive on the 18th Sam duck-hooks a 5-iron approach out of bounds. His triple bogey 7 means he misses the cut by two shots. From nowhere and with 71 holes safely negotiated, due almost certainly to Q School nerves, the dream is over for another year for another player. Sam's more successful counterparts at Chart Hills – Guy among them – will hear the story and know that, by the grace of God, it was not them.

Fleesensee, Bogogno & Moliets

Only one of the three First Stage Q School tournaments organised in the opening week of the event is on continental Europe. It takes place at at Fleesensee Golf & Country Club in Germany, but there were few signs of the local golfers on the leaderboard. Instead, the Scandinavian contingent was making its mark with Swede Kalle Edberg leading after round one; on days two and three, it was two different Danes who came to the front: Kasper Linnet Jorgensen and Knud Storgaard respectively. The two Danes eventually share the first prize, but the cruelty of Q School is never more evident than when Edberg, the initial leader, shoots 75, 77 and 70 to leave him three shots short of the cut for Second Stage.

In the second week of Q School, Bogogno in Italy and Moliets in France play host to tournaments. Italian Michele Reale is in control early on at Bogogno in a particularly cosmopolitan field, full of continental Europeans with a sprinkling of those from further afield such as South Africa, America and even Brazil and Chile. An opening 65 by Reale is followed by two more rounds in the 60s. However, on the last day he is pipped for the winner's cheque by 21-year-old Austrian Bernd Wiesberger who shoots the best round of the day, a 65.

At Moliets, the assembled field is more than a half filled with either French or Spanish players. However, one of the joint winners is an English pro, James Morrison, who takes top spot along with Spaniard Carlos de Corral. They both finish on 16 under par and head a total of 34 qualifiers.

Moliets is noticeable for the best last round performance of the First Stage. Thirty-two-year-old Frenchman Sarel Son-Houi, who had failed to make a cut in any of his Challenge Tour starts up this season up to this point, shot a remarkable last round 64 to sneak into the final qualifying position. This kind of last-minute low score was what Martyn Thompson and so many other First Stagers were hoping for on day four of their Q School tournaments this month. Not surprisingly, such performances are incredibly rare.

St Annes Old Links

The most dramatic of the tournaments in First Stage turns out to be at St Annes Old Links on the Lancashire coast, not least because it is dogged by heavy rain and high winds, weather that misses all five of the other venues. In the first three days it blows a hooley and there are bursts of rain so fierce that Blackpool Tower – just a couple of miles away – is lost from the horizon. This week, St Annes is a place for hand warmers, thermal underwear and double-thickness wind jackets as some of the scoring goes skywards. On day two alone 2mm of rain falls in just five minutes and visibility is down to a few hundred yards at best. Unusually, the tees are even moved forward because the wind is gusting at over 30 mph.

This all takes place on one of Britain's classic links courses. St Annes Old Links is a fabulous example of an English seaside course with a classic clubhouse, a mixture of red brick and pebble-dashed façade. The building boasts high-ceiling rooms, oak-panelling, a snooker room and enormous honours boards with ornate wooden sculpturing all set off by a large colour photograph of the Queen at her most regal.

The PGA Tour office is set up in the Ladies Committee Room where huge windows overlook the putting greens, most of the course and Blackpool Pleasure Beach in the distance. The dining room next door with its all-day breakfast, tasty carvery and Sky Sports on the TV is a perfect area for players to congregate. However, there is a certain irony in what the players want to watch: live coverage of the British Masters at The Belfry which taking place concurrently. This is actually the tournament they would rather be playing in because it is a full European Tour event with many of the star names involved and a reminder of the rewards that could be theirs. Every player in St Annes is dreaming about being at The Belfry in 12 months time; watching what-might-be will be inspiring to some and overwhelming to others as they wait to play today.

After head greenkeeper Stuart Hogg and his team have kept the tournament on schedule for the first three days, more heavy rain is falling on day four and the original start time of 7.25am is delayed. The players get hourly updates, but they can only hang around the clubhouse, nerves jangling, there is nowhere else for them to go; there is talk of the event drifting into a fifth day.

Tournament Director Kevin Feeney watches helplessly as the downpour continues. Although 95% of the course is fine, a few key areas are unplayable. Small amateur events can easily be abandoned for the day in such conditions, but not the pro events, not the Q School. Eventually, the weather relents and the first groups eventually peg it up at 12.45pm – more than five hours after their original start times. Hanging around drinking coffee with nothing to do but wait and worry is not ideal preparation, but it is part of the life of a pro. The last groups – including the leaders – may struggle to finish before sunset. Thoughts of possible missed planes or an extra night in the hotel are put aside; it is game on.

The players at St Annes include the usual mix of are Q School hopefuls, but also some much more experienced candidates. These are players of substance, men who understand how much strain this tournament can cause to the psyche. Scotland's Murray Urquhart knows his way around European Tour events; Q School has played a full part in the story of his career.

In 2002, Murray made it to Final Stage and a par on the last hole gave him the 32nd out of 36 Tour Cards handed out that year. He had been in 25th place before the final 18 holes and the extreme nervousness of the occasion is something he can recall in an instant.

"I was right on the bubble and the whole of the last round you're pushing and trying to be cagey as well. It's a horrible feeling. Going down the stretch you're numb, especially the last three holes, I had a double bogey on my 16th from nothing and I had to finish par, par and did that. But coming up the last you don't know what you need, whether a par is enough to get your Card or if you should go for a birdie. It is a unique experience. I've never had that feeling since. It's different from winning a tournament, a totally different kettle of fish. My last putt was from two feet and it felt like twelve."

Even five years after the event he laughs out loud; he can feel the tension of the moment even now. "It was a par 5 over water straight into wind; I didn't hit a great tee shot, just into semi-rough and had to lay up. My knees were shaking; I hit a punchy 6-iron and then a wedge into a tight, little green to a back pin. I knocked the first putt two feet past but somehow managed to get the next one in."

It was a dream come true, but Murray's season on the Main Tour was poor and he has returned to Q School every year since then; this is his 10th visit.

"It's getting harder every year, less spots available realistically. There are 1,000 entries, guys trying to do what they dream of doing. It doesn't matter if you're 18 and just turned pro or 34 like me and been doing it for 10 years, the incentive is there. The fact that I've been there and seen what it's like, that's an advantage. But it's a cut-throat business at the top level because there's a lot of money to be won."

For Murray, playing a full season on the European Tour has been the highlight of his career so far and he is intelligent enough to know it might stay that way. "To say that I've played at the peak of the game [is my career highlight] and I qualified to do that instead of getting invites."

But his view of Q School as an entry to the Main Tour has changed. "The Challenge Tour is the better way in because you get a better category and more starts. I got a Card in 2003 and got about 14 starts but not at the bigger events, so you're chasing your tail even then."

Murray also admits that attending Q School is now a strain on his family life. "I think I'll stop coming eventually; the cut-off is from domestic changes. It's harder being away from home. It's a young man's game and it's getting younger, more guys in their mid-20s, with 10% body fat and hitting it miles. Nowadays you have got to be fearless."

Murray's 2007 Q School adventure is not his best and he is tied 55th after day three. In the final round, he needs to push for birdies, but the course, the weather and nerves are a tough combination. "It's the old story that you should just go out and enjoy it, but I've still to discover how to do that. For something as important as this for a pro, you are ultimately trying to relax and, if you're holing putts and playing well, then you do enjoy it. But I've struggled on the greens all week, so enjoyment doesn't come into it; it's more of a grind."

Murray eventually cards a disappointing 75; not surprisingly, he flees St Annes as fast as he can. "The big cash has gone for a year. From my perspective, I have an exemption to the Scottish region and there are lots of pro-ams, but it's not my dream, not where I want to be."

Murray is right about Q School being for young men. Lloyd Saltman's younger brother Elliot makes it through by two shots and Walker Cupper Rhys Davies from Wales has an excellent 69 to finish fourth. These are boys by comparison to Murray.

Another player in the later phase of his career is Darren Prosser who is tied 10th after two rounds and then suffers a 77 in round three to drop to tied 33rd. A further plummet down the field looks likely on the final day, but sometimes experience is your friend.

Midlander Darren has never won his Tour Card, but has played in over two dozen events on the Main Tour during his 17 years as a pro. It is a source of pride. "I've been very lucky to play in so many Tour events and make the cut in some of them. Last year I qualified for the PGA Championship at Wentworth and played with (Jose Maria) Olazabal on the third day. A few years ago, I was fourth going into the final round of the English Open and played with Justin Rose and David Howell on the weekend. So I've played with the best players in the world and some guys have never done that."

Darren's desire is to play a full season on the Main Tour. "I want to know that if I had a good run at it, whether I could do some damage there." He finishes one shot inside the cut after a final round 68, one of the best scores of the day.

But for every celebration, there are far more players in Lancashire facing the kind of disappointment that was unthinkable at the start of the week.

Jamie Moul is one of three 2007 Walker Cup players at St Annes, but he is the only one not to progress. Like Prosser, the 23-year-old from Essex shot a third round 77; Jamie is making amateur-type mistakes – on par 5 holes where the pros usually score their birdies, he is over par for the week.

"I actually felt I've been hitting it pretty good which is the annoying thing. I'm disappointed, but hopefully I might get an invite or two on the back of the Walker Cup. I'd be happy with Challenge Tour next year. The plans are still there. I'll turn pro in the next few weeks; I'm ready. I've learned enough in amateur golf now. If you're not in contention in amateur golf, there's not a lot to play for. But as a pro, you're playing four rounds for something, for a reason. That's what I'm really looking forward to."

Including Rory McIlroy (who turned pro directly after playing in this year's Q School First Stage), a total of 16 amateurs progress to Second Stage out of 65 who entered. There are few 'career' amateurs at the top of the unpaid ranks these days, most are young guns heading for the professional's dream of Tour glory. Of course, only a small percentage will make it and Q School is often a first step in testing their talents in a professional environment, judging how close they are to being able to join the paid ranks.

Jamie represents scores of amateurs and twentysomething players who go home from St Annes and the other Q School First Stage venues with renewed determination. They have many more years in which to achieve success and their self-confidence is still high because at least they may still be big fishes in the amateur pool; for them, Q School is still an adventure.

By contrast, among the more fascinating stories from First Stage come from the golfers with the smallest chances of a Tour Card and therefore the biggest dreams.

One such player is Samuel Kemp, a former police constable from the Bahamas and self-taught pro golfer, who is making his second attempt at the European Tour Q School. He finishes 10 over after three rounds and has spent $5,000 (including travel expenses) for the privilege. He admits to never having played in winds as strong as those at St Annes. Plus the cold means he is forced to wear so many clothes that his golf game is hard to find. Somehow Samuel manages a giant smile before making a long trip home.

Another big-time dreamer at St Annes is Lee Nuttall, an unpretentious 48-year-old Lancashire ex-pat who has been working as a teaching pro in Spain for the last five years. Lee was talked into entering Q School by friends and members who thought he was good enough even though he had only ever played one other time on a links course. His opening 87 would be the worst round by any player all week and he finished 30 over par, 116th and in last place of those who completed three rounds.

However, some compensation for his disappointment was not far away; he fitted in a rare visit to his parents in nearby Bolton, something he had planned from the start. "I perhaps should've gone to France where the conditions are similar to Spain, but I wanted to see my parents because I don't have much contact with them any more."

But the most remarkable First Stage Q School tale is that of Joe Smith; a Romany gypsy, former bare-knuckle fighter and one of the most likeable guys in the whole tournament. In reality, the odds of him progressing to Second Stage were huge, his chances of a Tour Card simply astronomical, but Joe is undaunted because he sees Q School as a romantic quest.

Joe's story is neither sad nor desperate because his love of golf and his ambition are unquenchable. At Q School, he is like a child in a sweet shop; his every action, every conversation, every shot is filled with a joy of life. Joe has none of the airs and graces of so many pro sportsman of the modern era who live in a gilded cage of privilege. From him, there are no complaints about the bad weather, his lack of smart clothes and new clubs from a fancy sponsor or whether the greens are too slow and the bunkers too full. Joe is just happy to be alive and to be playing a game he adores. His Q School story – even if ultimate failure is almost inevitable – has the emotional arc of a movie script.

Refreshingly, Joe's ethnic background – unusual for almost any professional sportsmen – is not something he hides from; his golf balls are logo'd with the words 'Gypsy Joe'. In addition, he is proud of his past as a bare knuckle (and later licensed pro) fighter and even the fact that for long periods in his life he never touched a golf club.

At 36-years-old, Joe is no spring chicken, yet he has a genuine, appealing naivety. His enthusiasm to speak expansively about his game, to question other pros around him, to investigate his chances with even the most unlikely stranger – it all provides for a charming counterpoint to the rash of cookie-cutter young golfers he is battling against. Joe is what we sportswriters commonly refer to simply as 'a character'.

From the age of seven, Joe's chosen sport was bare knuckle fighting until his mid-teens, that is, when he took up golf. His family roamed around London and its outskirts, so Joe was able to join a club, Home Park (nowadays with new owners and re-invented as Hampton Court Palace GC). With just his natural talent and limited amounts of coaching, he won several prestigious events at the club as well as the London Junior title back in the mid-80s. But out of nowhere, his life as a gypsy caught up with him.

Joe was playing in a club tournament at Home Park and was given a plate of sandwiches to eat for free; he did not feel hungry so gave them to his father. Inexplicably, a club official challenged Joe's father about the sandwiches and asked him to pay for them. The seemingly innocuous incident sparked into a major row.

"I was victimised for being a gypsy. My father didn't feel he should pay for something that his son had given him. My father was reported to the club committee for not paying and he was asked for his resignation. We both left the club. I then had to go to a public course where the practice facilities were not very good and it had a bad affect on me. It was racism and it is still a bad memory. They thought they could stamp me out of golf and my way of life, but that's not happened." The memory still hurts Joe.

It was extremely difficult for Joe to devote himself to golf to the same degree after the incident at Home Park. His game suffered and although he turned pro at 20 and tried to make his way in low-level mini tour events, Joe's heart was not in it and he felt more like a Sunday morning hacker than a professional golfer.

By the age of 29, it was time to put down the clubs for a while. "I got to the stage with golf where I needed to let some steam off, I was becoming frustrated. I thought that I'd never know how good a boxer I was unless I tried, so I joined the IBA ranks and had 12 fights. And 12 wins." Joe won the London heavyweight title in 2003 and won back his self-respect. His commitment to golf also returned and the Q School dream began.

Joe has come to Q School for the last four years but has yet to make it past First Stage. He is at St Annes to test himself (his regular tournament golf these days is over two rounds on the Jamega Tour) and hope for a fairy tale week; even making the third round cut would be a major result for Joe. He opens with a 1 under par 71, but crashes to a 78 on day two, leaving him tied 67th. For Joe to survive into day four now means everything; for some, Q School success is more immediate than a Tour Card.

Joe shoots a 75 on day three and is one of the earlier finishers; he has to wait for several hours to see how the rest of the field performs. He nervously practices putting below the tournament office, regularly sending his children – one his caddie, the other a ball spotter – up the metal staircase to check the scores. As it turns out, his 8 over par score is right on the mark and he makes the final day.

The smile on his round, almost cherubic face is priceless.

The next day Joe would need to shoot a 63 to reach Second Stage and, in such unhelpful, cold conditions that would be a world class round by anyone's standards. So his chances are, at best, remote, but his enthusiasm is undimmed.

"Fairy tales do happen and I'll still be there with a shout. If I can get the flat stick working then who knows. Somebody shot a 64 on day three, so you don't know when 63 is your day. It just happens."

For his final 18 holes, Joe sets off in hope and his driving and approach work are both solid. He is hitting plenty of greens in regulation and there are birdie chances, but he is not taking them. Golfing miracles are very rare, mainly because when most of your game is in good order, a single part will fail you. So it is today with Joe; it is his putting, the flat stick that he spoke about fails to ignite and deliver the round of his life. He keeps his poise and tries his hardest, but it is not to be. He walks off the 18th green with a 3 over par 75, still smiling.

"It's frustrating, very frustrating. I shot three over; I hit 17 greens in regulation and the one I missed I had a bad bounce into a bunker, splashed out to 5ft and only just missed the putt. But I am happy because I played good. I was a bit off the pace, I suppose, and even the best round of the day wouldn't have got me in. But I could've shot 65 the way I played tee to green. This is the second time running that I made the fourth day. I was a bit closer last year, but all in all it's not been too bad. The Q School is like the FA Cup: we can all play, we hit it similar, some longer than others and we're all trying to find that magic button to press to turn the scores around. It's not a waste of a week; it was a great week."

By the time Joe finishes, sunset is less than 20 minutes away. On the other side of the course, the leaders are being urged on in near darkness by worried tournament officials; no one wants to come back tomorrow to finish a couple of holes.

Finally, at dusk under purple-pink clouds, Walker Cup star David Horsey completes a round of 68 to win him the event. Somehow, the officials have brought home the last group with about ten minutes to spare and despite the huge delays caused by the bad weather. First Stage is over for another year. While David checks his card in the scorer's office, Joe Smith is already on his way to Blackpool Pleasure Beach with his two sons. He has played his heart out over the whole four days, finished tied 81st out of 121 golfers and earned himself a good time among the autumn holidaymakers. Even at the First Stage of Q School, some losers are also winners.

CHAPTER 11 – October 2007

Last Man In, First Man Out

"When I got my Card back in 2002 I shot 67 and 66 on the weekend and that 66 is one of the best rounds I've ever had, probably not the best, but under the circumstances it's right up there." – Paul Broadhurst, Tour winner, Ryder Cup player and three-time Q School attendee.

Millions of armchair golf fans around the world are fed a constant diet of the game they love on the small screen thanks to the growth of cable and satellite television channels over the past couple of decades. Live coverage of the top European and American events is now part of the normal TV sports weekly watching schedule. Whereas once we saw only the Majors (and then often for restricted numbers of hours), we now see all the top international action and the biggest trophies being held aloft on the two main Tours in Europe and America.

But despite the many hours of live coverage and all the chatter from ex-pros and various commentators, the average TV fan is slightly misled. That's because the cameras quite naturally follow most closely the storyline of the winner of each tournament, yet as the season moves towards its climax, there are countless other under reported dramas happening out there. Certainly by October, the first prize cheque at each event is by no means the only story.

Right now, every Euro earned by each player can have a profound effect on his season. Tournament winners on the European Tour will get a huge chunk of the prize money each week – usually around 16% of the total – and the cheques gradually reduce until those finishing around 70th receive little more than loose change, a few thousand Euro. But every Euro counts as all the players are battling for a position on the Order of Merit (previously known as and perhaps more aptly described as the money list) and the higher you finish, the better the tournaments that you can play in next season. While the successful players look towards the titles and such, many journeymen pros are simply trying to hang on to their European Tour Card; for some a huge achievement in itself.

The trick to staying on the European Tour is to finish the season in the top 115 of the Order of Merit; such a position means a Category 7 guaranteeing a choice of entry to most of the biggest money tournaments and the much-sought-after ability to plan a complete schedule for at least 12 months. Finish 116th or worse and it could be the start of the slippery slope to golfing oblivion.

When you consider that over 350 players actually play in one or more European Tour tournaments during a season, then the top 115 is quite a select group in itself without even considering the hundreds of others on the outside trying to get in. The top 115 is also a group that is tougher to be in each year as standards rise and more young pros from all around the world aim for a spot among the elite. It is the after effects of Tiger Woods' emergence as a professional more than a decade ago – he has both inspired a generation of young players and also helped grow prize money in golf to previously unimaginable levels.

If golf isn't frustrating enough, imagine how a tournament professional feels when he has sweated through as many as 30 tournaments, scores of competitive rounds, thousands of drives, irons, chips and putts only to be told at the end of it that he's not good enough to come back next year. Each season, there is always at least one player who suffers an unpleasant fate at the year's final tournament – he is overtaken by a rival or two and finishes just one place away from retaining his Tour Card. That 116th Order of Merit spot is a deadly place to be.

While the Last Man In (115th on the list) spends the winter planning a new assault on some of the world's richest tournaments, the First Man Out – 116th – suffers a Q School examination.

In 2007, things were slightly complicated because the official Order of Merit – as often happens – includes some players who are affiliate members of the Tour not full members and therefore not eligible for next season's Tour Card. When this happens, the affiliate members are ignored when the 115 Cards are handed out. This year there were two affiliate Tour members well inside the 115th place, so the Last Man In this year would actually be finishing officially 117th. Even though the rules seem convoluted for some fans, the players know exactly who is in the most precarious position of Last Man in. As the last tournaments unfold, it is Lee Slattery from Liverpool.

The last two tournaments of the European PGA Tour season are staged in the Mediterranean, this year both are in Spain – the penultimate on the mainland in Madrid and the final one of all on the island of Mallorca. Madrid's top Tour Card story is Emanuele Canonica of Italy, one of the longest hitters in Europe. His 6th place finish in Spain's capital is his best showing of the year and takes him from the 120s in the Order of Merit to 110th – that is Tour Card safety with one week to spare.

England's Sam Little is a player well used to end-of-season struggling for a Tour Card. In 2005, Sam made an up-and-down from a greenside bunker on the final hole of the final tournament to get his Card and then hoped he would never be in that position ever again.

However, it has been a miserable season for Sam only made memorable because his wife gave birth to twins in August. As the season draws to a close, Sam has had one top 10 finish all year, so tied 7th in Madrid earning almost €20,000 was most welcome. He moved up to 153rd in the Order of Merit and now needed a top 8 finish in Mallorca to save his Tour Card once again.

Sam was not alone in hoping for a near-miracle. Another Englishman, Richard Finch, had been showing signs of a return to form. A determined character from Hull, Richard is 124th in the Order of Merit and needs a top 10 finish in Mallorca.

There is a lightning delay during the first day of the tournament and Niclas Fasth (himself chasing the top spot in the Order of Merit) is the early leader, but Sam is forcing himself into a position of reckoning and potential glory. He is 4 under after 16 holes of his opening round before hitting a driver out of bounds to drop a shot. A magical 4-iron to one foot on the par 3 18th gets the shot back and he is just one behind the leaders. Astonishingly for a man under such pressure, Sam's post-round interview shows a golfer enjoying a rare spiritual calm. "You've got to enjoy it because if you don't enjoy it, you're going to play badly. The last two months have been difficult for me, but the last three weeks I've played great, trying to enjoy golf and I'm getting the rewards."

Days two and three pass without more weather delays. As for the Last Man In story, Lee Slattery is in trouble; he misses the cut, as does Sven Struver (121st in the Order of Merit) and Patrik Sjoland (127th). More unlucky still is Scot Alan McLean (116th) who was not eligible to play In Mallorca to defend his position and did not receive an invite from the Tour organisers. Needless to say, Alan is not a happy camper.

Still in with a chance, however, are Ian Garbutt (117th), Alessandro Tadini (118th), Jarmo Sandelin (119th), Steven O'Hara (123rd) and Robert Rock (130th) who all make the cut along with Germany's Marcel Siem (139th). Just 11 months ago Marcel celebrated winning the WGC World Cup with partner Bernhard Langer; such are the vagaries of golf.

When the third rounds are completed (actually on the morning of day four because of the earlier delays) Sam and Richard are both well-placed tied for 5th, but the next 18 holes will be among the most stressful of their careers. They have a chance to save their whole year.

The problem is, do they attack for birdies or just avoid bogeys? Do they risk the brave shot or play for the centre of each green? Strangely, it is Sam and Richard whose minds are most likely to be in a turmoil about strategy while Garbutt and company know that there is no alternative but to play aggressively. However, early birdies take the pressure off both Sam and Richard.

But success is not supposed to come easily in golf and Richard follows his birdie with a precise approach to 3ft on the 6th only to somehow miss the putt. Meanwhile, for Sam, there are birdies on the 8th and 10th taking him to 2nd place on his own; he is now beginning to regain control of his destiny. Richard is still well inside the top 10 after an outrageously good lob wedge recovery on the 10th to save par.

The final holes at Mallorca are known to be tough and birdies are not littering anyone's card, so one for Richard at the 14th is of more-than-normal significance, especially as water is a real danger for the approach. Both he and Sam – playing in the same threeball – now almost have Tour Cards in their pockets.

Nevertheless, the rollercoaster continues – Richard cannot get any pars as he approaches the finish – he double bogeys the 15th then holes a 30ft putt for birdie on 16 only to bogey the 17th after missing from 20ft. At this point, Richard is joint 10th – good enough – but a final hole bogey would drop him to tied 16th place and lose his Card. Somehow he lands a perfect 4-iron on the par 3 18th and sinks another birdie putt. Richard's final six holes read: bogey, birdie, double bogey, birdie, bogey, birdie, but his 2 under for the last three holes saves him – anything less and he would be back at Q School again. He finishes tied 7th – jubilation.

Sam is a little more conventional in his finish; he birdies 15, pars the next, then pulls off a majestic 70yd chip to save his par on 17. There are no last hole dramas required and his final score is a 3 under round of 67. Three weeks ago, Sam was 164th in the money list, but with €222,220 for this 2nd place he is catapulted to a staggering 76th place on the Order of Merit. Richard pockets €48,700 to move him up to Tour Card safety in 110th place.

Watching the players close-up in these situations you cannot help but empathise with the pressure and read it on every expression on their face. After Sam's round, he is interviewed live on Sky Sports and is choking back tears. The enormity of what he has achieved – one of the most gutsy rounds of the year – is beginning to dawn on him. "Take a minute," says Sky's Tim Barter who had followed Sam's progress and can sense the player's bottled-up nervous energy that makes it so difficult for him to speak at all.

Eventually, Sam sums up how he feels. "When I holed my putt for birdie on the 16th I actually thought I might have a chance of winning the tournament, but this (Tour Card) is a wonderful consolation. I can't control what other people do,

I can only control myself and because of that, I am really proud of myself for coming through this week. This was my great escape."

Richard is bubbling after his remarkable last few holes, almost too pumped up to express himself fully in the immediate post-round interviews. "One minute I was thinking 'Fine, I can do it' but now and again I was hitting shots and thinking 'What am I doing?'. I was really proud of the way I battled back. When I walked from the 17th green to the 18th tee, everything went through my mind and to hole for birdie from 15ft at the last was just superb."

To perform so well when there is no other alternative is remarkable. It is one of the ultimate tests of guts and heart. What Sam and Richard – and others who have done the same thing in the past – will always wonder is this: how does a player find such form under the most intense pressure but not in other tournaments early in the year? If any golfer ever finds the answer, then they will bottle it and make billions. Most pros will tell you that winning a golf event comes when your game is in good shape, so performing under this kind of end-of-season pressure is all the more remarkable. In a way, the accomplishments in Mallorca by Sam and Richard are straight out of the Q School handbook.

However, not everyone can be a hero this week. Robert Rock, Steven O'Hara and Marcel Siem all fall well short of their targets for the final day. Jarmo Sandelin is luckier, he finishes the tournament a lowly tied 50th to win just €8,600, but it proves to be enough. Jarmo creeps into the Last Man In spot at the expense of Lee Slattery who is suddenly €77 short of the Swede. Now that is heartbreaking.

The stories of Ian Garbutt and Alessandro Tadini are only a little less sad. Ian drops three shots in his final two holes, shoots a last round 74 and ends up one shot behind Jarmo. It is the kind of finish that causes sleepless nights and he is €188 short of a Tour Card. Alessandro is right on course for his Card when he reaches the last hole and makes a bogey; he also comes up one shot short of a Card.

Yet again, the nature of golf at the journeyman end of the spectrum produces moments that will either haunt players or provide them with the biggest of adrenalin rushes. It seems to happen every year.

The difference between Last Man In and First Man Out can be agonisingly small over the course of an entire season; in playing terms, it can be a single bad swing or one lucky bounce. Either way, the smallest incidents translate into prize money which is the measuring criteria and that's when players see how a mid-season change of putter or the search for a more compact backswing will have either worked or failed. In the worst case in recent seasons, the monetary difference between death or glory has been less than a tenner, in fact £9.39 (€14 in Tour currency). A pro golfer's career is thrown into chaos all for the price of a round of drinks.

The man to suffer this fate was Australian Jarrod Moseley in 2004. One of many Aussies on the European Tour, Moseley had enjoyed a decent amount of success after bursting onto the scene in 1999 with a stunning win in at the Heineken Classic in his native Australia only 18 months after turning pro. A rising star, he then settled into life on the Tour earning money and plaudits.

But 2004 was a bad year; he played 25 events – more than enough to keep his Card usually – but made only 10 cuts. He had started the season brightly, yet through the summer slipped inexorably down the Order of Merit.

By the final tournament – this year it was the Madrid Open – Jarrod was in desperate straights at 114th on the Order of Merit; he first had to make the cut in Spain and then hope that a handful of rivals would not outscore him. In 2004, Last Man In would be 116th, so a dramatic finish to the season for Jarrod was guaranteed. Of course, when form is lost it will not magically reappear on demand and Jarrod missed his 15th cut of the year in Madrid and then spent the next two days watching three fellow pros try to pass him in the rankings, their own careers on the line.

It was like death by a thousand cuts to see both his and their fortunes rise and fall with each shot: South African Richard Sterne, Wade Ormsby (another Australian) and Sweden's Robert Karlsson. All three men had done what Jarrod failed to do: make the cut. Sterne, in fact, was in the best form of his pro life and went on to take the title by two shots with final rounds of 66 and 65. The €166,660 that he won didn't so much as edge Sterne past Moseley as rocket him from a place in the mid-130s to 70th.

Ormsby, meanwhile, who was in his rookie year on the European Tour, did his fellow countryman no favours. He shot a remarkable 66 on the last day for tied 6th place to earn his second biggest pay cheque of the year – €30,000 – and also shoot him past his Aussie friend. Both those performances under such pressure would be appreciated, even by Jarrod, but it was Karlsson's performance that hurt.

Karlsson, the immensely tall Swede who had five Tour titles to his name, had been out of touch for several of the preceding seasons; at one time he even contacted a life coach to help him relax both on and off the course. But the changes had yet to bear fruit (two years later he would win twice more and make the European Ryder Cup team); tied 16th was his best finish of 2004.

In Madrid, Robert sneaked into the weekend right on the cut mark of 1 under par and then shot two very ordinary rounds to finish tied 77th, joint last but one. To the horror of poor Jarrod Moseley, that clumsy finish to Robert's season allowed the Swede to celebrate while it devastated the Australian. The difference between Robert's season-long income of €145,868 and Jarrod's €145,854 was the aforementioned €14.

To make the whole episode even more excruciating for Jarrod, the player who finished dead last – Spaniard José Rivero - earned precisely €14.50 less than Karlsson. Therefore, if Rivero and Karlsson had swapped places then Jarrod would have been the one to keep his Card, but only by the even more agonising amount of less than a single Euro.

To be a successful pro golfer, it pays to keep a level head. Moseley is a case in point because this whole affair had a happy ending – the Australian turned up at Q School a few days later and, to his eternal credit, shot a 70 in the final round to earn the 25th Tour Card.

The trials and tribulations at the lower end of the Order of Merit are just one example of how each tournament – in fact, each Euro won by each player – contains any number of sub-plots.

There is the battle for the Vardon Trophy – that is, No 1 on the Order of Merit – or a top 15 place on the money list that is important because it means automatic entry into all four Major championships. Then there is the fight for a top 60 end-of-season finish so that a player gets invited to the money-fest that is the Volvo Masters at Valderrama (€4 million in total prize money and €15,000 even for finishing last). Is there more pressure at the top end of professional golf or the journeyman end? The question has many answers, but the whole Q School experience always gets a special mention.

Even many current Tour high-flyers more concerned with the top of the money list know how difficult it is to be at the other end of the golfing rainbow. For Nick Dougherty, for example, the most stress he has felt on Tour did not come when he was fighting for a title. "The most important shot I've had was in the German Masters when I was struggling to keep my Card, not when I've had chances to win. It's about when you play for your career. Q School is a huge amount of pressure; the enormity of what it means is actually what holds people back."

Nick knows how lucky he was to pass through Q School so young and on the back of a Walker Cup winning effort as well. "I finished third in Final Stage in 2001 and it felt almost straightforward, but knowing a bit more now and seeing guys who've gone back and forth there, it's not that easy. I was fortunate. I can see that the more you go there the harder it is. And for guys who need to make a living and have a family to feed, you have to go back; I hope never have to because it's not something I'd cherish."

Barry Lane is a player who has been forced back to Q School several times, seven to be precise. But Barry is now one of the European Tour's elder statesmen and has won a veritable fortune in prize money – including the $1 million in the 1995 Accenture World Championship of Golf.

"Q School's an absolute nightmare. I got my Card four out of the seven visits, but it is so nerve-wracking. You have to be fit and playing well for the whole of the tournament. It's even tougher now because you may have to play through two qualifying rounds, but in my days you pretty much only had to enter and you were through to the final that was only four rounds. I remember missing by a shot and waiting for another year to have another go. Horrible."

And for the 47-year-old Lane and many fellow pros, that is the overriding problem with Q School – lose a little form on Tour and there's always next week, but if your game crashes and burns at the School then you will almost certainly fail and have to return in a year.

"It's a daunting prospect because it is your whole livelihood," says Barry, now happily able to play on Tour because of his position in the top 40 Career Earnings List. "That one week means everything. The pressure is unbelievable and so the golf that is played is fantastic. It's so easy to miss your Card. I have admiration for all the guys who do it because you look around the Tour and almost everyone has been through it. There's more than 75% of the Tour has had to go through Q School and I think it's a fantastic idea."

Paul Broadhurst is an inspiration to Q Schoolers because the Englishman is one of the few to win before *and* after a visit to Q School.

Paul's first time among the Q Schoolers seemed like a breeze to the then 23-year-old West Midlander. He turned pro in September 1988, in the days when there were only two pre-qualifying Q School tournaments and eventually won the 18th Tour Card.

The next few years were a dream as he won three times and even made the 1991 Ryder Cup team. But 9th place on the Order of Merit in 1996 proved to be a summit that he would fall from quite dramatically. His Order of Merit finishes in the next three years were 25th, 35th and 47th before in 2001 he slipped to 157th mostly because of a hand injury.

By now the previously free-wheeling bachelor Broadhurst had been replaced by the family man with three young children who was also closer to 40 than 30. He was forced back to Q School and failed to gain a Tour Card; his career was in jeopardy and his pride was badly bruised.

"In 2001 I went back to the School with no confidence whatsoever, didn't expect anything, completely different circumstances than the first time. I was 15 years older with a family to provide for and the pressure was really on. Going there not playing well is really difficult. I made the four-round cut, but finished nowhere." His experience was similar to what Phil Golding went through five years later.

On his return from the School, Paul felt an understandable numbness, but his standing within the Tour was not forgotten. "Afterwards, I didn't know what to expect. I was hoping I'd get a few invites on the basis of playing Ryder Cup and winning a few times. I had a few days at home of not knowing; I wasn't sure what was going to happen. Then I had a call from Ken Schofield (then Executive Director of the PGA European Tour) who said not to worry. I played about 20 events the next year on invites and was grateful for that."

However, the 2002 season was not auspicious and, despite the assistance, another Q School visit was almost inevitable. "I didn't play particularly well that season, but found something in the last few weeks. So I went to the School with a bit more confidence and finished 17th. Touch wood, I haven't been back since and my career has moved on a bit since then."

In fact, Paul is living proof to many Tour pros that a comeback via Q School – even in your late 30s – is possible. His return to the big time was confirmed in 2005 when he won the Portuguese Open, a title he went on to defend in 2006. But the pressures of winning and those of Q School are not comparable for a pro like Paul. In his first School visit, there was time on his side. "I felt a lot of joy to get a Card in my first year. There was no Challenge Tour, so it was either get through or twiddle your thumbs for 12 months."

Thirteen years later, Paul suffered the infamous fear of the Q School and he now knows the difference between the stresses and strains of regaining a Card against picking up a Tour trophy. Is being in contention to win on Tour more pressure than Q School? "Not even close. When I got my Card back in 2002 I shot 67 and 66 on the weekend and that 66 is one of the best rounds I've ever had, probably not the best, but under the circumstances it's right up there. To play six under when you know your livelihood is on the line, I took a lot from that. Maybe Q School is not as much pressure for someone who's just starting out because they have plenty of other chances, but for someone like me it is. I'd been out on Tour for nearly 15 years by then and I had nothing to fall back on."

For those pros who only just failed to secure their Tour Cards this year (Slattery, Garbutt and the rest), they will at least have the consolation of being exempt from Second Stage and going straight to Final School. That applies to anyone between 115 and 145 in the money list.

Meanwhile, neither Andy Raitt nor Sion Bebb managed to make the month of October memorable; they both played just one tournament (the Open de Madrid) and failed to make cut. They will play now Second Stage and be joined by Euan Little (who dabbled in the Challenge Tour, but found no real form) and Guy Woodman whose season has been almost at a standstill for weeks. Phil Golding – as a Tour champion within the last 10 years – will vault past Second Stage straight to Final Stage. He has failed to find any consistent sharpness as the season closes and will now only have the six rounds at San Roque to overturn the effects of two torrid years and the threat to his whole career.

Another long and tiring golf season is almost over, yet those still involved in Q School will be playing their most important events of the year. Time is running out, but hope still remains.

 **– November 2007**

Second Stage

"There are certain people who won't get through [Q School]. A lot of people are just not good enough or they have a full-time club pro's job or other aspirations. But if you dedicate your life to it then it can happen. The people who are passionate about golf and who give it the time, they are the ones who should keep trying at Q School" – Nick Dougherty, multiple Tour winner and Q School graduate 2001.

If First Stage of Q School is a crazy place sprinkled with odd golfing characters, then Second Stage is a kind of twilight zone that all golfers wish to pass through as quickly as possible, hopefully successfully. Second Stage is a bit like the middle film in a trilogy – think Lord Of The Rings, The Two Towers: it is a dramatic movie featuring a terrific battle, but you know all along that more drama and an even better battle will follow in the final instalment. Second Stage, therefore, is full of the usual agony and ecstasy, while Final Stage will be the same with the volume turned up.

Second Stage is distinctive for one particular reason: playoffs. First and Final Stage tournaments operate a system whereby players can be tied for the final spot and still succeed. For example, Tour Cards are given to those finishing 30th and tied and First Stage progress is given to those tied on the cut mark. However, the four Second Stage events need to send through exactly the right number of players to fill the 156 places available at Final Stage, so there have to be playoffs to sort out who moves on and who goes home. Second Stage playoffs are perhaps the cruellest of all ideas invented by golf administrators.

Second Stage tournaments develop an atmosphere of fear that is different from other parts of the Q School journey; you are still a long way (10 rounds) from a Tour Card, but making it this far is no compensation. You can wear a Final Stage appearance as a badge of courage, but no one remembers you being at Second Stage.

There is only one significant absentee from Second Stage and he will not be playing in Spain this week for all the right reasons. Rory McIlroy turned pro the week after he got through First Stage at The Oxfordshire two months ago and proceeded to play on the European Tour via invitations organised by his agent. In just his second start as a pro, the remarkable Rory finished second at the Alfred Dunhill Links Championship, pocketed €211,000 and promptly won his Tour Card for 2008 without further recourse to Q School. Golfers in the four Second Stage tournaments hear McIlroy's news with a mixture of admiration and jealousy; if only they had such invites maybe they would also be avoiding this month's trip to Spain.

The four Second Stage tournaments take place this month all during the same four-day period, six weeks after First Stage. The courses are on the Mediterranean coastline of southern Spain to provide a climate with plenty of light and, hopefully, some sunshine and warmth.

Three of the four venues are familiar to regular Q School attendees: Costa Ballena, PGA de Catalunya and Sherry Golf in Jerez; only the fourth, Arcos Gardens (also near Jerez), is new. It is impossible to choose four courses which are precisely the same, but the PGA Tour acts fairly and allocates players to each venue not by preference but in an effort to balance each event with similar strength of players. So the 198 First Stage qualifiers are spread evenly across all four courses while the same happens to the 109 new players joining straight from the Main Tour (players who finish outside the top 145 in the money list) or Challenge Tour (players between 45th and 90th in the end-of-season ranking). That makes 307 players fighting for 64 spots, approximately a 1 in 5 chance of qualifying. Not the greatest odds, especially because the average player at Second Stage is a much more hardened tournament pro than at First Stage. Every player at the four venues truly believes in their chances of a Tour Card and many will have achieved that feat previously. No-hopers have already gone home. Second Stage golfers are just that bit more professional, but many are also more nervous. To miss out now would be like losing in a semi-final and no player, in any sport, enjoys that.

Arcos Gardens

For Guy Woodman, Second Stage is not foreign territory, but he has yet to progress beyond it. He believes he is now good enough and is drawn at the new venue, Arcos Gardens. This could be a benefit because, like most players, he is playing it for the first time.

Since First Stage, Guy has continued searching for his mid-summer form. He has been forced to spend more time working in the pro shop at Stoke Park to make up for all the hours he spent at early season EuroPro Tour events. He has been putting in up to 50 hours a week in the shop and is now short of practice and confidence. A trip to the EuroPro Tour Championship at St Andrews Bay in Scotland was disappointing, not just because his own form led to a tied 46th finish, but very heavy winds shortened the event to just two rounds and blew away chances of positive practice.

His preparations might have been far from ideal, but he comes here with determination and belief. However, those qualities look inadequate when Guy sees the near-7,500yd-long course and the wind that accompanies it. This track is for the big hitters and Guy is not among them; in practice rounds, he is 50 yards behind other players. "On one uphill par 5 into the wind, I'm hitting driver and my best 3-wood and don't get there in two; the young German guy I played with hit 5-iron for his second shot onto the middle of the green. I'm hitting driver then 3-iron or rescue club into lots of par 4s and there are not many par 4s like that on the EuroPro Tour. I'm not as used to it as some of the other guys. I am surprised about how far some of these kids hit it. It's out of my comfort zone."

Early on, Guy realises that he has to step up to a considerably higher level in class and that it will take his very best game to stay in touch. Despite the lack of distance off the tee, his opening round begins brightly and he is 2 under after nine holes. Then the first disaster strikes – a four-putt at his 10th hole (the 1st on the course) for double bogey.

The course is now testing his entire game under the most intense pressure – he cannot drive far enough, he is hitting long irons into most greens and now his putter is ice cold. His round ends unimpressively when he finds water with his second shot on a par 5 that is even reachable for him in two hits. Guy had hoped to pick up a shot, but instead drops another; a possible 73 turns into a 3 over par 75 to leave him tied 53rd. Only 19 spots are available for Final Stage here and Guy is four shots off the pace already.

Day two is the same tale of woe – very windy and too many multiple putts. A 74 is a slight improvement, but Guy is going backwards against the field, he is tied 61st. The young Englishman is still in with a chance and he is hitting the ball better, but he has to tighten up every aspect of his game, particularly his putting.

He grits his teeth for one last effort; unless he can shoot well under par, his Q School efforts this year will be in vain. Guy tries to stay calm and search out memories of his best golf to inspire himself, but all his problems remain: length off the tee, approach shots not close enough and the trickier greens. Guy cannot stop the three-putts and his third round never catches fire. He finishes day three tied 53rd, eight shots off the cut mark. Guy speaks to his parents and almost admits that he now has no chance of progressing; he deals with some of the inevitable disappointment a day early

Desperately wanting your dream is one thing; playing well enough to achieve it during one specific week of the year is another. With only pride to play for, Guy's body-constricting desire is eliminated and he shoots his best round of the week, a 2 under par 70 including five birdies in the last 14 holes. It is still nowhere near enough.

"I had it going at times, but nine three-putts and one four-putt throughout the week was what killed me. I'm standing over a 6ft putt with a foot of break on a really quick green and I'm not as used to that as the others playing on better tours. It's a huge disappointment, but it's another experience where I came away thinking I could have done it. My comfort zones need to change and I need to compete at that level more often. I believe I can do well at this level, but I haven't played enough big tournaments. I would make faster progress playing this kind of difficult course more often; it would either bring the best out of me or I'd fail miserably."

Guy actually felt good on the last day of the tournament. "That was how I needed to be from the first hole of the tournament, I struggled to get into that state. I double bogeyed my fourth today and I knew I was pretty much done after that. You so desperately want to do well, you're over-trying, you get tired and over-analyse instead of just getting on with it. I had one of the better scores on the day. It's ironic; you come away thinking 'What if'. I've got to learn from it, but you think how many more learning lessons have I got to have? I've improved this year, got the win and achieved some of my goals. The frustrating thing is that now I've got to wait another year. Maybe a shot better every round is what it comes down to."

While Israel's Birgir Hafthorsson wins, among those out of Q School at Arcos Gardens are Michele Reale, David Horsey and Lloyd Saltman. Like all those three and others, Guy is doing everything he can think of to keep improving – his technique, fitness, mental game – but the Q School does not lie; this year, Guy is not good enough. He hides behind a veneer of hope, but the kick in the guts that Q School administers is hard to take. Guy is a classic case of the young player whose dream is continually a finger-tip out of reach, yet he will not be deterred, he wants to come back for more. "I'm still desperate to play on the European Tour, I think I can compete there. I'm going to continue pursuing the dream. I'm not going to give up."

Costa Ballena

Over in Costa Ballena, there are no obvious favourites in what looks like one of the more open fields. A seven under par score from Northern Ireland's Damien Mooney gets everyone's attention and shows that this course can be tamed. By day two, 10 under is leading after two 67s from Australian Adam Bland. After round three, Bland is joined by French amateur Adrien Bernadet at the head of the field on 13 under. With 20 places for the 81 players, the final round brings the usual stories of triumph: Bland wins on 17 under and Bernadet takes second; Mooney only gets through by a shot despite leading on day one; 46-year-old Welshman Mark Mouland (a former World Cup winner with Ian Woosnam) snaps up a place with four solid rounds; Lee S James (202nd on the 2006 European Tour Order of Merit) never looks in danger and finishes fifth; while Scot Craig Lee shoots the best round of the final day – a 65 – to burst into the top 20.

However, there are more stories of disappointment: Adam Frayne of England, a consistent performer during the EuroPro season can only manage one of the alternate spots after a six-man playoff; the younger Saltman brother, Elliot, crashes out along with confident Walker Cupper Rhys Davies; Darren Prosser cannot get back into the race after a 3 over par first round; likeable Aussie Terry Price never looks close and Englishman Edward Rush (who bravely gained his Tour Card last year with a gutsy birdie-par finish at Final Stage) has a horrid four days to finish a lowly 72nd. There are some very solid tournament pros heading for the airport after day four.

Catalunya

At Catalunya, Andy Raitt is in the smallest field (just 72 players) which means less places available, just 17 (compared to 18, 19 and 20 elsewhere). Although this slightest of differences seems inconsequential at first sight, it will be significant to someone at the end of four rounds. That someone will be Andy himself.

The London-born golfer enters Second Stage after a season of wild inconsistency, not something his pre-injury golf had prepared him for. To start Q School with so little form is a problem for many players; if they had enjoyed a good season then they probably would not be there at all. Andy hopes that his experience of eight previous Schools will ease him through to Final Stage where his previous year's heroics would bring back good memories. However, he suffers the mother of all starts.

"I hit 3-wood off the 1st tee fairly far right; it's quite thin rough over there. I was a bit edgy. I hit a provisional ball, just in case, and then couldn't find the first one. I couldn't believe it. I made triple bogey; I mean, the first hole of the tournament; it's very stereotypical of the way I've been playing." Somehow, his experience and patience prompts some birdies and he reaches 1 under after 13 holes before eventually finishing level.

During the second day, Andy has a horrific Groundhog Day moment. With a two-tee start, he begins his round on the 10th and gets to 4 under after six holes; he is starting to feel confident when he reaches the 1st hole again.

"I hit a 2-iron off the tee this time. It went right again, but it looked like it was just off the fairway in light rough. I got down there and couldn't find it. I thought I was going crazy. I had to walk back up the hill to the tee and hit another. I took double bogey." Five shots dropped on the same hole over two days and yet Andy proves his skill by fighting back to 1 under for the day and the tournament.

By now he is right in the mix. While the leaders have reached 11 under, Andy is in a group of no less than 11 players in joint 13th place. With 17 spots to play for, the Catalunya tournament is going to be a tight affair.

Day three and another 1 under score means Andy holds his position and lies tied 14th with four other players. He expects his Q School experience on day four to make the difference, plus he hopes for better luck. Andy has had plenty of bad luck recently – in life and on the golf course – so surely it is his time for some good fortune.

On the last day, the previous horrors on the opening hole evaporate as he holes a birdie putt on the 1st green. However, Andy's loose shots are never far away with his tendency to 'lose' the club on his down swing and he makes four bogeys on the front 9, slipping to 1 over for the tournament and a long way from the cut.

Andy knows a birdie blitz is the only answer – he gets them on 10, 11 and 12. He still really needs another birdie, but misses from 4ft on 15 and from 15ft on the next. Then Andy has putts that lip out on both 17 and 18; that little bit of extra luck has eluded him again. His fate now rests in the hands of others. "When I putted out on the last I thought I was on the mark. Then I looked closer at the scores and thought it was 50-50. There were five groups behind and, basically, I needed a couple of those to mess up." Unfortunately, no one did mess up.

Andy's 1 under finish is one shot short of the mark. If just one of those first-hole horrors on the opening two days had not happened, then he would have been inside the mark quite easily. But despite his level head and his belief that experience would prevail, Andy is left wanting. Immediately afterwards, Andy is in a state of shock; so much has happened to him and so much of it has been bad. Another slap in the face seems almost normal. He tries to understand intellectually while keeping his emotions in tact.

"Ten years ago I missed at Q School a couple of times by a shot or two and, in those days, I really wanted to play in those big tournaments. I was more disappointed then, it really hurt. This year I don't feel so bad. Maybe compared to the other issues I've had in my life recently, it's no big deal really. I'm surprised

I don't feel so upset. It isn't as painful as I thought it might be." Andy is probably fresh out of tears for his situation. He takes the loss of his livelihood like a man and there is a little consolation in being made 5th alternate for Final Stage after a one-hole playoff. This means he will need five players to drop out of Final Stage in the next week for him to take up an unlikely place at San Roque. One or two dropouts perhaps, but never five. For Andy Raitt, it is the end.

Among those who finished ahead of Andy were Spain's Gabriel Canizares who shot a best-round-of-the-week 65 on the last day to take first place; Scotland's David Drysdale who won his Tour Card last year, but never found consistent form during the season; and England's Andrew Marshall who had finished 73rd on the money list in 2006, but dropped to 150th a year later.

And among those who failed at Catalunya were Wales's Alex Smith, so impressive in finishing second at First Stage at The Oxfordshire; Julien Foret of France, another 2006 Q School graduate; Stuart Little of England, whose 15 years as a Tour pro could not save him; and David Porter, a young pro tipped for better things who had to retire after three rounds.

For Andy, it is time to reflect, especially because the next day, he starts to feel the hurt. "Competing is probably over for me now. I don't have a stock shot or a stock swing or a stock grip. When I play social golf I might finish a couple under par because I'm relaxed. But on Tour, every day has been a struggle. In my heart of hearts I know next year I will struggle as well even if I had got my Card; I'm not suddenly going to grip a club and feel it is secure. I do play better than I used to on occasions, but I won't ever be able to play at my best. Everyone else is getting better and I'm struggling day-to-day."

Talking to Andy is not like talking to any other professional on Tour. His story is unique and you cannot help but feel sympathy for him and his bravery in trying to battle back. But Q School 2007 may be a landmark; he has to decide if he ends his dream of glory on the Main Tour. Andy could be one of the many golfers whose pro tournament career ends after crashing into the Q School buffers just one time too many.

"Every shot's a struggle. There's no natural element in my game any more. It felt like hard work all season and yet I thought it was going to be easier and easier this year with all the surgery I've had. I've had significant improvement with my arm and shoulder and I do have good days, but as far as building my game again? Well, I don't have the same strength through my wrist to know where the club face is and I'm using the index finger to grip too hard and that relates to my shoulder."

Andy can explain all the technicalities that only fellow pros might truly understand, but essentially a player of his ability will know the direction of the ball immediately on impact. A top pro's feel for the club is finely tuned; a blocked shot or a duck hook is instantly apparent. But with Andy, he has lost that feel, that close relationship with the clubface that took thousands of hours on the range to develop.

"Everyone has tendencies and fears a particular shot, but no other pro would hit a shot and not know where it's gone; they could tell you if they've hit it left or right. But because of my wrist, I don't know where the ball is at impact. I've been working on the premise that if my shoulder is neutral then I can swing neutral and allow my body to control the ball without using the strength in my hand. But at the end of the day, it's such a disadvantage. Now I tee up waiting for a mistake. Maybe it's rose-tinted glasses, but I never used to feel that way; I'd look at the fairway and try to hit it instead of just trying to avoid the big error."

There is a sadness in Andy's voice and he sighs when he recounts the details of his troubles, but he never asks for sympathy or that anyone make allowances for his injury. His personal life with Lindsay is a huge bonus, but his money troubles are now back; he earned just €50,000 in prize money this year, not enough to cover his expenses. He takes responsibility for who he is and what he has done; how many other people – let alone other professional golfers – would go to the same lengths to continue their dream? His courage is admirable. But perhaps at Catalunya at the Second Stage of Q School 2007, a veil has been drawn over his European Tour career.

"It's a nightmare having to bring it to an end like this. If I'd given up a few years ago, I'd be in a different frame of mind. I've had a chat with Lindsay my girlfriend about what I'm going to do, maybe I should do something else." The decision will be the most difficult one of his life.

Sherry

At Sherry Golf Club, there would be more playoffs, but the drama would be heightened and would provide proof that life – and golf – is neither fair nor predictable. The playoff will leave one player stunned to the point of incoherence, a second in near-tears despite success and a third thankful for at least a handful of hope.

Sherry has the look and feel of a new course, it was completed only three years ago. It is very open and relatively flat (just the 1st and 10th provide real uphill walking exercise) with manageable Bermuda rough and sparse trees close to the fairways. There is, however, plenty of water on the back 9 and the course can bare its teeth with a tad of wind. For three days, however, there is hardly a breath of a breeze and it all suited one man – Sion Bebb.

With newly-acquired bagman Gary Marshall at his side, Sion's passage to Final Stage is virtually secured by round two. His opening 65 is paired with a 68 and he is already six ahead of second place. The Welshman has gained so much confidence from his top 10 finish in Switzerland in September and looks a different player than 12 months ago. On the course, he walks like a winner and so it proves; a 70–73 finish takes him to an easy victory at 12 under. None of the other four Q School Second Stage events are so dominated by one player.

But while Sion Bebb strolls masterfully around Sherry, Euan Murray is at the gut-wrenching end of proceedings thanks to a shaky opening 75 that leaves him tied 53rd. For someone with so few competitive rounds towards the end of the season, such an opening is not surprising despite Euan's renewed love of practicing. It is the old story of the difference between hitting on the range and 'match' fitness, that is the cut and thrust of a real tournament. Euan is already in a position where every shot will count and he admits to himself that he feels nervy and unsure of his game. Nothing could be worse than missing Final Stage, yet he has straight away put himself into that place.

His preparation was sound and one masterstroke was to employ an experienced Tour caddie, Martin Rowley. This veteran carrier is one of the masters of his trade; Martin was with Ian Woosnam for eight years and has even been head of the caddies association for almost 20 years. He gained fame – but not fortune – in Lawrence Donegan's seminal book on the caddie's job, Four Iron In The Soul. If Q School progress comes down to one correct club choice or the lining up of a particularly tricky putt, then Martin is as good as anyone to have at your side.

Second Stage caddies are not here to make lots of money, most will be friends or family doing the job for free; even the full-time Tour bag men will pick up just a few hundred pounds in wages plus expenses. Euan is a friend of Martin's and the master caddie sincerely wants one of the nice guys on Tour to succeed, but at the end of the day this is business and all that matters is securing one of the 18 Final Stages places on offer. Martin will speak his mind and risk upsetting Euan rather than let this Q School tournament end in failure for the player.

Martin's words can be harsh, but he is an experienced caddie who wants to get his player's attention. "There's no point in not speaking the truth and that's my way of motivating the player; if they want someone just to save them carrying their own bag, then they should employ someone else."

Euan leans on "Rowls" heavily as he recovers after his first round. A second round 68 and third round 70 are the perfect antidote to his opening horror show. Martin's diagnosis is full of caddie-style black humour. "Euan's problem is that he needs a frontal lobotomy. He thinks too much sometimes. He's got the talent and he just has to be patient. Players at this level aren't always good enough to force it, but they can all get birdies. It's what they give back to the course that counts." Euan takes Martin's tough words in good heart. They both want the same result, after all.

To add to his nervousness, Euan is having problems with his swing, there is a lack of completion to his turn that means his hands are working too hard and the ball is shooting left. It is mostly tension that are causing the problem (is it ever thus at Q School?) and by the final day, with Euan one inside the mark at 3 under tied 14th it will take all the efforts of both player and caddie to hold on to this position.

Given that this is probably the strongest of the four fields, Euan has his work cut out. By the end of round three, many of the would-be Sherry qualifiers are crowded together in a tight bunch; there were 29 players at one under or better plus a further nine on level par and all these men know they have a very decent chance of making the top 18 who will go on to Final Stage.

On the range before the start of day four, the talk is of 3 under (Euan's current score) being the mark if the wind stays away and probably 2 under if it blows (although it has not done so all week). Martin thinks par for Euan will be enough and he highlights holes like the par 5 5th, the awkward long dogleg 11th (another par 5) and the driveable par 4 16th as the potentially "smelly ones" for Euan. The last hole is also no pushover and all the back 9 pins are in totally brutal spots – either very near water hazards or the back fringes where overshooting would mean killer downhill chips from nasty lies – so there will be no easy pathway to Final Stage here. Patience and calmness will be the watchwords.

Euan starts confidently with two pars; he is playing with experienced Frenchman Olivier David (who starts on 4 under) and a young Italian pro Lorenzo Gagli (3 under). As it happens, Euan's counterparts begin brightly, especially David who is soon racking up birdies and heading for a safe score. Euan, meanwhile, is playing safety-first golf with his putting being particularly cautious (no one is rushing anything three or four feet past; it's all dead-drop speed). The early irritant is the pace of play; delays start on the second tee. This would be a long, tiring day.

On the par 5 3rd, Euan comes alive. His drive unluckily finds the rough and an uphill lie means no chance of going for the green, so he clips a 9-iron to around the 115-yard marker and then flicks a gap wedge to 10ft. "Keep you head still," says Martin before the putt gently drops for a neat birdie. Four under is undoubtedly good enough, so to get there this early is great news. No problems at the par 3 4th, so it is on to Smelly Hole No 1.

Euan had suffered at this hole before, yet his drive this time is sound, down the right of the fairway leaving him a 4-iron to the green. The smelliness is in the approach; water down the left and a bunker right at the front of the green; a high draw is the ideal shot to take both hazards out of play. What happens instead bears little resemblance to that plan; Euan jerks his shot into the water some 70 yards short of the green. Neither player nor caddie is impressed, but Euan plays a delicious recovery chip to 6ft. One putt for a par, surely he can do this. The problem is that Euan's previous putts have all been a little edgy, so he decides to hammer this par attempt home rather than simply tap it gently forwards. To Euan's disgust, the putt lips out only because it is to pacey. Bogey and back to 3 under. Martin's raised eyebrows speak volumes. Tour caddies have a few very raucous sayings to describe the play of their employers and Martin delivers one: "If you play like a c***, then expect to get f****d". Harsh, but fair.

Euan looks a little shocked; he begins to pull away from shots, unable to settle. It is a sure sign of nerves. Martin is giving him strong advice and Euan is definitely listening, but the enormity of the day is weighing on the player's shoulders. He needs to get to 4 under again and provide himself with a cushion because the wind is starting to blow much stronger than it has done all week. This is bad news for every player fighting to get a Final Stage spot and particularly so for Euan because the back 9 is the toughest section of the course; those who had started at the 10th will have a definite advantage. It means even a few of the 10 players who started the day on 1 or 2 over will now have a chance. Euan's battle just got tougher. However, pars on 7, 8 and 9 dilute some of the tension.

After the 9th, the players are met by a scorer who asks their current number for the tournament so it can be entered on a makeshift paper scoreboard. This is primitive stuff and the players take no mind as they walk to the 10th tee, but the few spectators can at least see how the day is progressing. Over par scores are in black, level par in green and under par is red on the large sheet. Black is the most popular colour as the early starters are falling back. Only two men of those who began on the 10th – John E Morgan and Marcus Higley, both of England and each with lots of Tour experience either in America or Europe – are making a move. Morgan is 4 under after nine holes and Higley has moved to 2 under. With the easier front 9 ahead of them, they are now in the cat-bird seats. Meanwhile, those who began the day close to the cut mark are mostly holding their positions. Euan's 3 under – level for the day – is now right on the button. He and Martin are both still thinking that a level par final round will be enough.

On the 10th tee, Euan strikes a fabulous drive and then a towering 8-iron level with the pin only three feet away; this is his moment to push for home and leave the dramas behind. However, the putt that Euan eventually nudges towards the hole is hit with no confidence and falls away to the left. His par feels like a dropped shot; Euan may not get any easier birdie chances on the tough back 9.

Setting aside such disappointments is never easy at Q School and it is doubly difficult when Smelly Hole No 2 follows immediately. Euan hits his tee shot at the 11th right into a sand trap on the corner of the dogleg. When he arrives at the scene of his crime, the shot looks even worse because the ball is in a plugged lie near the face and he can only hack it out some 30 yards. This leaves an extremely difficult, long third shot into a narrow green with water all down the right and a sucker pin near the wet stuff.

Euan takes plenty of time and stays well left, but is short and also just off the green. The noose is tightening as Euan's fourth shot – a short chip – comes up 12ft short. There now follows a long debate as both Martin and Euan read the crucial par putt differently. The player eventually bows to his caddie and Euan strikes the ball firmly into the hole. This is a huge let-off. Two pars in the last two holes, but totally different feelings for Euan. Not surprisingly, he is now playing very cautiously. Had Euan known what was happening around him, his guts would have been even more in turmoil.

By now, the early finishers are coming into the scorer's office. John E Morgan is in the first group home and scores a remarkable 67 leaving him 4 under for the tournament and on his way to Final Stage. John has surprisingly taken one of the 18 spots thereby cutting the odds of players like Euan who are still right on the mark at 3 under. Marcus Higley, however, cannot convert his chances on his last 9 holes and level par for the tournament is well short; he dropped two shots on his easier back 9 rather than picking two up.

Euan's place at Final Stage is now in his own hands. Holes 12 to 14 are completed with relatively standard pars, but at the 15th his drive finds another bunker, his second is 40 yards short and he summons up all his courage to hole a 4-footer for par. He knows that too many knee-knockers like this will eventually catch up with him; he wants tap-in pars not scrambles. Of course, it does not help when those around you have all the luck. Also at the 15th, Olivier David hits an even worse drive than Euan, almost goes out of bounds with his second, plays a poor lob wedge onto the green, yet holes a 45ft putt for par. Oliver comes off that green looking like a man whose death sentence has just been reversed. Instead of drifting back towards the cut mark, the Frenchman is 6 under and just about home and dry. Euan has not had a long putt drop all day and somewhere in the back of his mind he feels like he deserves one.

Another rudimentary scoreboard on the 15th green shows that Euan's chances are narrowing. Twenty players are now 3 under or better. The message is simple – Euan's 3 under score will be in a playoff for a Final Stage spot; the 2 unders look certain to be going home.

At the driveable 16th, no one takes a driver. Euan elects for a 5-iron, but immediately cries "big bounce left" after hitting it. The shot is certainly no disaster, but lands in the rough where he will have little control of his second shot. In addition, the pin is cut so close to the water at the back of the green that it looks almost in the lake. It will be a brave man or a complete idiot to mess with this pin. As it turns out, Euan is neither, but there is no glory in a slightly-duffed chip that almost comes up short of the green let alone the pin. Euan's first putt from 40ft is not much better; he leaves himself another nightmare 4-footer. To his great relief, he strokes the ball into the middle of the hole. By now Martin is trying everything both to keep him calm, but also to urge him on for the par 5 17th and a par 4 18th now ahead. "Eight more shots," is how Martin predicts the next two holes; that will mean a birdie-par finish and definite progress on 4 under.

It looks good when Euan hits a long, bold drive down the right on 17. The green is certainly reachable from 260 yards with his 3-wood, but Euan fats it horribly and the ball comes up short, 40 yards from the hole. Now with an awkward hanging lie for his third, Euan's best option is to finesse the ball to the middle of the green and two putt. His birdie chances are low because the pin is so near the back of the green as to be almost impossible to attack. After the chip, however, even his par chances are not good; it is another 24-handicap shot (as described by Martin) and Euan's ball is not even on the green. His fourth shot is a nervy stab and Euan has another knee-knocker for par, this time from 6ft.

This is classic Q School, a case of a man stumbling over the line. Somehow, Euan is unaffected by his three previous poor shots and thumps the putt home, right in the middle of the cup. Heart-in-the-mouth stuff.

The 18th at Sherry – like so many of the courses used by the PGA in southern Spain – is an accident waiting to happen. There is water all down the right for the drive, but plenty of room on the left, where only mounds and lots of thickish Bermuda grass await. Euan has been hitting his driver pretty well all day and does not hesitate to pull it out of the bag once more. His natural draw avoids the water, but also the fairway on the left; he is left with a slightly hanging lie for his second shot. The pin is well back on the top half of a two-tier green with heavy rough and water to catch the overly bold approach. By now, Euan is almost praying for par to finish on 3 under and probably a place in a playoff. Birdie is unlikely, especially as he has picked up only one shot against par today and that was 15 holes ago. Bogey and, surely, he goes home.

The approach shot causes another debate between Euan and Martin, both expect the ball to fly out of the rough, so an 8-iron rather than a 7 (which brings the water into play at the back of the green) is the club of choice.

The club swings, but it is not Euan's best effort; he catches the ball slightly fat and sends it straight into the bunker just short of the green. The last thing Euan needs is a 30yd bunker shot to a back pin with water (aka disaster) awaiting beyond, but he makes a good fist of it and flies the ball to the top level, but still 20ft short and the putt will be a double-breaker.

"Do you think I need this?" asks Euan. "I know you do," is the best that Martin can say. There is much studying, but although the putt just reaches the hole, it breaks 2 inches to the right and leaves Euan with a bogey.

You can almost see the air being sucked out of Euan's body. He believed that if the putt went in then he was off to Final Stage and if it stayed out, well, he was out of Q School for another year. The bogey is only his second of the day, but it drops him to 2 under and at this time that is one shot too many.

Euan strides to the scorer's office to discover the worst – as it stands, there are exactly 18 players on 3 under; all spots for Final Stage are taken and only the 12 leading players are yet to finish, all of whom had started the day on better scores than Euan. The next group to finish is probably Euan's only chance; if one of them drops a shot at the last hole, then Euan might still have a playoff for a Final Stage place. It is Englishman Justin Walters – who began the day on 4 under – who is being sucked into the drama; he is 3 under for the tournament after 17 holes.

Justin is a friend of Euan's and, like the Scot, he knows a par on 18 will be enough. He is an emotional player on the course; on the 11th tee he hurled his driver away in frustration after blocking the ball into water. On 18, he tries to remain calm, but a poor 4-iron tee shot is far too short to provide an easy second. He tugs a horrible approach off to the left and is finally left with a 5ft downhill putt for par. It slides past. He slams the putter head into the palm of his hand and curses. He has slipped to 2 under. Euan Little has been thrown an unlikely lifeline.

There are no cameras here, no computerised scoreboards, so news of Justin's bogey is slow to reach Euan who has been thinking the worst. He cannot talk, he cannot think, he wanders to the car to find some quiet. His mobile phone is already screaming with voice messages and texts from friends and family. They are checking the European Tour website for scores, but the slowness of the rounds and the impending playoff have delayed the results being posted. Euan is unable to call anyone; he sends one text to his mother saying that nothing is finalised yet and he will phone later. "I can't speak to my parents. I know the disappointment for them will be terrible." As he speaks, he believes he is in a playoff for an alternate spot.

After a few minutes, he wanders back into the bar area and overhears the rumours that he is in a playoff with two other guys for the 18th and final spot to Final Stage. The Tour office is guarded, not releasing the information until every player is signed in, but it is true: Justin Walters' crash on the last hole has opened up the last qualifying place. Justin, Euan and a young Austrian Florian Praegant, who had shot a creditable 1 under final round score, have all finished on 2 under.

To keep a clear head Euan goes to the driving range. A fellow Scot and long-time friend, Scott Henderson joins him along with Martin. There is not much to say except that Euan is the most experienced of the three and that must be to his advantage. The playoff is sudden death with one player going straight to Final Stage, one to be handed the 2nd alternate spot and the third to receive the 6th alternate position which is, realistically, a ticket home.

Martin tries to bring some levity to the proceedings as all three players arrive on the tee; he takes a driver from his player's bag and pretends to hit the first shot. "I'll pay the green fee," he jokes. Half smiles only. Euan is still trying to tune out of everyone else's emotions. "Some guys were cheering and hollering in the clubhouse because they got through and you've got to respect that because it's fantastic for them. But I didn't want to be around that." In fact, it is only on the tee that Euan realises for sure that he is playing for a Final Stage place and not just an alternate spot.

After drawing lots, Euan will drive second. He is the shortest off the tee, but strikes a solid approach to the back right hand corner of the green and gets his par. His opponents both show nerves, but also scramble fours.

They move to the 18th. Euan's two rivals both hit irons off the tee, but the Scot hits driver again almost to the exact same shot as in regulation. He is in the best shape of the three, but he fails to take advantage with a poor approach that he tugs left. The tension is too much for all of them; Euan misses from 8ft for par and three bogey fives are all they can manage. Back to the 10th.

Euan has wasted one golden opportunity while the other two are feeling relieved. Luck will enter into the equation at some point and maybe Euan has wasted his opportunity.

Adrenaline is now in short supply; all three look sunken-eyed and exhausted. They each have supporters with them – Justin has his wife as caddie; Florian is followed by fellow countryman and qualifier Roland Steiner; and Euan has Scott Henderson – but there is little that anyone can do to lift the players' spirits. There is little joy in a Second Stage playoff even for the winner; the key feelings will be either relief or despair.

At the third playoff hole, Florian hits a short hook left and Justin a massive block to the right. Euan hits his best drive of the playoff down the middle and is again looking the man-most-likely; he even manages a smile after his second shot finds the heart of the green. Yet, somehow Florian and Justin continue to scramble successfully; both eventually hole par putts leaving Euan with his third chance to wrap up his place at San Roque next week. It is a 25ft putt and he has already seen Justin's effort which is on a similar line. Rather than risk going a few feet past, however, Euan tries to drop the ball in with dead weight and it shaves the hole through lack of pace. The excruciating playoff goes on.

At playoff hole No 4, Euan's driver again overpowers the iron shots of Florian and Justin off the tee. The approach shots of Euan's rivals then open the door once more; Justin can only hit his second to 50 yards short of the green while Florian blocks a shocking 5-iron into the lake. Surely, Euan can grab this chance. But the tension has become unbearable and he misses the 18th green for the third time today; this attempt flies left leaving him a difficult chip out of a scrubby lie.

Florian's mistake is fatal and he is heading for a six, but Justin recovers. He needs a rudimentary chip-and-a-putt from the back of the green for a five. The chip is poor and he has a short, downhill putt (similar to his attempt in regulation) to at least put some pressure on Euan who has just chipped his third shot to within 6ft. When Justin misses, Euan has two putts to take his place at Final Stage. He uses both putts and his face looks empty; the well of emotion is almost dry. There are a few perfunctory handshakes before the other two players move on to settle the alternate spots.

Euan finds it difficult to make sense of a crazy day and the wild playoff. "I've had it all, I've really been through the ringer. I felt I had an edge with the Florian, but I know Justin well and know he could play. Those two guys were playing the wrong tactics; they should have gone for it (on 18) because there was only one spot. You can't play irons off the tee there, it gives you too much to do. It's driver, 7-iron. In a way, they gift-wrapped it for me."

But honesty about his own struggles is not far from the surface. "I've played poorly myself, though, and still got through. That's golf. After all that, you're not tired, it's like a great empty feeling when you think you nearly missed it and then someone gives you half a carrot; it's not even a full carrot. I was so convinced I could do it and I really wanted it; I thought somewhere down deep inside 2 under had a chance. Everybody said last year 'you only missed by one shot', but you miss by one shot because of yourself and what you do. I got sucked to the cut line today and maybe that's something I've got to rectify in the future. I definitely let my mind get carried away out there because it's tough not to; I'm thinking of my coach, my family, my best friend. I probably don't look happy, but it's incredible the feeling I've got inside, I could run a marathon. I'm elated. I'm not ready for next week, but I soon will be."

Euan's 2006 experience when his final putt lipped out was agonising and today almost ended with the same emotion. The fine line between triumph and disaster is as thin as ever. The Scot is relieved, euphoric, tired and shell-shocked all at the same time. As a professional, he is already thinking ahead to San Roque, but the scars of days like today sometimes heal slowly.

Meanwhile, Justin Walters misses another short putt at the next playoff hole and allows the young Austrian to take the 2nd alternate spot. Justin walks away as 6th alternate and knows that it is tantamount to goodbye to Q School.

As he packs up his clubs and leaves the clubhouse with his wife close by, Justin's face is deathly white and his brave words are not enough to hide momentous disappointment. "I played good all week, but I've pretty much come up with nothing for the year. It's tough. You kind of beat yourself up (after dropping into the playoff) and then have to pick yourself up again. I wasn't really nervous. I've been a pro for five years and you get used to it. The hardest part about it is knowing the consequences."

The 18th at Sherry GC will never be on Justin's top 10 list of favourite holes. "Me and 18 are like oil and water. I haven't figured out how to play that hole yet. My biggest mistake was my fourth shot (on the fourth playoff hole), the chip. It came out soft; it was probably the nerves. If I put down a bag of balls there, I'd probably get it up and down 90% of the time."

Not surprisingly, tears are starting to form in his eyes. "I don't really know what I want to do. The hardest thing to ask yourself is 'Where do I go now?'. I missed Q School First Stage in the US by one shot and now this. I've got my wife here, so it's not the end of the world, I guess." His remark is slightly unconvincing as this job of tournament professional that he has chosen has just stuck a knife in his belly. His dream of playing on the best golf tours in the world has taken him across continents and is the most important thing in his life. Will there be tears, he is asked. "There probably will," he says and walks quickly away.

To contest a Second Stage playoff takes immense strength of character; it is a level of intensity far in excess of what a normal club golfer might experience. This is golf at its most brutal. The rewards loom large when the putts are there to be holed and the consequences of missing would cause many to curl up and hide.

Coincidentally, 12 hours earlier in China at a European Tour event, Phil Mickelson, Lee Westwood and Ross Fisher are involved in a playoff for the title. The difference, however, is clear: the winner (Mickelson) takes home a trophy, a massive cheque and lots of World Ranking points, and even the two playoff losers bank €300,000 each. By contrast in Jerez after the Second Stage of Q School playoff, Euan Little wins an invitation to six more rounds of nerve-jangling golf; Florian Praegant receives an outside chance to join him; and Justin Walters walks away with absolutely nothing. Justin is now effectively nowhere on golf's professional tournament map. Yes, he will play on the third-ranked Sunshine Tour in Africa and he will also receive a few invites to Main Tour events, but it is odds on that Q School 2008 will be his most important tournament in the next 12 months. Justin – along with hundreds of other pros – will have to wait a whole year to try to hoist his career back on track. No wonder there will be tears in Jerez.

 **– November 2007**

Final Stage

"Final Stage of Q School is one of the only weeks of the year when I wished I had an ordinary 9-to-5 job!" – Simon Hurd, Q School graduate 2004.

Day One

"The Tour School is the ultimate reflection of you as a golfer. When you don't match your expections then you have to realise your game wasn't good enough and you go back to the drawing board." – Murray Urquhart, 12-time Q School attendee.

Southern Spain in the second full week of November 2007 is dazzlingly sunny and warm, just as the Q School Final Stage golfers ordered. The two San Roque courses are in excellent order and 156 top class golfers are ready to start the six-round tournament to decide which 30 of them will receive full exemption to the 2008 European Tour season.

A total of 876 began this journey and exactly 720 have fallen by the wayside. Final Stage is where the want-to-be-heres meet the don't-want-to-be-heres. For the Q School rookies, just progressing to the San Roque tournament is a remarkable achievement; this week will be a journey of discovery for them because such an intense six-round event like this is not on their CVs. They are desperate to prove themselves. For the seasoned Tour pro, there is a reluctance about making the trip here; these veterans are trying to bounce back to the place where they believe they belong – the European Tour – and Q School is just an annoying hurdle they have to jump.

Both sets of players will endure Q School rather than enjoy it and, by the end of it, everyone will have suffered through some of the agonies and ecstasies top-end sport can deliver

The field is a strong one, certainly on a par with anything in recent years. The highest ranked player is Alan McLean of Scotland who watched helplessly from his home in Ontario as his place in the top 115 of the Order of Merit disappeared in the last three tournaments, none of which he was invited to play in. Alan's Sony World Ranking is 251 and illustrates the level of the Q School contestants – these are players of high quality, yet they still have to strive to be among the very best. To play regularly on the Main Tour, the modern pro golfer cannot just be good, he has to be truly exceptional. In all there are 22 players at Q School inside the top 500 in the world; Sion Bebb is 426th and Euan Little 485th.

The 156 men playing this week arrived in one of 13 different ways: most recently, 75 won through from Second Stage; 15 qualified from the Main Tour by finishing between 117 and 145 in the Order of Merit; twenty six are from the end-of-season Challenge Tour rankings between places 16 and 45; three places each are allocated to leading players from the Asian, Sunshine and Australasian Tour money lists; two are either a Q School winner or Challenge Tour winner from 2006; and one is on a medical exemption (Raymond Russell of Scotland). But the most interesting category of player is the winners on Tour from the last 10 years.

This year there is a total of 21 former champions, the most high profile being ex-Ryder Cup players Andrew Coltart of Scotland and Joakim Haeggman of Sweden. Others include more Scots Dean Robertson and Andrew Oldcorn, England's David Carter and Gary Emerson, David Park of Wales and Jarrod Moseley of Australia. Phil Golding also qualifies in this way as the winner of the 2003 French Open.

Coltart is the main spokesman for this group of former champions. "I am here to win and I am strangely looking forward to it because I am hoping this can kick-start the career again," he says during practice. "I still haven't achieved all that I want to achieve; I have lots of unfinished business."

The former winner of the Qatar Masters and Great North Open has over €5 million in career earnings, but at 37 he returns to the School for the first time since 1993 after finishing 168th on the money list with just €127,000. Coltart knows how to create a confident mental attitude, but he is currently struggling with his Game and will need a steady start.

"Mentally, I'm fine being here. What has been frustrating has been wanting to improve and get better, still having goals, dreams and ambitions and getting further and further away from them. You hear about how hard the guys who are doing well are practising, but you can practise hard and not do well. Practise makes perfect? That's not necessarily true. Perfect practise makes perfect."

Another interesting group here is the 13 Tour Card winners from last year's Q School (including Sion Bebb) who have returned to San Roque this week. A further nine of the successful class from 2006 – such as Andy Raitt, the joint winner from last year Alexandre Rocha of Brazil, and Scotland's David Drysdale who finished third – have already been knocked out this year.

Meanwhile, three Q School reserves are hearing good news. England's Ben Evans is 1st alternate and replaces Alvaro Velasco who flies home to Argentina four days before the contest begins because of the death of his brother. Austria's Florian Praegant – who lost so dramatically to Euan Little in the playoff at Sherry – gets a starting spot when England's Ian Garbutt drops out with an eye infection. Then on the morning of the first round, Sweden's Oscar Floren finds himself in the tournament because of a wrist injury to Italy's Massimo Scarpa.

Praegant is particularly surprised, especially after his dramatic loss in the playoff. The 25-year-old Austrian with a fine amateur record broke his neck in 2006 in a swimming accident putting his career in doubt. But he recovered and has been learning his trade on the Alps Tour. "I am obviously a little bit surprised to be playing here, but I am not nervous. It would be amazing if I got my Card because my year was not really that good. My best finish on the Alps Tour was only 5th place," says the Final Stage rookie.

However, although three alternates had their wishes granted, the next man on the list, 4th alternate Adam Frayne who had hung around during the practice days, quietly hoping he might be needed, makes the depressing journey back to England. Fifth alternate Andy Raitt never actually left home; he always knew his chances of playing were somewhere between slim and none – and so it proved.

On the morning of day one, the conditions are benign – temperatures in the mid-to-high 60s – although the forecast is for the weather to deteriorate towards the end of the tournament. The experienced players have brought along winter clothing and wet weather gear because they remember the awful conditions in 2006 when the event suffered two days of postponements due to torrential rain plus a last round storm delay of almost two hours. So the opening day tactic for most players is to make hay while the sun shines, get some early birdies. If the weather forecast for days five and six are true, then today is a perfect time to get below par.

The main questions for every player before the opening round are firstly about what score will ultimately be needed to earn a Tour Card and, secondly (and on a more sub-conscious level), can they finish in the top 30?

To answer the first question, you only need look back at a few previous Q Schools: even if the weather stays benign, level par over six rounds will not be far away, while anyone shooting consistently one under each day will walk it.

The second question is harder, but the Q School veterans think they have the answer. It is their accepted wisdom that one fifth of the 156 players have no chance; these players are surprised to be here and are already half-expecting to fail, albeit it gloriously. Another fifth are just not in good enough form including many who finished low in the Tour money list or who are returning former Tour winners. That leaves about 90 players to worry about.

The Q School vet will say that another fifth will lose out mainly because of either fatigue or nerves or both; these players just do not have what it takes to be a top pro. That leaves the number of potential Tour Card winners at 60. This is how the experienced players will think as they stand on the first tee while the rookies may be in awe of the situation or be gobbled up by the stresses and strains of the tournament as it builds to a pressure-cooker climax.

Those with Q School experience also know that not every player who will get a Tour Card at the end of the week will play to their very best potential. Q School calls for steady golf, a different kind of playing tactic than normal because there is absolutely no safety net. Those who make the fewest errors (like three-putts or visits to the various lakes and hazards) and are able to grind through the tough holes are most likely to succeed. The players with the cast-iron self-belief, those who can compartmentalise the consequences of failure, these men will triumph.

Having said all this, there will still be some surprising names among the 30 or so Tour Card winners, after all, that is the joy of sport. Some rookies will hit a rich vein of form and some veterans who looked odds-on to return to the Tour are stopped in their tracks by an unaccountable attack of anxiety.

Q School is not meant to be easy and, the fact is, it keeps getting harder. The standards of golf keep rising, while the players get younger and fitter. Plus, the potential rewards on Tour keep growing along with the players' hopes and expectations and that all adds to more nerves. But in the final analysis and whatever predictions the veterans might make, if there is ever a time to bring your 'A' game into play, then Q School is it. After all, it is one of the toughest tests in golf.

Unlike First and Second Stages, Final Stage of Q School feels like a real European Tour event. The field is bigger, the course set-up is more challenging, there are far more pro caddies around and you can even count a smattering of spectators.

The format is simple: each player will play two rounds on the New Course and on the Old Course – both par 72s – over the next four days; the field is split in half and the players alternate between the two courses. In addition, there are two tee-off starts each day to forestall any possible weather interruptions.

The players are placed in the same threeballs for the first two days after a random draw and then there is a re-draw for days three and four. After four rounds, the top 70 and ties will go through to the fifth and sixth rounds; tee times will then be decided on scoring, so that the leaders start off in the last group of the day. After the final round, the top 30 and ties receive Tour Cards that provide full exemption for European Tour events throughout 2008.

Of the two courses, the Old is considered slightly more difficult, perhaps by one or two shots, but both are set up in similar fashion each day to avoid benefiting one group of players over another. The greens will be cut to run between 10 and 11.5 on the stimp metre depending on the wind; if the worst blustery conditions prevail then the speeds will be towards the slower end of the scale.

A contingent of full-time European Tour officials and dozens of local volunteers are on hand throughout the six days led by Mike Stewart who has been Qualifying School director since 2001. Mike does his level best to make the week as fair for every player as he possibly can and both he and his team offer up as much encouragement or sympathy as and when it is needed.

Today, the tournament office is fielding lots of questions while the driving range, practise putting greens and chipping areas are all jam-packed. The players are trying to smooth off the rough edges to their game and clear their minds for the marathon ahead. Everyone wants to get off to a solid start and no one intends to play themselves out of the tournament after the first 18 holes. This is a crucial day and, along with day four and day six, is the most nerve-wracking.

Sion Bebb is off in the very first threeball on the 1st tee of the Old Course at 9.00am; Andrew Coltart has a similar honour on the New Course, but off the 10th. Phil Golding is also an early starter on the New (9.10am) while Euan Little is off the 10th at 10.30.

From the very first hole, Sion carries on where he left off at Sherry less than a week ago. He is bursting with confidence and begins with two birdies. This kind of start allows Sion to play the kind of game he prefers: steady golf to reduce any chance of a major error. Gary Marshall is on his bag again and they are making quite a formidable team; in just two tournaments together they have had a fourth and a win.

The Welshman's drives are long and straight, his iron play more than adequate and he is holing his share of putts, especially the sneaky short ones. It is these kinds of putts that require so much attention and Sion gets quite animated over them. He has a habit of moving a little quicker than normal when lining up his key putts and is apt to lie flat on the ground in an effort to read the breaks on the subtle San Roque greens. Putts like the three and a half footer for par on the 17th are classics; both Sion and Gary get low to the green before deciding on line and pace. Sion holes this putt and goes on to record a 71. He is angry that the four par 5s did not give up a single birdie, but 1 under par is bang on his target.

Phil Golding is playing his first competitive round since the Kazahkstan Open in September on the Challenge Tour when he finished tied 51st. He has been working particularly hard with his coach Jason Banting – who will also caddy for him this week – on his short game and suspects that he might feel a little off the pace to start with – as proves to be the case.

He is level par at the turn, but then suffers a horrible four-hole stretch; bogeys on 12, 13 and 14 are followed by a double bogey on 15 – he is only partly through his first round and is already 5 over. This is the nightmare that everyone is trying to avoid. Five over on day one is not fatal, but it piles on even more pressure than the player is already feeling and rocks the confidence. Phil's lack of tournament golf – better known as match fitness – is undermining his chances.

The 16th, however, on the New Course is an inviting par 5, especially with a quiet wind. Phil takes his opportunity and reduces the damage with a birdie; a par on the short 17th is always a good score and now to the famous final hole, the 453-yard 18th that is a disaster zone for so many Q Schoolers. Phil knows that this is probably the most nerve-inducing hole on the course – especially on day six – so a birdie here would really lighten his mood.

Phil hits driver, 8-iron to a relatively comfortable flag; he is 8ft from a birdie and his putting stroke has looked smooth all day. Phil sees the line clearly and eases the ball straight into the hole for a three over par 75. It is certainly not good enough, but the manner of his golf in the last three holes as the pressure began to mount augurs well for later in the week. Phil has definitely started slowly, but he needed a competitive round to shake off some cobwebs. Five under would have seemed like Everest; 3 under and two late birdies reduces his task to something more like Kilimanjaro.

You might think that Euan Little would still be on a high from his playoff drama, but that is far from the truth. He hardly had the energy to celebrate on the night of his triumph and, instead, collapsed into a 12-hour sleep once the adrenaline had subsided. Next day, he drove down to Cadiz and met up with is sponsor, Willie Crowe from the Tipperary Golf Club in Ireland. Euan's pre-tournament routine at San Roque has amounted to just one practice round because these are courses that he already knows well. There is no need to pound the driving range in search of his swing; all that work is done. Euan feels like he is ready. He is staying in a beautiful apartment a few miles away overlooking the ocean and Willie is providing both moral support and his cooking talents, he was a head chef long before becoming course director at Tipperary.

However, despite the assured build-up to Final Stage, Euan is giving the sponsor a few heart attacks today. The par 3s are causing Euan some problems; he drops three shots on them. However, there are also plenty of birdies out on the New Course and Euan grabs four of them to finish at 1 under par. There is no Martin Rowley on his bag (instead another experienced Tour caddie, Brian McFeat, a fellow Scot, has been hired), but Euan has made a confident start.

As day one unfolds, there is plenty of drama already both good and bad. The round of the day is on the New Course where England's Robert Coles cards a six under par 66, two better than the next best. Robert says a new putter and becoming a father for the first time just six weeks earlier are possible reasons for his good form. Meanwhile, the Old Course is proving tougher and 68 is the best score by four players. Andrew Coltart manages a level par 72 and says a 69 was possible, but is happy with his opening 18 holes.

There are plenty of steady rounds of golf – 29 players hit the most popular score of the day, one under par 71 – and there were some disastrous rounds as well. France's Jean Pierre Cixous shoots an 80 and England's Gary Clark a 78, both on the New Course, while another Frenchman Raphael Eyraud also shoots 80 on the Old Course with four others on 79 including one of the former Tour champions, Raymond Russell who has been suffering all year with injuries.

As dusk approaches, the driving range and the putting greens finally empty. The first step on the latest part of the long Q School journey is complete but, whatever the first day score, a peaceful night's sleep is not easy to come by. All the players – those who have scored well and those who have played badly – know that golf is the most mystifying of sports and everything could change tomorrow.

Day Two

"This is probably one of the worst tournaments you can play, it is hard to be focused over six rounds." – Sven Struver of Germany, three-time Tour winner and seven-time Q School attendee.

Day two is all-change day at Q School because the players who teed it up on the Old Course yesterday move to the New and vice versa. It is also an all-change day in terms of the weather. There is a definite increase in the wind strength as the day progresses and both courses are suddenly considerably more tricky. Both New and Old Courses need wind to protect them and today the prevailing easterly starts to blow for the first time this week, a distinct disadvantage to rookies who practised in the calm conditions.

The contrast between the two courses is now more apparent. Whereas the Old requires greater driving precision, the New is a place to open your shoulders a little more. In addition, both courses have their horror holes – the Old is dominated by the stretch from the 5th to 8th while the New is memorable for the 16th to 18th. By the end of the today, these will be the holes that most players will remember, either for the happiest or saddest of reasons.

Today Phil Golding is under pressure. Yes, he knows that Q School is a long week and, yes, an opening 75 is retrievable, but the time to play well is now. Phil cannot contemplate another 'sabbatical' year, not now he is in his mid-forties. He is one of many players whose career is on the line this week; no Tour Card and the next few years of his career could be full of corporate days, pro-ams and coaching rather than the glamour of European Tour events.

Phil begins on the Old Course at the 10th with two experienced pros, David Drysdale and Robert Rock. Phil looks the part of a European Tour regular, his demeanour is that of the accomplished professional he has been for many years. He knows both David and Robert and chats easily with them during the round. Phil's momentum from yesterday's final holes holds good and at the turn, he is 3 under for the day and back to level par for the tournament. He is hitting the ball with precision, notching up easy pars and giving himself plenty of birdie opportunities. This is perfect Q School golf. His 20 yard chip to the hole-side on his 8th hole (the 17th on the course) is proof that his short game in particular is sharpening up.

His back 9 is less spectacular – only one birdie - and his only bogey of the day arrives after he finds a bunker at the par 3 7th (his 16th). A 69 on the more difficult course on a windy day sends Phil's confidence soaring; it is one of his best rounds of the year. He is now level par, tied 51st.

Phil is still cautious about too many celebrations afterwards and sticks to the routine that he and Jason have set up: he practises elsewhere rather than at San Roque so as not to remain immersed in the tournament tension and only hits balls for a short time either before or after his round; then he reflects quietly on his day, has a bite to eat and gets an early night.

In addition, Phil is studying old journals that he has kept from previous tournaments in which he makes notes of feelings or physical aspects of his game. He reads about slight changes that he has made to his game in the past, perhaps a different posture or his position to the ball at address. He then incorporates the feedback from tournaments past into his present day feelings about his swing. It is an unusual thing to do, but shows his dedication to finding a solution to his poor showing at Q School last year. Phil is in a comfortable mood.

Also on the Old Course, but starting at the 1st is Euan Little. He tees off at 9.20 while the wind is at its calmest, but fails to cash in on his good fortune. He is hitting good drives and flushing his approach shots, but no early putts drop. Instead, bad luck is following him and any poor shot or swing is being punished. He finds bunkers on the par 3 3rd and the par 4 6th and suffers a bogey each time.

His back 9 gives up a birdie on the 10th and there is no more damage done in the last eight holes; he finishes on a 73, level after two days. Euan is frustrated because he would normally expect to make more than one birdie in 18 holes, but tied 51st is safely in the pack.

Sion Bebb, however, is enjoying the extra space available on the New Course. Again, he starts fast, three birdies in his first seven holes. But, as the wind blows stronger, Sion's golf becomes slightly ragged and two three-putts on his back 9 from just 15ft and 20ft leave a sour taste in his mouth when he signs for another 1 under par 71. He is 2 under for the tournament and in tied 18th place.

Compared to Sion's start at Q School last year (he was 6 over par after two rounds and in tied 110th position), he is in great shape. His routine is like Phil's, that of a veteran of Q School: very little practice, a quiet evening with some supper and, by a little after 9.00pm, he takes to his bed almost unable to keep his eyes open. The mental demands and levels of concentration are as tiring as the physical demands of playing so many consecutive five-hour rounds. Sion knows surviving the fatigue is one of the keys to a successful week.

By the end of today, every player has sampled both courses and the leaderboard is starting to take shape – Spain's Pablo Larrazabal is on top after shooting a best-of-the-day 66 on the New Course for a 7 under total. There are already 50 players at 1 under or better and some surprising names are making a move including first alternate Ben Evans, aged just 20 and a two-time winner in the Faldo Series who only turned pro on the opening day of the tournament.

Ben actually says he felt more pressure at First Stage than he does this week, but the thought of a Tour Card adds a serious tone to his voice. "It would mean everything if I got through," he says without hesitation. Ben looks even younger than his 20 years; his body is still filling out and his face is that of an adolescent. But he talks with authority for one so young and his talent is obvious; he definitely has the eye for a birdie and only needs to keep those errors to a minimum to have a good chance.

Of the other Final Stage rookies, Austrians Florian Praegant (69 today) and Roland Steiner (71) are well inside the top 20; Craig Lee of Scotland, a survivor of the horrid First Stage weather at St Annes Old Links, cards a 68 to lie tied 5th; and England's Gary Boyd (one of only two amateurs still in the field) manages consecutive 71s for a 2 under total and tied 18th.

But not everyone is settling into the six-round marathon. Andrew Coltart shoots a torrid 77 on the Old Course and is now tied 120th on 5 over; unsurprisingly, his mood of optimism is no longer apparent. Other past Tour champions like David Park (5 over) Malcolm MacKenzie (7 over) and David Carter and Raymond Russell (both 9 over) are already staring into the void.

However, Australia's Peter Senior is showing that there is life in the oldies; his 67 moves him to 4 under for the tournament in his first ever visit to the European Tour Q School. The event's oldest player at 48, Peter is warming up for the Seniors Tour more than he is in desperate need of retaining his Card, but it would be a considerable blow to his pride if he failed here and he intends to fight hard the whole week.

Two players in particular feel the full force of the difference between days one and two. Robert Coles's opening 66 was a great start, but Q School is like a man-trap waiting to snare unsuspecting victims and the Englishman slumps to a catastrophic 79 on the Old Course today.

"My 66 was a surprise, but not as much of a surprise as this. It was a bad day. I've had a massive high and a massive low now. I had a four-putt and a three-putt early on and was giving away shots too easily. It's difficult to get those shots back at Q School," he says. Coles was leading by two shots yesterday; today he is tied 66th with 16 others.

At least Robert was not alone in his agony; Sweden's Frederik Orest followed a 68 with a second round 80 and fell from joint second to tied 109th.

Golf is no different for these experienced tournament pros than it is for millions of amateurs – just when you think your game is sorted, it turns around and bites back. And this is only day two.

Day Three

"If you don't get your Card one year, then you don't know if you'll ever make it back on Tour again." – Alastair Forsyth, Tour winner and four-time Q School attendee.

Sometimes the pain that golf imparts is just too much. Euan Little is one of the best-humoured and chattiest players on Tour. He is a hail-fellow-well-met guy who has a word for everyone and knows how to enjoy life. But day three of the Final Stage of Q School is one golfing disappointment too far.

For much of Euan's third day, he is in control of his game. He is playing well within himself on the New Course again and is steadily pushing into the very heart of the event. He comes off the 9th green 2 under for the tournament; Euan is starting to play to his potential.

Then comes some of the most upsetting few holes of his career. The wind has been blowing from the start, but like any Scottish golfer, Euan is used to such conditions. However, from nowhere, his good form turns turtle. There is a needless three-putt bogey on the par 5 11th and two double bogeys on 14 and 17. Euan finds himself fighting a fault in his swing; he is getting stuck underneath the ball at impact and relying on his hands to get him out of trouble. Like at Second Stage, he is over-analysing the problem and it is sapping his confidence. As he picks the ball out of the hole on 17, he suddenly feels slightly light-headed; it is the tension, the intense concentration, his overwhelming desire for a Tour Card. Q School is taking its toll and proving it really is no ordinary tournament.

Euan had put himself into the top 20 after 9 holes and then stumbled through 41 shots (5 over) on the back 9. Only one player all day (young Englishman Seve Benson who was on his way to a 14 over par three day total and second-to-last place) played a worse 9 holes.

This is precisely the wrong score at the wrong time and Euan's 75 means he has gone tumbling backwards; even a par score today would have moved him up the field.

When golf is your life, you learn to take the blows. There is only ever one champion in a tournament of 150 or so players. Even the perfect round or simply the perfect shot, is sometimes unobtainable. Most of the time, players understand that golf is simply a game of imperfections; they do not hit their irons quite crisply enough, they mis-read some putts or their driver misbehaves. There is little room for error in modern-day golf because the courses are so long, greens incredibly slick and the rough too penal; but the players learn to cope.

For the first time in over a year of talking about Q School and his dreams of returning to the Tour, Euan is almost speechless. He is angry with himself, numb in his body and sick to his stomach. He says only a few words outside the scorer's tent before leaving. "That's as mad as I've ever seen him," says one of the Scottish golf writers Jock MacVicar who has known Euan for many years.

Euan has plenty of support – Willie Crowe, his sponsor, has provided his accommodation here; Euan phones Bob Torrance, his coach, most evenings; and friends from the Tour like ex-Ryder Cup player Philip Walton are constantly calling and texting best wishes.

But no one can console him today. Euan is now tied 77th on 3 over along with nine other players and the predicted four round cut mark is most likely to be two under. Missing the cut here provides almost the same limbo-land ranking as failing at Second Stage; it is an outcome that Euan cannot contemplate. His mood had been sunny before today, but Q School just got deadly serious.

He is now caught up in the chasing pack instead of hunting with the leaders. A handful of these players on the fringe of the cut will come through tomorrow, but will Euan be one of them?

Euan is not alone in falling foul of the last few holes on the notorious New Course at San Roque. Fellow Scot Andrew Oldcorn ends with a 76, leaving him at 4 over; Robert Coles does not match his day one 66 on the New and limps to a 73 for a 2 over total; and Oscar Floren's good luck at being the last alternate to get a place at San Roque runs out with a 75 to take him to 5 over.

On the Old Course, Andrew Coltart's struggles begin to overwhelm him as a 75 has him at 8 over and with one foot on the plane home; David Carter is even worse off on 12 over after the same third round score. David Park keeps himself in the hunt with a 71 for 4 over and now, like Dean Robertson (also 4 over) and Andrew Marshall (5 over), needs to find a round in the 60s just to play the last final days.

Even for hardened pros, poor rounds of golf at crucial times like these are tough to accept. For the amateurs, missing out on the monthly medal with a three-putt might mean an extra pint in the bar afterwards to drown their sorrows, but the pro has to immediately eliminate negative memories and move on to the next round otherwise they would be paralysed with fear of making another mistake. There will be dozens of golfers fighting for their livelihoods and careers tomorrow and tonight they are all looking for the answer. There are no free spaces on driving range this evening.

At the other end of the scoreboard, Sion Bebb is moving relentlessly upwards and completes his first nine holes (the New Course back 9) in one under par. The re-draw has put him in a threeball with two young hopefuls, Florian Praegant and Gary Boyd and both are displaying their potential. While Gary starts well, his luck eventually runs out and he finishes with a 75. Meanwhile, Florian is relying almost exclusively for his putting on a local retired English stockbroker named Barry who is a long-time friend of the Austrian golf team coach Anders Forsbrand. "Putting is the weakest part of Florian's game," says Barry as he shoulders the bag for another stroll along a fairway. "I'm reading every one of his putts for him because I know the greens better, I've played here a few times." The father-and-son-style partnership is working as Florian holes some unlikely putts – even one from the fringe of the 16th for birdie – and finishes with a 67 to climb up the field into a tie for 3rd on 7 under.

Sion is shaking his head as his inexperienced partners play carefree golf and on the back 9 he has a crisis of his own. A sudden gust of wind and a bad kick sends his 6-iron tee shot on the par 3 4th into a hazard and, after a penalty drop, Sion writes up his first double bogey of the week. All the good work of the first part of the round is now cancelled out. He gathers himself and drains a good 4-footer for par on the 5th, but then misses a 6ft birdie on the next. Sion is grinding and almost ready to settle for level par today; then the unexpected happens. He hits a sand wedge to 5ft on the 7th and a 4-iron tee shot to 1ft on the 8th for two easy birdies.

Sion's drive on the 9th ends up behind a tree to the left of the fairway and he decides to gamble with a 7-iron from 186 yards and over water. A slight draw and he is in the hazard, but the strike is perfect and the ball lands 15ft away. A third birdie on the bounce gives Sion a 69; out of almost nowhere he has one of the best scores on a very difficult day.

Sion is now tied 9th halfway through the tournament, but absolutely refuses show complacency. A couple of friends congratulate him, yet he chooses to deflect the praise and talk about how hard he needs to concentrate tomorrow. A few practice putts as the afternoon ends and Sion is off to watch some football on the TV. Another day over, another good job done.

Phil Golding's day three was always going to be a profound test of his character. On day one, he showed inevitable rough edges while on day two he was assured and silky-smooth – so which side of his game will show up today? A bogey-birdie start on the New Course has Phil still wondering what the answer is; when he three-putts the par 3 4th for a second bogey, then he is left shaking his head.

However, Phil finds some answers. On the back 9, two birdies and an eagle reverse his fortunes and he finishes with his second consecutive 69. His iron play is outstanding – almost pitching in for an eagle on the par 4 14th – and he is setting up plenty of birdie chances.

But putting is so often the key and Phil is particularly pleased with his showing on the greens especially because he gambled with a change of putter before the tournament began. Phil rarely changes his putter, but explored his garage five weeks ago and re-discovered an old White Hot Odyssey he had never used before in any tournament. According to Jason his coach, the Odyssey sets his hands slightly forward and in a better position for a more consistent stroke. In golf, the smallest adjustments can mean the biggest improvements.

Phil now lies joint 13th on 3 under for the tournament and, considering he was 5 over just 39 holes ago, he has definitely come to the party. Two Spaniards – Pablo Larrazabal and Luis Claverie – lead on 8 under while only Praegant's 67 and Claverie and Joakim Bäckström of Sweden with 68s shoot better than Phil today.

This is the first day of thick, low clouds to match a gusting wind; many players dress in black or other dark clothing as if the more mournful weather reflects their more serious mood. Yes, the wind has become a factor, but there are also a few Q School quivers. The scoring reflects the growing anxiety among the golfers. On day one, 58 players broke par, today just 33 players managed the same feat.

There will be a veritable cavalry charge tomorrow by all the players just outside the predicted cut mark, all desperate to make the last two days. A round under par tomorrow might eventually be worth a great deal of money and even save a career.

Day Four

"Not making the cut at Q School was the worst feeling ever because you basically get no playing rights and it meant I had to go back to playing EuroPro events." – Graeme Storm, Tour winner and four-time Q School attendee.

Q School is such a compulsively fascinating event because there is tension in every single shot and every single player will have a significant story to tell by the end of it. Day four of Final Stage is probably the second most awful day for the players; if they fail to make this cut then, not only do they miss the final two rounds and contest the top 30 spots for a Tour Card, but they are also denied any worthwhile playing category for next season.

The other cruel drama of day four of Q School is the interminable end-of-the-day wait to see who leaves and who stays. The main scoreboard near the outdoor restaurant and bar area of the San Roque GC is the focus all week for the hundreds of players, caddies, friends and family. The cut mark will move up and down during the day in keeping with the fluctuating fortunes of the players and the tension at this wailing wall is palpable. Some very capable players will be packing their bags today, their livelihoods suddenly in jeopardy.

As dawn breaks with bright sunshine and no wind, the cut mark is 2 over par. Seventy six players are on that mark or better as the players tee off and the chatter in the locker-room is speculation about whether 2 over will still be the cut mark at the end of the day. The general consensus is that 1 over will certainly make it, 2 over might be cause for anxiety; and anyone on 3 over will almost certainly need to settle their hotel bill. So, the strategies are clear: those players inside the cut need par at least; those around 2 over will want to shoot under par just to make sure; and anyone further back will need to go low.

Euan Little begins the day on 3 over and tees off on the Old Course in the first group on the 10th tee. He knows what he needs to do. His mood is one of concentrated calm; he now needs a convincing start.

However, everyone's nerves are tweaked after Gary Lockerbie's opening drive; somehow, on one of the easier driving holes, the Englishman hooks his first shot out of bounds. Lockerbie – playfully nicknamed 'Disaster' by his contemporaries – eventually takes a double bogey 7.

Any knot in Euan's stomach might have twisted a little after seeing a ball go OB, but his own first tee shot is fine and he reaches the green in a regulation three shots, has a 6ft birdie chance, but pulls it slightly left. A par. No worries, no dramas. On his third hole, he picks up his first shot against the course; he is now 2 over. Four more pars follow and Euan is looking composed and confident.

There is, however, an emerging problem. The third player in the group is the young German Benjamin Miarka who is living up to his reputation as one of the slowest players on any tour. Inexperienced tour pros are not always in tune with speed of play at the top-level tournaments. They sometimes still use elaborate pre-shot routines that should be left on the practice range or they want to spend extra time visualising their shots or they slow to a crawl when weather conditions are poor. A few decades ago, a threeball would race around 18 holes in three and a half hours; nowadays, rounds of professional golf too often last for over five hours and the younger players know no better. Slow play is seen as a cancer within the sport and the senior pros are irritated – even angered – by it. For some, the slow play is tantamount to cheating.

The rules state that players are allowed one minute to complete a putt and 40 seconds for all other shots once it is their turn to play, but Miarka is taking almost twice his allotted time on some shots. The threeball is put on the clock by an official after only a couple of holes and they manage just seven holes in two hours. Miarka is eventually personally warned about slow play. To be on the clock is the kind of disturbance no Q Schooler needs and is especially frustrating for the two players innocent of any infraction. Euan stands away from Miarka at every opportunity; he tries to relax into his own space to guard against letting the situation get the better of him.

By the par 5 17th (the group's 8th hole) Euan hits what caddie Brian calls a 'Bing Crosby' (a drive that flies straight down the middle). The Scot then lays up with his second and hits a 129yd wedge for his third to give himself a 12ft birdie chance. He holes it and is back to 1 over. After another solid drive on 18, he has almost the same wedge shot as the previous hole; the ball lands 20ft from the pin this time and Euan grabs another birdie. He now stands at level par for the tournament and last night's dark mood is far from his mind.

Euan is feeling a little more relaxed, but the more difficult 9 holes now await him. It is a long walk between the 18th and the 1st and, on the way, he chats about the weather. "Beautiful day," he says to no one in particular as the group walks behind the scoreboard outside the clubhouse restaurant and towards the 1st tee. Euan does not give in to the temptation to check any scores; he is thinking only of holding his newly-found form, especially on the greens. He is thankful for a putting tip he received last night. Euan complained of feeling a little trapped in his putting posture and a fellow pro suggested he move a couple of inches backwards, away from the ball. The tip seems to be working.

The problem holes on Euan's next 9 are likely to be the 6th, 7th and 8th, none of which seem to fit the eye of the majority of the players including him. The strategy is to build up a head of steam in the first five holes, hang on through this three-hole stretch before a final birdie chance on the par 5 9th.

However, trouble can also come from elsewhere. The 1st is an ordinary par 4 with a fairway slanting wickedly to the right away from a massive bunker in driver range on the left hand side to catch the overly cautious tee shot. In addition, the end of the driving range – an out of bounds area – is just to the left of the bunker. The required shot (for right-handers, anyway) is a driver or 2-iron towards the right edge of the big bunker with a touch of fade. At best, the ball will find the short grass; at worst, a short iron second shot from sand to a slightly elevated green is none too difficult.

Euan takes driver and is first of the group to hit. As soon as he strikes the ball, he knows something is wrong. Instead of heading for the right hand edge of the bunker, the ball is hooking to the left, heading towards a cart path. The ball appears to veer sharply even further to the left on landing and no one is quite sure where it finishes. Something freakish has happened and Euan hits a provisional tee shot just in case.

He shakes his head softly after his second tee ball lands in the fairway bunker. Euan has spent the previous nine holes repairing the damage of the previous 24 hours and now he might have undone much of the good work in one shot.

After trudging up the fairway, Euan hopes for a miracle. He scans the bunker and the rough around it, but is now fairly certain that his first tee shot went out of bounds. After a couple of minutes, he sees his Titleist among a bunch of practice balls on the driving range. His ball actually hit the corner edge of the cart path and shot 40 yards offline. Being out of bounds with his first drive means a two-shot penalty and Euan is now staring at a double bogey. Sure enough, one sand shot and two putts later and he writes '6' on his scorecard. He is back to 2 over with the toughest part of the course still to come.

The words of Euan's coach Bob Torrance now come to his mind. Bob is his mentor and Euan respects everything he says and, as well as coaching his swing, the older man knows how successful golfers overcome adversity. Euan can hear Bob's voice: "Head down, bum up, plough on." It is now or never; Euan must get himself out of the mess he has got himself into.

A birdie chance on the 2nd from 8ft misses just to the right, yet he unexpectedly holes a birdie from 20ft on the par 3 3rd, the ball falling into the cup with its very final ounce of energy. Back to 1 over. The 4th (a short par 4) and 5th (a reachable par 5) both provide more birdie chances, but Euan misses the crucial putts by a fraction each time. On the 5th his putt actually sits on the very edge of the hole and refuses to drop.

Now his margin of error is small. Euan needs four pars to finish on 1 under and make the cut, but if he drops just one more shot then 2 over is likely to mean the end of his tournament. If he should somehow fall to 3 over, then that score would definitely be too many. Euan has to dig deep. Unfortunately, three of the last four holes have been absolute bitches all week.

The 6th hole on the Old Course is a relatively short par 4, but both the drive and second shot require precision. The tee shot is a long iron or rescue club because the landing area for driver would be in the middle of the fairway lake. A bunker on the right of the fairway catches plenty of tee shots and there is a drop-away bank to the left, so the fairway is quite tight, no more than 20 paces at best. Euan aims right and his ball bounces through the fairway bunker and onto a grassy downslope; actually being in the bunker would make for an easier second shot.

The green is elevated with a deep bunker cutting into the front left edge, plus it is two-tiered and the pin is invariably on the top level. From the fairway bunker side, Euan has a tall cork oak 50yds away slightly blocking his shot so he tries to hit a 6-iron with some fade to the back of the green. He decides to grip slightly down the shaft because of the downslope, but that takes a crucial few yards off the distance and the ball finds the deep front bunker. It is not an easy sand shot and Euan's ball gets no backspin and runs 15ft past the pin. The par putt then slips past the hole on the right. Bogey. Two over.

Play grinds to a halt again as the group reaches the 7th tee. Euan's dropped shot may be partly a product of the pace of play; he likes to play at a much faster pace.

Ironically, he now has to stand and wait again which only gives him more time to reflect on his dropped shot. Now he feels he must get another birdie. However, par on the 7th hole – his 16th – would be a good result today never mind a birdie. The pin is back left and Euan tries to draw a tee shot off the right hand side. The ball does not obey his command and holds its line, landing on the fringe of the green. He has an improbable 40ft chip for a two and the ball comes up 4ft short. With no hint of nerves, Euan makes the short putt for another par and remains 2 over with just two holes to play.

Euan has been in plenty of tight situations over his 11-year pro career, not the least of them last week at Second Stage, but these closing holes are testing even his nerve.

The 8th hole is another beast. Again the tee shot has been causing problems all week. There is another right hand side fairway bunker which is attracting plenty of drives and, further to the right, light rough drops into a small swale with a couple of wild olive trees; anywhere here is bogey country. On the left is out of bounds, a place that is proving increasingly magnetic to any player with a slight hook.

Luckily for Euan, the obvious shot here is a draw, his stock shot. He aims over the right hand bunker so that his normal amount of draw will bring the ball back onto the fairway; this tactic takes the out of bounds on the left out of play. However, the tension of Q School is causing Euan's swing to lack authority and, although he avoids the left hand side of the fairway, he still makes a mistake: he blocks his drive away out to the right. His body was moving a little too quickly through the swing and he got slightly ahead of the ball that negated any draw spin. He has not hit a drive like that all day and the shot takes him by surprise. He has no certainty where the ball has landed; all he knows is that he is the swale beyond the right side of the fairway. Things are not looking good.

As he walks towards his ball, Euan ponders that with even half-decent luck he could escape with just a mid-iron to the green; after all, there is only light rough down in the swale. But when he gets closer and sees the damage, he shakes his head in disbelief. The ball has landed right under a small olive tree; Euan can maybe get a wedge on the ball and punch it back onto the fairway, but not much more. Again, he is staring at a bogey. He needs to get as much distance as he can with his second shot. He studies his chances and thinks he can play a clever chip shot past one of the other trees nearby and get close to the green. He thinks it is a risk worth taking.

Euan clips the ball firmly, but it hits an olive tree branch and the ball ends up back in the rough only about 60 yards away. His third shot is a gap wedge that flies over the flag and lands in the first cut of rough at the back of the green. He is then faced with a chip onto a green sloping away from him and with the pin tight at the back; it is one of the hardest shots on the course and, although Euan makes a good fist of it for his par, the ball stays above ground. Another bogey. Three over.

This is now a dire situation. The scoreboards are indicating that even 2 over might be too many, so Euan has no option but to at least birdie his final hole. At least it is a par 5, so there is even an outside chance of an eagle.

Euan's final hole drive is long and straight but a couple of yards too far to the right; a fairway tree will partially block his second shot. He will now need to fade the ball which is not a shot that comes easily to Euan who tends to draw the ball. After plenty of thought and extra consultation with Brian his caddie, Euan tries for the fade, but instead he gets a "double cross" and the ball turns over to the left rather than swinging to the right. There is another long walk before Euan finds his ball yet again in an unappealing spot: partly buried on a grassy slope to the far side of a greenside bunker. His next shot will be with the ball little slightly below his feet, making it even more difficult. Add in what is at stake and it takes all the restraint he can muster not to scream at the golfing gods about his lack of good fortune over the last few holes.

Now it really is all or nothing for Euan. If he can somehow chip in, then he will have eagled the hole and finish on 1 over for the tournament, definitely good enough for two more days. A chip and a putt will leave him on 2 over and a 50-50 chance of staying in the tournament. Anything else and another Q School dream dies.

Bob Torrance told Euan last evening that all he could do was give his best on every shot. Euan is determined to do just that and again takes extra time; it is too late for any official to worry about slow play because the whole field is moving at a crawl. He carefully studies the 50ft chip shot and contours of the green; he will land it about half way and let the ball roll to the hole. To give himself a chance of the eagle, he needs to be a little more aggressive than usual. After several practice strokes, he settles over the shot; one last look at the pin and he is ready.

The ball comes off the clubface a tad thin; it has a low trajectory and is a little more speedy than Euan wants. He stands up off the shot quickly and watches the ball approach the cup; he waits for his miracle. For a slow second or two, he watches the most important shot of his whole golfing year. Just 12 months ago, Euan's Q School ended with an 18th hole drama and here he is again. Will the result be different?

The ball misses the cup by a couple of inches and runs off the other side of the green onto the fringe. It was a shot of great difficulty, a high tariff attempt that he may have been able to hole one time in 20 attempts, but this was not one of them. Euan's face and body twitch almost imperceptibly as he walks to his ball. No chance of a 1 over finish, but he has a 10ft putt to get to 2 over and a sliver of hope.

It is a relatively easy putt, but the ball will travel over at least 3ft of fringe; that means a slightly less than perfect surface for another enormously important shot.

Euan gives the shot the full treatment – he is low on his haunches studying it from all sides; he looks carefully at the edge of the hole; he has not given so much attention to a putt all day. Finally, he strikes the ball firmly, but it bobbles on the fringe. The ball misses by an inch to the left; there is no birdie. Euan taps in for par to record a 72 for the day and 3 over for the tournament. He knows his Q School is over. In 2006, Euan left San Roque desperately upset; 12 months later and nothing has changed.

Euan leans on his putter and stares into the middle distance. He shakes his head very slightly and his face looks tired and empty. He completes the formalities of handshakes with fellow players and caddies and his walk to the scorer's tent 20 yards away is slow and sad.

A year ago, he had made the four-round cut before suffering his crushing, last-round failure – a missed 8ft putt denied him his Tour Card by a single shot. Then his dream was almost in his grasp; this time he has fallen well short. Whatever, the desolation is real, almost physically painful. Euan sits on a bench in the shade and tries to make sense of the last five hours.

At level par with nine holes to play, he looked a certainly to move on to days five and six. But then a cocktail of bad luck and bad shots has ended his season. For the second time in 24 hours, Euan is finding words hard to come by. Any tears can come later; for now he tries to understand what happened intellectually rather than emotionally.

"I am totally deflated. I really tried to overpower my negative thoughts in the last few holes to come up with what I needed, but I was just misfiring and I don't really know why. I would love to play without nerves and today I think I coped with them and I felt very comfortable after nine holes. But the result is the same as last year. I'm gutted."

Euan thinks that his 2006 experience has actually prepared him for today. "That was the worst I've ever felt on a golf course. To get so close and not get a Card; that was a new experience. I let myself down and my family down. Right now, I guess the feeling isn't quite as bad. I'm not as suicidal as I thought I might be. I think 2006 taught me something."

These are brave words; it is less final half an hour after another cruel let-down and he is searching for words and reasons for what happened. "I'm actually still furious about yesterday because I let it get away from me in the last few holes. At one stage I got really light-headed and I thought my head was going to explode. There were doubts in my mind. I was hitting bad shots that I hadn't seen for months."

There will be some beers tonight with Willie, his sponsor, as yet another player tries to comprehend what happened to his plans, his dream of the Tour. Euan struggles to find his normal sanguine self; this man, who is so open and chatty, is now drained by another tortuous Q School in which he came up short.

"I suppose there's more to life than getting yourself wound up about this. Things just didn't work out." Like most of his professional golfing counterparts, Euan tries to see the best in every situation, but Q School has dealt him another blow and full recovery will be a slow process.

By contrast later in the day, Sion Bebb and Phil Golding are both smiling broadly, especially the Englishman. Phil shoots his third successive 69 including a hole-in-one at the 7th hole on the Old Course. He is now 6 under par for the tournament.

It would be the only ace of the week and Phil is slicing through the field at a rate of knots. Given that he was 5 over par after 15 holes on day one, his streak of good form is even more remarkable. He is tied 11th and no player has scored better over the last 54 holes.

"I got a bit edgy on the back 9, so I've still got something to work on," he says afterwards. "I'm going to keep the same routine: a bit of putting and then hit 30 balls or so and get some rest. I'm still reminding myself it's process, process, process; no punching the air. It sounds a bit boring, but even on the hole-in-one – it was a 4-iron, two bounces and in – I just shook hands with Jason, kissed the ball and moved on."

Sion – playing the New Course – matches Phil's score and is now in third place on his own at 8 under. But after each day he looks a little more fatigued. "Every shot is mentally draining out there," he says after his round. "Another two rounds to go; I'm happy with my score, but I'm not smiling until Tuesday." He returns to his apartment for tea and pizza plus as much sleep as he can get.

Lee Slattery hits the round of the day, a 64. He started day four at 1 over par, on the fringes of the cut, yet is now 7 under and tied 4th. In the lead is Spain's Pablo Larrazabal and Thomas Aiken of South Africa, both on 10 under.

But the story of the day is not about the leaders, it is of those around the cut mark. Back in the scorer's tents, Jenny Janes and Carmel Treacy of the Tour's Field Staff are not only acting as official recorders, but also official deliverers of sympathy and advice to players who are on or near the mark. As the afternoon progresses, those on 2 over are increasingly in danger of missing the cut; the calm conditions are allowing a few extra birdies. Once the first few groups sign their cards, the level of anxiety at the giant scoreboard grows steadily.

England's Andrew Marshall is one Tour veteran on the edge. He has just shot his best round so far – a 3 under 69 – and is one of those on 2 over. But he is worried and already talking of other options if his Q School implodes.

"Every day's been a few too many for me. I was 4 under with three to play and shot a 69; it should have been 6 or 7 under. I needed another birdie,

I suppose. It's tougher here every year and not making the cut will be hard to take."

As the hours tick by, still no one knows for sure if 1 over or 2 over will be the cut mark. The top 70 players and ties will remain in contention and, by 3pm with plenty of groups still playing, the cut looks like falling at 1 over. Then just an hour later, after a few nervous players drop shots towards the end of their rounds, 70th place moves to 2 over. Andrew Marshall and about a dozen other players standing at the wailing wall breathe a sigh of relief.

But the drama is not over as everyone waits until the final group reaches the scorer's tent. In the end, a late birdie by Robert Rock – one of the last players to finish – kills off the chances of no less than 16 players on 2 over. Seventy one hopefuls finish 1 over or better and will contest rounds five and six while 85 players will be leaving San Roque earlier than planned.

There are plenty of dreadfully sad stories. Frenchman George Plumet and Björn Pettersson of Sweden both double bogey their last hole to miss by one; Van Phillips of England, a former Portuguese Open champion, slumps to a 78 and a 6 over total when even par today would have been enough; the 2001 PGA Champion Andrew Oldcorn cannot make a comeback and finishes 7 over; Brazil's Alexandre Rocha, who was joint winner of last year's Q School, is also 7 over; Dean Robertson of Scotland suffers from too little competition in top tournaments and cannot break par during the entire week, yet still only misses by three shots. The list of quality golfers falling at this hurdle is a long one and includes several former Tour champions: Darren Fichardt of South Africa, Steven O'Hara and Raymond Russell of Scotland, David Park, Mark Mouland and Mark Pilkington of Wales, ex-Ryder Cup star Joakim Haeggman of Sweden and Wade Ormsby of Australia.

The leader on day one, England's Robert Coles, and Sweden's Fredrik Orest, who was joint second after the opening round, are both going home after today. But perhaps the most heart-rending story is Andrew Coltart's.

The 37-year-old from Dumfries in Scotland should really be in his prime golfing years; he has two Tour titles and one Ryder Cup appearance to his credit. He is well-liked by his peers and by the media, but this season's form has been dreadful, no top 10s and 18 missed cuts in 29 starts. A fourth round score of 73 leaves him 9 over par and 138th in a 156-man field. The tough Scot with the Sean Connery accent is still in a state of shock straight afterwards. "I haven't played well for a while and it continued in that vain this week; it's not enjoyable. No one department, it was just pretty poor in general. I didn't play well in the 2nd round (a 5 over par 77) and that gave me a lot to do. I couldn't get anything going."

His eyes are hidden behind reflective sunglasses, but it is clear that Andrew is angry to find himself in this unexpected situation after 15 consecutive seasons on Tour. His words are clipped with disappointment. "I never envisaged missing out on my Card at all and I thought that was a good tactic, but it backfired subsequently. What now? I have no idea, some invitations, I suppose," he says. "I'll have a wee think about it in a week or so when my head has cleared a bit."

This was Coltart's first visit to Q School since 1993, but with so much talent bursting through every year, it may not be his last.

Day Five

"I think all pros should spend a year on Challenge Tour, but Q School is one of these things where you get a chance of creating something for yourself. It's a lot of pressure to live with and a lot of pressure to play under." – Thomas Bjorn, multiple Tour winner, Ryder Cup player and two-time Q School attendee.

Q School is noticeably quieter on its penultimate morning. There is a sombre mood in the practice areas. The odd player who missed the cut or a newly-unemployed caddie amble around the tournament office looking for travel advice or information on other golf events. The players remaining in the hunt for Tour Cards acknowledge the fallen and offer good luck wishes and a handshake. But there is not really much anyone can say.

There is plenty of room on the driving range and practice putting greens as the contestants get ready for Moving Day. In a regular golf tournament lasting only four rounds, Moving Day is day three – the halfway cut has fallen and, if a player is going to win, then now is the time to make a move. At Q School, Moving Day becomes day five.

All 71 remaining players now have a chance of a Tour Card; even those who scraped through on 1 over are just three shots off the crucial 30th place. Those towards the back of the field will definitely need to beat par today because no one wants to leave everything to the very final round. There is much debate about what score will be required by the end of tomorrow and 30th place looks likely to fall at 3 under. If the weather deteriorates (which is what the forecasters predict) then 2 under or even 1 under might be enough. Basically, all the players know that pretty much anything can happen over the next 36 holes.

The Old Course will be the site for today's action with the New Course providing the ultimate test tomorrow. There is always a little doubt about how the courses will be used on days five and six, but Mike Stewart, the PGA tournament director, made the decision yesterday afternoon. Tradition dictates that the New Course is left for day six and he is happy to stick to the normal plan.

On day five, the players are placed in new threeball groups in order of scoring, but will still start from two tees The leading players will play from the 1st and tee off later while those at the back of the field will play from the 10th and begin earlier. The opening shot takes place at 9.00am and there are 10-minute gaps between the groups so that there will be plenty of light left at the end of the day in case of unforeseen delays (dusk falls around six in the evening here).

The day dawns with zero wind and blue skies. Although this is mid-November, the sun will still be quite intense by mid-afternoon, with temperatures well into the late 60°s and even early 70°s. With the surprisingly pleasant weather making the golf a little easier – despite the large amounts of nervous tension in the air – controlled aggression is likely to be the tactic of most players.

Phil Golding tees off the 1st at 10.10am in the fifth group from last and gets off to a dream start; after three holes he already has two birdies under his belt. Right now, he can do no wrong. Pars at the 4th and 5th keep him on track and at 8 under his name will appear on the leaderboard for the first time.

The course is set up for someone to score low and one of Phil's playing partners – Terry Pilkadaris of Australia – birdies all of the first three holes; it is definitely going to be somebody's big day.

Sion Bebb tees off in the last threeball of the day on 8 under with two 24-years-olds, Pablo Larrazabal and Thomas Aiken, who are leading by two shots. Larrazabal and Sion are the only players to have scored under par on each day, while Aiken (a regular this year on the American PGA's Nationwide Tour) is the kind of player with his supreme length who could take either of the San Roque courses apart.

The styles of the two young men and the more experienced Welshman could not be more different. Larrazabal and Aiken are both firing for the pins and thinking about winning Q School while Sion has an out-and-out no-risk philosophy, reckoning par as a good score on each hole long before he thinks of a birdie.

Sion seems a little out of sorts today; he is not hitting his irons close enough for birdie chances and his putter is luke warm. His conservative tactics have been working so far, but his two young partners are soon picking up shots around him while Sion starts to drift backwards after a clumsy bogey on the par 5 5th where he bunkers his wedge third shot and then three-putts. He needs to find his rhythm.

Up ahead, Phil negotiates the awkward par 4 6th in par, but at the short 7th he tugs a 4-iron tee shot into the left hand bunker and cannot get up and down in two. It is his first bogey of the day. Nevertheless, another par on 8 is followed by a fourth birdie on 9. Phil is 8 under at the turn with only five players ahead of him. It has been a remarkable run.

While Phil remains calm, Jason his caddie cannot help his mind from racing ahead; surely they can push on from here, he says, the trickiest part of the course is behind them. If proof were needed, Pilkadaris dropped five shots at the 6th, 7th and 8th compared to Phil's one.

Back in the final group, Sion actually comes through the same tough three-hole section unscathed and is only 1 over for the day. His frustrations are building however, because his young playing partners are thrashing the ball all over the course and still improving their scores. Some of their recoveries are startling and together Larrazabal and Aiken pick up five birdies and no bogeys on the front 9. At 7 under now, Sion has actually dropped below Phil and is off the leaderboard. Meanwhile, Austrian Martin Wiegele is showing what can be done – he has five birdies of his own in the opening nine holes and has burst into contention on 12 under.

The back 9 on the Old Course seems to be at the mercy of the players, but just to keep the leaders honest, the wind starts to freshen a little as they reach the 10th. Nevertheless, Phil Golding pars 10 and also 11. The 12th is a different matter: he three putts for a bogey and then repeats the mistake on the 14th. Just as Phil was expecting to push on, the course takes back a couple of shots. Then on the par 4 15th, he gets greedy and tries to flush a drive across the right-to-left uphill dogleg. The changing wind fools him and he finds trouble. Suddenly, Phil has wracked up three bogeys and he is 1 over for the day (5 under for the tournament) in the middle of the same kind of poor run that he had on day one.

At the same time, Sion Bebb's lack of birdies means he is also being caught and passed by rivals. His day is summed up on the 10th where he plays his conservative three iron onto the green of the par 5 and settles for par. He can only stand and stare as Aiken slams a 330yd drive (with a 3-wood) to the middle of the fairway and then a 4-iron to 12ft before holing the eagle putt. Larrazabal is almost as impressive; he snags a birdie despite a wayward second shot into some trees level with the green.

It is now 2pm and the final threeball has played just 10 holes in three hours. As predicted, the wind is getting up and play slows to a snail's pace. While Sion looks tired, his young rivals are feeding off pure adrenaline. Sion continues to grind out the pars while fireworks flash around him: Larrazabal finds water on the 11th for bogey and drops another shot at 12 while Aiken – all 5ft 8ins and 155lbs of him – seems to be in his version of The Zone and is heading for an excellent score.

Meanwhile, Phil is coming towards the end of his round and the constantly changing wind is causing him problems. The crucial score of the 30th placed player is moving inexorably towards 4 under and Phil – who was 8 under at the turn – is now just one shot better than that at 5 under. Whereas two hours ago a Tour Card looked odds-on, now he is in real danger.

He has three holes to complete and is looking desperately for one more birdie. He manages an easy par on the 16th while on the par 5 17th Phil has a better chance from just 15ft, but the putt slides wide left. His confidence on the greens is disappearing.

On the 18th, Phil hits rescue club for safety and finishes in the far corner of the dogleg where he can hit a 4-iron approach. He completes the shot and his ball lands on the back left fringe of the green. He is 35ft away and would love to sneak in a long birdie. He hits his birdie attempt with accuracy and it misses by less than an inch. Phil gasps and is unconcerned that the ball slips two and a half feet past the hole. A near tap-in and he will end the day with a 1 over par round to leave him in the top 20 and at least one shot inside the Tour Card mark. Then the unthinkable happens: Phil misses the putt. It was an absolute tiddler by a pro's standards, a gimme in matchplay. Phil has not flunked a putt this short in any of the previous 89 holes; he is in shock.

The broad smile of the previous three days is replaced by a face full of anxiety. Q School is playing its usual tricks, creating drama where there should be none. Phil is back to 4 under and right on the mark for his Tour Card at tied 24th along with eight other players; now he has no room for manoeuvre, no margin for error.

About one hour later, Sion approaches the last hole. The Welshman's back 9 has been a par-fest, eight in a row and he is still 1 over for the round. Even Larrazabal and Aiken have dropped a few shots as their luck slightly ran out in the increasingly windy conditions. However, Sion senses that many other players in the field have been scoring below par (especially because the last group suffered the worst conditions) and he really wants a birdie to finish with a level par 72. He has been averaging at least 3 birdies per round, but has had none so far today.

Sion hits his driving iron off the tee, but his approach comes up 20 yards short of the green. It is a bad mistake, the wind has fooled him and his concentration is running low as he has now been on the course for almost five and a half hours. Sion's chip shot up the green is workmanlike and rests 10ft below the hole; no birdie, but a likely par. After a delay while Aiken holes out for double bogey (he has found the lake with his approach), Sion and Gary his caddie prowl around what they hope will be their final shot.

Sion tries his trademark full-body horizontal position in one last effort to see the line. Then he sends the putt forward at a good pace expecting it to break slightly from the right. It looks set to drop and then lips out on the right hand edge of the cup. Sion is bent double with disappointment as if someone has kicked him in the guts; a second bogey of the day when he really wanted a birdie. His 74 – the same score as Phil – is his worst of the week. While 41 of the 71 players break par today, Sion and Phil are among a handful of the leaders to falter and fall back into the pack.

Sion's 6 under total for five rounds still leaves him tied for 11th, but 30th place is only two shots worse off at 4 under. Another 74 and Sion could ruin his week and all the hard work that he has put in. He had started the day on 8 under and level par today would have left him tied 5th going into day six, not only 90% certain of a Card, but probably a very good Card. Now four days of hard work is forgotten and the 10ft missed par putt floods his mind.

"I'm goin' home," is the full extent of Sion's post-round press conference. He waves everyone away and instead talks things over with Gary near the putting green for a few minutes before heading for the car park. He is seething. His Tour Card seemed secure until today's 74. Now he feels like he has to start all over again from scratch.

Phil does not leave the course quite as swiftly as Sion, but he is also pondering his week so far. He had enjoyed some luck – like the only hole in one of the tournament – but has also fallen foul of bursts of bogeys. He now he faces one of the most challenging rounds of his life. Will the fact that he has played very little this year come back to haunt him or can Phil remember the good times and find the kind of form that made him French Open champion three years ago.

As predicted, it was someone's big day. That someone was Martin Wiegele whose 64 leaves him on 15 under, worth a four shot lead from Aiken (who reached 14 under himself at one stage) and Larrazabal both on 11 and Lee Slattery two shots further back on 9 under.

Today has seen a few players fall totally out of contention for a Tour Card and even fewer at the very top of the leaderboard basically book their places on Tour next season with 18 holes of the New Course still to play. But Q School is the cruellest of tournaments and tomorrow it will demand plenty of heroes but also a few fools. Unfortunately, there is no certainty tonight which players will fill which roles.

Day Six

"You can miss out at Q School and just get lost forever." – Tony Johnstone, multiple Tour winner and 20-year European Tour pro.

The final day of any professional golf tournament is payday; in a normal four-round event, the last 18 holes decides how the prize money is split up. Q School is slightly different. The pros are not really playing for today's prize money at San Roqueas much as the prospect of riches to come. Yes, the £15,000 cheque for finishing first today is nice to win, but you might win a hundred times that amount in a couple of successful seasons on Tour.

The last day of Final Stage is all about where the 30th player finishes. If you can beat him – or at least tie with him – then you have secured your Tour Card for 12 months. Finish below him and you will have to survive on a smaller, much less lucrative Tour or maybe live for a whole year off a few pro-ams and last-minute invitations or you might give up pro tours altogether.

So whole careers are at stake again today and, if that was not cause for enough tension, then a howling easterly wind and predictions of thunderstorms add an exclamation mark. The strong breezes earlier in the week will feel like gentle zephyrs by the end of the day if the forecasters are right, so tournament director Mike Stewart takes no chances. The worst of the weather is due after lunch, so start times are moved up by 30 minutes to 8.30am. Given that it is still dark at 8.00am, this is as early as day six can start and means that the first couple of groups off the tee have less than half an hour of daylight in which to warm up. However, after five consecutive days of 5 hour 15 minute, sweaty-palm rounds, there are not many contenders in a fit state to pound endless balls on the range this morning. Golf pros are used to rolling with the punches of weird weather conditions and, although they might not always agree with every decision tournament officials make, this one seems a sound idea – get the whole thing up and running early and take out the possibility of a day seven. The early start is good news for those players around 30th place because they will start early and most likely enjoy the best of the weather while the leaders teeing off later will suffer the worst. Thirtieth place is currently on 4 under, but the bad weather means the Tour Card mark may drift backwards to 3 or even 2 under, so those players at the very back of the field feel they still have a chance.

The New Course at San Roque, so neatly designed by Pete Dye and Seve Ballesteros, seems almost built to showcase today's prevailing easterly wind and among the two holes most affected, are the 9th and 18th. These holes are hugely under appreciated in the world of golf because they provide some of the sport's most dramatic moments.

The 9th and 18th run parallel to each other and are similar in many ways and, without the addition of wind or Q School tension, they are fairly ordinary: just long-ish par 4s needing a bold tee shot and a precise approach. Today – as in every other final day of Q School at San Roque – the 9th and 18th greens will be places where more heart-busting triumphs and head-hanging tragedies will occur in the shortest time frame than any other European Tour event.

The 453yd 18th hole will be particularly under the spotlight as all the leaders and most of those players around 30th place will finish there. It is a blind drive a fairway that is reasonably generous with only a few scattered nearby trees and no rough to speak of. But when players reach the brow of the fairway hill and feel the fierce headwind blowing into their faces for the second shot then the knots tighten in their stomachs. The approach shot can be anything from a 2-iron to an 8-iron and, all the time, the small green with its slight back-to-front slope sits waiting. There is the lake all along the right hand side and a small valley to the left and at the back; it is both uninviting and intimidating. Plus there is a cart path dangerously close to the green on the left; even that area will likely come into play today. The 18th at San Roque might not compare in European golfing folklore with the 17th at St Andrews or the 18th at Carnoustie, but in Q School history, it has broken many hearts and today it will break some more.

It is another two-tee start and as the 8.30 groups hit their opening shots, the general mood is subdued as everyone – from the volunteers around the course to all players and caddies – knows how much is at stake. Only a couple of players are really without hope today – Fredrik Widmark of Sweden and Jordi Del Moral of Spain who shot 78 and 77 yesterday and are 4 and 5 over respectively. Benjamin Miarka of Germany and Andreas Högberg of Sweden are next worst on 2 over and then seven players stand on 1 over including Tour stalwarts Robert Rock, Gary Emerson and Patrik Sjoland along with Gary Boyd, the only amateur left in the field. Somebody always bursts through the field on the final day of Q School; a 4 under par score of 68 might be enough for these six back markers. And they all know it is possible.

By contrast, Sion Bebb and Phil Golding are inside the top 30 and even par rounds of 72 will probably be good enough for them. They both suffered highly annoying bogeys on their final holes on day five which had soured their evenings. Sion says with great understatement this morning that he was "cheesed off" because he had slipped right back into the pack of players scrambling for Cards rather than being at the head of the field contesting the winner's cheque. He reports a poor night's sleep. "I had butterflies in my stomach because you're thinking of the good things that happen and the bad things as well."

Sion desperately wants another year on the Main Tour and if he fails now after such a great start, it will be terribly hard to swallow. Deep down he understands that today could go either way – another stepping stone to a solid career on Tour or a return to the nowhere-land of Challenge Tour and regional golf. His nightmare is another frustrating 74 like yesterday's, but Sion believes everyone is allowed one bad day in six rounds and he is determined not to put himself through another. His mood is one of quiet confidence.

Phil is a little more difficult to read this morning when it comes to his emotions. He is good at dealing with disasters intellectually and his years on Tour make him guarded about showing his disappointment. However, his coach and caddie Jason knows the true suffering of Phil's final hole yesterday. "That 3-putt really hurt him on the last," Jason says this morning. "We were 8 under after 12 and all I could see was us finishing another one better than that or at least the same." Phil had fought his way into the comfort zone with just six holes to play, yet now he starts in the danger zone instead. Only eight players shot worse than 74 yesterday, so Phil's career is once again teetering on the edge of collapse. A second so-called sabbatical year could be tantamount to early retirement for him. He cannot allow it to happen.

The Englishman is off in the third group of the day from the 1st tee at 8.50am with Terry Pilkadaris of Australia and fellow countryman Lee S James, all of them on 4 under. There are some forced smiles among the group, but this is a day destined for endurance not enjoyment. Phil needs a solid opening few holes, but when he hits his first drive of the day it is everything he does not want. He pushes his shot badly to the right into a copse of cork trees, the ball coming to rest behind one of them; there is no other option but a chip-out.

How often does this happen to even the best pros? All the experience, all the rehearsals, all the muscle memory and they start a crucial round with a horrid shot. It happens even to the very best (remember Tiger Woods' first shot in the 2006 Ryder Cup hooked directly into water?). Phil is already deep in thought and walks extra-slowly down the fairway. If nerves were not already bothering him, then they will be now.

After the chip out, Phil hits a very brave third just over a bunker to within 10ft; he tugs the putt slightly and it misses left. A bogey start is just what he and every other Q Schooler does not need on day six.

However, the dropped shot seems to get Phil's attention and ramps up his concentration level. The par 5 2nd hole gives up an easy birdie to him, so the damage is immediately repaired. Solid pars on holes 3, 4 and 5 show that Phil's head is dealing with any demons. He is slightly helped by his two playing partners making similar errors to his own – almost no one is free from sin on the last day of Q School. Lee is continually over-clubbing his irons and Terry is also making mental errors and dropping shots. Q School, true to form, is working its evil spells.

On the 6th, there is another birdie chance for Phil from 6ft, but it is missed. The player lets out a big sigh; Jason grimaces. One third of the round gone and no real sign of how his day will end; he is still on the mark at 4 under.

Meanwhile, Sion is in the 7th group off the 1st tee, playing 40 minutes behind Phil and, by contrast, his game is transformed from the day before. Instead of being unable to hit approach shots close enough or not holing mid-range putts, Sion has turned both parts of his game around. Despite predictions of nerves – he birdies the 2nd, 3rd and 4th to suddenly re-appear on the leader board at 9 under. His 25ft putt on the 4th for the third consecutive birdie is particularly welcome because it is just over an hour into his round and the first really heavy gust of wind blows in followed by a few spots of rain. Spectators start to unroll their umbrellas.

The weather forecasters have got it right. The leading group of Thomas Aiken, Pablo Larrazabal and Martin Wiegele are still on their first hole and the wind and rain is starting. The more birdies you have in the bag by now, the happier you are. Sion is in control of his own destiny again; he is five shots clear of the Tour Card mark (4 under) and does not need to press from this position. He can return to his tactic of pushing gently forward, accepting any birdies, but avoiding the slightest chance of a round-busting mistake.

By contrast Phil has no such safety net and a bogey 6 at the par 5 7th means he has slipped out of the top 30. Then, another mistake: Phil's tee shot comes up short left of the par 3 8th when anything right is safe. It is a second bogey on the bounce and Phil has fallen to 2 under, in danger of slipping into all-out reverse. Jason starts working overtime on re-focusing his friend's mind.

The 9th is into the headwind that is now gaining power and Phil's tee shot is another push, not dissimilar from his opening drive. Yet this time lady luck smiles and he hits a tree trunk, bouncing into the middle of the fairway. He then draws a 4-iron approach shot in to 30ft, leaving him with a relatively calm two-putt par.

Phil turns in 38, 2 over par for the day and 2 under for the tournament. At this point there are 30 players on the scoreboard at 4 under or better, so the cut is right where it began the day and Phil is outside it. There is no sign of a burst of birdies from players behind him, so Phil is by no means out of contention. It is too early to predict the final cut mark, but Jason is keeping his eyes and ears open. When it comes down to the last few holes, Phil will need to know exactly where he stands.

Sion's story could not be more different. The smelly 6 that Phil took on the 7th is put into context by the now back-in-form Welshman who gets another confident birdie and is 4 under for the day and 10 under for the tournament. Sion has made as much progress through the field as anyone and is feeling confident about a high finish. Around him, however, there are raw nerves; Aiken, the young South African, drops four shots in his first six. More wind and rain means birdies are now at a premium, even for the leaders.

Meanwhile, a three-hole downwind section begins the back 9 for Phil; it is a great chance to recover his position. The long walk from the 9th green up a sharp incline to the 10th tee gives him time to reflect. He is walking well behind his playing partners spending considerable amounts of time selecting clubs and studying his yardage book. This unhurried pace helps him concentrate; he knows his score can still be turned around particularly after Jason reminds him he is averaging four birdies per round and he has achieved only one so far.

The rain has now stopped and the sky is actually brightening, but the wind is freshening and gusting, so choosing the right club is now a difficult job. Phil gets his club selection just right on the 10th with a steady par and follows that with a birdie on the 11th thanks to his new, trusty Odyssey White Hot # 7 putter.

On the 12th Phil has an outside birdie chance from 33ft. As he surveys the putt, he thinks of his six-year-old son Lucas and a conversation he had with the boy the previous night after his annoying fifth round. "Why are you grumpy, Daddy?" asked Lucas. "You've had a hole in one and some birdies. Don't be grumpy." Phil's mind is filled with the picture of his son's smiling face; Lucas loves his daddy whatever happens on the golf course. Freeing his mind from the strain of the game, Phil drains the birdie. He is two-thirds through his last 18 holes and back to 4 under for the tournament. Phil recognises the atmosphere of unpredictability from previous Q Schools; a potential disaster is around every corner. Yet with conditions growing ever more windy, he now has a score that will definitely be good enough. But this is a classic Q School day – bewildering and topsy-turvy; there are no easy holes and Phil will do well to hang on.

While Phil's 13th passes without incident – a tap-in par – Sion's bandwagon is wobbling again in the worsening conditions. The three holes after the turn are supposed to be birdie chances – being downwind – but Sion finds a bunker off the tee on No 10 and three putts for a bogey. Then on the 11th fairway, Gary his caddie suddenly falls to the ground with a cry of pain; bizarrely, he has stepped into a drainage pipe hole covered only by a piece of replaced fairway turf. It is like a booby trap and Gary's first thought is that he has broken his leg. The hole is several inches deep and he badly gashes his left shin; there is blood everywhere. Gary wonders whether he can actually continue, but adrenaline soon kicks in and the Scot gets back on his feet after a few minutes, albeit limping quite badly. His leg is very painful, but there is a job to finish. The scary thing is that the hole was very near Sion's ball and the player probably missed suffering the injury himself by only a few inches.

Despite his reassurances, Gary is a little rattled and so, naturally, is Sion. The two men have formed a close working relationship in the last few weeks and this is their first real crisis of any kind. A bogey 6 almost inevitably follows. Then on the 12th, Sion three putts for his third bogey in a row. He has fallen to 7 under and his slide has to stop right now. Sion is annoyed, so Gary reminds him that he is playing well; just go back to the old routine of fairways-and-greens.

By now, the wind is a factor on every single shot, even the putts. Gusts well over 30mph mean that players are backing off shots and their golf balls are being swept off course through the air; even balls on the greens are in danger of being blown off their spots. Of all the types of weather conditions, a strong, gusting wind is the most disliked by pros. PGA referees around the course are carefully monitoring conditions and three reports about balls oscillating on the green will cause a delay. Little did anyone know on the course but this near-gale has already blown over the event scoreboard near the clubhouse and will later divert flights away from nearby Gibraltar Airport. A gripping climax is about to begin.

With five holes to play and at 4 under, Phil Golding would settle for a run of no-nonsense pars, but golf is rarely a game of serene, untroubled progress. The 14th is a par four that is almost a rehearsal for the horrid 18th – the distance is almost the same, the headwind is in the player's face and there is a lake on the right of the green. Phil hits another powerful drive that leaves him with a 4-iron second shot that he can draw in from the right to the pin positioned left. "We need one more birdie," says Jason, but when the approach shot is in the air, no one is thinking of a three.

Phil pushes his ball a little too far right and shouts "Get down" almost immediately. He and Jason are frozen as they watch the ball hang out over the lake for a couple of seconds and Phil's Q School chances hang with it. Somehow, a slight draw and a little wind work in its favour veering the ball slightly to the left to land on the fringe area around the green less than two yards from the water. With a true sense of drama, Phil's lucky Titleist # 3 (he has played the same number golf ball each day) then rolls another few feet before stopping less than two feet from disaster. It could just as easily have taken a hop into the lake or carried on running a little further, but the golfing gods give Phil a big break. The word 'relief' hardly describes his emotions at this point. Phil has not mis-fired a shot into water so far this week and this is about as close as he wants to get to it. The margin for error on that shot was far too close for comfort; the strain is beginning to show and a par is a blessed relief. But still the rollercoaster will not stop.

Phil's drive on the 15th is too close to a tree and requires a sliding cut shot for his second to a pin on the front of the green. Phil comes up short with his approach and decides to putt over a very bumpy fairway area. It is the right shot and the pace is perfect, but the ball bobbles six feet to the right. He fails to hole the par putt and the luck he enjoyed on 14 deserts him. Back to 3 under.

There are now 35 players on Phil's score which means he must par the last three holes for his Card. A relatively easy task on any other day but today. The par 5 16th actually offers a birdie chance and a cushion; Phil hits a super drive and then a solid 5-wood that comes up just short of the green. He chips on to the top tier within 5ft and the putt drops. Sensational – a birdie and 4 under again; surely his drama is over.

The crosswind on the 17th is Phil's next problem and club selection is the key. What he does not want is to bring the huge bunker on the right into play. Phil and Jason spend an age choosing a club because the wind is now switching direction almost by the second. Amazingly, however, Phil commits the cardinal sin of playing the one shot he was aiming to avoid. He hits a perfect rescue club for distance, but the ball dribbles into the sand to the right of the green.

It is not a difficult bunker shot, but the circumstances make it so. In addition, Phil and many of his fellow players dislike the San Roque bunkers because they contain tiny crushed marble rather than normal sand; shots from these hazards do not deliver the same amount of spin as the players are used to. Nevertheless, his 25yd sand shot flops majestically out of the bunker and comes to rest three and a half feet from the pin. All seems well, but the slightly downhill par putt lips out. Phil has just blind-sided himself and created yet more needless anxiety.

Back to 3 under and the treacherous 18th will now play a full part in Phil's journey. He must at least get a par; there is absolutely no leeway. He has hit 425 golf shots over six days, some fabulous, some ugly, some that deserved better and some that seemed plain jinxed. Now he has to place every one of those shots to the back of his mind, focus on making two good swings, a couple of good putts and grabbing that Tour Card. "Trust it" are the words of advice from Jason's lips.

Phil's driver fires the ball long and straight; first job done, he has given himself every chance of a par. He will have a 4-iron from the middle of the fairway. He is still seems outwardly relaxed and, as he reaches his ball, he can see the small crowd gathering at the scorer's tent. He can also feel the monstrous wind blowing almost directly into his face.

Phil continues to take his time; he removes his visor for a moment and bends down to snag a few scraps of grass and throw them into the air to check the wind direction. Meanwhile, Jason is fighting his nerves and reminds Phil that this 4-iron is just like the one he successfully hit onto the 9th green; he says that this is what Phil has been training and practising for; this is his time. Everything seems to be moving in super slo-mo; real-life action is happening at the speed of dripping treacle.

Phil studies the shot some more; there is no rush. This 4-iron could define the last few years of his whole career: he is desperate to return to his glory days of high Order of Merit finishes, even another Tour win; he wants his peers to recognise that he truly belongs among European golf's upper echelon and that 2007 was just a blip. Phil is a proud man who has spent the last 12 months trying to understand his career stumble. At San Roque a year ago, he failed at Q School and stood in a kind of fog, unable to believe what had just happened to him. It has crossed his mind in the last 18 months that perhaps his time as a star of the Tour would never return.

That feeling of potential loss is what drives him today. Phil wants a place on the Tour again, probably much more than he can ever admit to himself. His position as a European Tour professional is what defines him as a person. His next shot will either re-launch his career or send it into an almost unstoppable downward spiral.

Somehow, like so many pros in similar situations, Phil zeroes in on the immediate job ahead; his concentration is now total. He eyes up the green for a final time and remembers Jason's words, "Trust it". Too aggressive and the ball will find the lake on the right; too cautious and he will risk a tricky up-and-down from the unpleasant valleys of rough on the left; the pin is far to the back of the green and certainly not offering any easy option. The wind blasts one final strong breath. Phil slightly grips down the shaft of the 4-iron and tries for a low, penetrating ball flight. There is no fear in his swing, it is grooved and fluid.

When a pro hits a good golf shot, there is a soft thudding sound on contact and a "whush" just after the ball leaves the clubface and bursts through the air. The pro will know within a millisecond of making the connection whether the ball is on target. This shot has to be perfection or damned close to it and Phil knows in an instant.

The Titleist is in the air for between three to four seconds. There are no tell-tale signs from Phil about where it will land. Often, if the ball is going right, the pro will lean left in an effort to pull on some invisible string to bring it back on line. If the ball is on its way to the left then the body will lean the other way. If the shot looks short, then the pro will to urge it on with words like "get up" or "big bounce"; a shot that seems too long would prompt a swift "get down".

None of these body movements or words are required. Phil's ball is on a perfect path to the green; it lands in the right half and bounces forward a couple of times to come to rest 25ft below the pin.

There is applause around the green. None of those watching know what Phil's score is right now or the tension that pre-empted that shot, but they definitely recognise great golf under pressure when they see it. Phil's chest puffs out ever so slightly as he strides to the green and marks his ball. He knows that the approach was his best shot of the day, especially given the circumstances.

There is some delay while his playing partners chip onto the green and Phil stands on the fringe by the lake calming himself for what should now be the final two shots of a successful 2007 Q School. He needs a solid lag putt and a tap in. He has done this is a millions of times.

Phil gives the first putt due attention, clears his mind and taps the ball forward. It rolls confidently right on line before pulling up a foot short. Phil nods to himself and taps in for that vital 4. He has finished the tournament on 3 under par. All the scoreboards indicate this is exactly the Tour Card mark. Phil has made it by the skin of his teeth. He has hit 429 golf shots in four days and if he had hit 430 then his current smile would be replaced by a face filled with anguish. He has bloody well done it; the weight of a whole year of expectation is lifted; the persistence of one of European golf's most regular visitors to Q School has won through.

Phil is triumphant; he extends his arms into the air after the final putt. There is real joy in his whole face and he shares the moment with Jason who walks forward to give his friend a huge hug. There would be no more honest or touching celebrations on the 18th green today. The accomplishment is shared; everything that the two of them had done during the last six days has been justified: the routine they adopted, the continual words of encouragement from Jason, the goal-setting and the focus on the short game. This is only the seventh time in 18 attempts that Phil has won his Tour Card at Q School. To make a comeback at his age and with so little golf during the season is a tremendous achievement. Many others far younger and with far better tournament preparation have finished well behind him. This is one of Phil's proudest moments.

As he and Jason walk off the green with arms around each other's shoulders, tears of relief – as well as of happiness – flood into the caddie's eyes. Jason wears his heart on his sleeve and he can control his emotions no longer. Phil retains his professional calm, but Jason will not be the only person to cry at Q School this afternoon because the emotional cost of either triumph or tragedy here is overwhelming.

The pro is taught to control his feelings in the golf arena, but those around him are more apt to release their emotions. It is the parents, wives, families, friends, sponsors, coaches and, yes, even caddies who more often display what Q School means to the player who must remain in control. This week, for instance, Jason has been Phil's entire support team – caddie, coach and friend – and if he did not shed a tear after the unpredictable ride that the two of them had shared then he would not be human. It is a poignant moment.

Phil signs his scorecard, receives congratulations from some colleagues around the 18th and is interviewed by a TV crew. He is still smiling. He is back on Tour and how he deserves it.

As Phil's celebrations are beginning, Sion is reaching his crucial last few holes; he is now battling both the elements and the inevitable nerves. However, the nerves he can cope with, but the wind is out of his control. The advantages of starting early are now apparent. Francois Delmontagne – who began on the 10th tee in a two-ball group and sped through his last round finished about one hour before Phil. The Frenchman had begun the day on the borderline at 3 under, but shot a 68 to easily gain his Card. His score would be the joint best of the day.

Elsewhere, the best most players can do is just hang on. South African James Kamte manages a 72 to finish 3 under and Marcel Siem of Germany (the player who won golf's World Cup 12 months ago) signs for a 71 and the same crucial 3 under score, exactly on the mark. Marcel is another who weeps with joy on the final green today.

But for every success, there are more tales of woe. South African Doug McGuigan bogeys his final two holes to drop to 2 under; Peter Senior fritters away three shots in the last three holes and ends at 1 under; Bristolian John E Morgan cannot complete a dream week for his soon-to-be-born child and leaks five shots in the last five holes to complete the tournament on level par. And still Sion is on the course.

The pace of play is slower than ever as the conditions worsen. Club choice is almost guess work and there is the first report of a ball oscillating on a green. A couple more and the tournament will be delayed.

At the turn, Sion was in the top five on 10 under, but those three bogeys in a row sent him even out of the top 10. On the 14th hole, he suffers another bogey and the advantage of his four early birdies has been completely cancelled out by four dropped shots. Now 6 under, Sion is not alone in dropping shots, but he can only guess about this. All he knows for sure is what the scoreboards tell him: who lead the tournament and 3 under gets a Tour Card.

Sion gathers himself on the 15th; he hits a superb wedge to the green from behind a tree and holes an unlikely downhill putt for birdie. Sion can think positively again; he wants three pars at least and a high finish to give him the best Card possible. Now he is back to 7 under and only the golfing equivalent of a horrible car crash will wreck his dream. But such things happen regularly at Q School.

In the group ahead of Sion is Derby's Stuart Davis who began the day in confident mood at 5 under; he had just shot his best round of the week on day five – a bogey-less 67 – to make a strong move for his first ever Tour Card. A Challenge Tour regular, Stuart just needed to stay calm to complete his most successful year since turning professional in 2004.

But Q School devours a few players every year and, unfortunately for Stuart, it is his turn. Stuart had battled bravely all day, but bogeys on 16 and 17 were perhaps understandable as the pressure mounted. With one hole remaining, he is on 3 under; a par for his Tour Card. What happens next would send a chill through every pro who has played Q School's last hole with a Card beckoning because they know it could so easily be them.

Stuart hits a reasonable tee shot on 18, but then viciously hooks his approach to the green; it bounces wildly on the nearby cart path and leaps 70 yards offline. Stuart's mind is in turmoil. Less than half an hour ago he had a two shot cushion, now he suddenly has to find a miracle chip onto the 18th green and hole the putt for a par or his Tour Card dream is over.

Instead of a miracle chip, Stuart airmails the green and the ball plops into the lake. A penalty drop, three more shots and it is a triple bogey 7. Stuart had one hand on a Tour Card almost all day and now it has vanished after five dropped shots in three holes. There are no words that can console a player like Stuart as he walks away alone from the scorer's tent. He is known for his fiery temperament and all those gathered around the 18th green leave him to his thoughts. It is hurtful even to try to talk to him right now. A wound like this will not heal overnight, but Stuart will be back at Q School next year if that is what it takes; being a golf pro is his life and he is not prepared to give it up. He will hope that next time a Tour Card is in reach, he has built himself one extra layer of courage that will allow him to grab it.

In the group behind Stuart is Sion who witnesses some of the devastation. However, the Welshman is made of sterner stuff these days and the par 5 16th is probably still a birdie chance despite the conditions. He hits driver, 2-iron and finds the green; two putts later and he picks up the shot he wants. Sion is back to 8 under. But the New Course is not finished with him just yet.

Sion hits a good 7-iron downwind to the par 3 17th green, but it is a tiny bit short and rolls back down a severe slope at the front. His chip is adequate, but he requires two putts and so writes another unwanted bogey on his scorecard. Sion is seven under again and still has four shots in hand with only the 18th to complete. He is not thinking of triple bogey disasters; he wants a final par to underline his improvement from last year and win a top 10 Tour Card. The way Sion finishes Q School this year means a lot to him and he is as focused now as he was for the first shot on day one.

Last year Sion won the 14th Tour Card, but although it was a major achievement for him, he often found himself on the reserve list for tournaments because the players are ranked 1 to 30 in Category 11b of the European Tour exemption list depending on their finish at Q School. That means the winner at San Roque gets first option of tournaments among those in the 11b category and the other Tour Card winners follow in sequence. If Sion can finish even a few places higher this year then it could mean a vital two or three more tournament entries. So his very final hole this week has hidden, additional importance: every place higher up the Q School ladder can put more pounds into your bank account. Plus, no pro likes ending a tournament with a bogey, it leaves a sour taste in the mouth.

Sion hits a decent drive off the 18th and faces a crucial question with his second shot: does he aim for the tricky pin in high winds with tension building by the minute or is there a smarter move. In the group ahead, Stuart Davis's bold approach proved fatal to his chances, so Sion reverts to a tried-and-trusted tactic and it is a lesson in smart golf.

The top pros believe in their talent and Sion knows that bringing the water into play is foolish at this stage; he needs to play the high percentage shot. Tournament pros will admit that they hit very few drives or iron shots with maximum strength; the vast majority of long putts are lagged rather than raced at the flag; such tactics are why they score so well so often. Sion does not need to witness the meltdowns of others to understand that now is not the moment to throw all his good work away. He has plenty of talent and this is the time to show it.

His best option is to play his approach towards the shallow hollow short left of the green, chip close to the flag and then single putt for a four. He remembers the 2006 Q School when he completed par in just the same way. Believe it and it will happen. It sounds so obvious after the fact, but San Roque on the last day of Q School can muddle the mind.

Sion asks Gary for the club that will put him in the shallow hollow and he is handed a 3-iron. His swing is full of confidence and the ball flies perfectly towards his target before nestling in the almost perfect spot for his planned third shot. He now has the easiest of chips to the flag, plenty of green to work with and no risk of water. This is the work of a pro's pro.

The pitch and the 6ft putt are completed with a certain inevitability. It has been a fine round; his 71 today is beaten by only one golfer finishing in a later group. Sion is tied 6th for the tournament and will receive the 9th Tour Card. He has succeeded at Q School for only the second time in 12 attempts, but this year he has looked the part of a European Tour player. It is a commendable return to The Big Show particularly because of his consistency – only one round over par (only one other player – Pedro Linhart of Spain – matches that feat) and only one double bogey all week.

Q School is often less about the birdies a player shoots and more about what he gives back to the course in terms of bogeys or worse. The spectacular shots are all very well, but they are risky and pros do not like risk. Sion's performance has been a Q School masterclass. Immediately after finishing his round, he shows only a small smile of satisfaction. No fist-pumping, no high-fives. This is a quiet man on the course and a sincere, family man off it who cares for others. Sion knows that dancing with joy is inappropriate as the dreams of some of his friends are being crushed. His celebrations will be elsewhere, in a more private place. He knows how to let his hair down, but it will not be now.

He is reflective afterwards and still has just enough energy for some dry humour. "It's a crazy game, golf; and those were horrendous conditions. Level par is a great score today and it helped me that no one was able to come up through the pack. I got to 4 under for today, but it was obvious that the conditions would mean a bogey run at some stage. The six-footer on the last makes me feel better. I'm absolutely delighted. It could've gone either way. You see friends missing Cards. It's not nice. I'm happy inside, but I don't jump up and down because I know how other people feel. I'm looking forward to a relaxing week at home. A couple of beers tonight; I think I deserve them." Only a couple? Probably not.

Sion has reached an age where he has seen the best and the worst of what golf can throw at someone. It is hard to put into words how much this Tour Card means to him. His is a grown-up response. To him, the Tour Card is the financial security of his wife and young daughters, it is the deep respect of his fellow Welsh pros, it is the happiness in the eyes of his whole family, it is the proof of his talent to his late father.

Perhaps the most telling part of Sion's last words is that "it could've gone either way". On some days you control golf and, on others, golf seems to control you. Sion's self-belief had increased so much over the past couple of months that he had vast amounts of control of his game, of his emotions and of his career. In fact, he is already thinking of his first Tour event of the 2008 season. This is a very different Sion Bebb than at Q School 12 months ago.

There were several players who began the day in better positions than Sion Bebb, but they could not convert their chances. Two new young pros, Tiago Cruz of Portugal and England youngster Ben Mason, had both started on 7 under; they each had a four-shot cushion, but it was not enough. Cruz stumbled to a 5 over 77 while Mason's few short months as a pro were not enough to prevent an 8 over par 80. Mason is not tearful, he now knows he can compete in the world of pro golf and, like any 20-year-old, is already excited about the future. He is a star in the making.

The Q School 2007 almost claimed another higher profile victim. South African Thomas Aiken was 11 under on the 1st tee at the start of the day, in joint 2nd place, but the more holes he played, the more ragged his golf became. The wind, the nerves, his relative inexperience: it all combined to turn Aiken's day into a near-catastrophe. He dropped four shots in the front 9; managed a couple birdies on the 11th and 12th, but then went spiralling out of control. By the time he stood on the 18th, he was just 4 under for the tournament (a frightening 7 over for the day). He was suddenly in grave danger of an unimaginable plummet from being in contention to win Q School to missing his Card. A Stuart Davis-like disaster – even a double bogey rather than a triple – and his week would be wasted. His final drive was adequate, his second just crept onto the green, his lag putt was over-hit and he took two more to complete his round – a bogey five and Aiken would finish plum last of the Tour Card winners with a final round of 80. And golf fans wonder why players at Q School lie awake at night worrying.

But while Thomas Aiken's post-round smiles were of relief, those of England's Paul Waring and Craig Lee of Scotland were of unfettered elation. Both men had begun their Q School journeys at First Stage – Waring at The Oxfordshire and Lee at St Annes Old Links. Before this year, neither player had even reached Second Stage let alone Final Stage. Today their stories are among the most remarkable.

Paul's grandfather – the man who had introduced him to golf – died three weeks earlier while the young golfer was out in Spain practicing for Second Stage. Paul had to choose between continuing his dream or returning home for the funeral. His family was adamant – stay and play because that is what your grandfather would have wanted. He qualified easily from Arcos Gardens.

At the turn on the final day at San Roque, Paul was 7 under, but running out of steam. However, there was a guardian angel helping him hold on and finish on 3 under to achieve a most surprising Tour Card. "I know my granddad's looking down on me now. He was a sport maniac and looked after me a lot when I was younger. I was asking him to guide me through. I think about him a lot and he'll always be there. He taught me that there are worse things in life than missing a 4ft putt on the last hole. I've already had a few tears and I'm sure there will be a few more later."

Craig Lee was originally determined not to attend Q School this year. He started doing more golf teaching early in 2007 and also opened a custom-fitting club centre. Craig was building a new life away from tournament golf, he had turned his back on his dream of a place on the European Tour. He celebrated his 30th birthday and was enjoying a settled existence than the one of a tournament golfer. But many pros whose lifelong desire is to compete with the best players in the world are fooling themselves if they think they can give it up so easily. Craig kept Q School in the back of his mind even while his life was changing and sent in the entry forms almost on automatic pilot. He certainly did not entertain any serious hopes. Nevertheless, Craig took his place at First Stage and finished 3rd.

"Before Q School, I didn't practice much or play well in local tournaments in Scotland. Then a retired local businessman gave me £2,000 to enter and I had nothing to lose, but my form at St Annes was a surprise." He then went to Costa Ballena at Second Stage and managed 4th place. There are only a few days between Second and Final Stages of Q School, so Craig had little time to worry about what might now happen to him.

"I didn't know what to expect here (at San Roque), so I didn't really have a plan. I just tried to play the best I could and see what happened. I've been up and down all week, but adrenaline kept me going for the last round; it was definitely very tough. This is a completely new way of playing golf, being defensive rather than pushing for more birdies. Today I just held on."

Like any first time Q School qualifier, Lee can hardly fathom what he has just achieved. "High as a kite" is how he describes his feelings and the thought of being on the practice range with the likes of Monty, Padraig, Sergio and others almost makes him swoon. "This is just the best feeling ever," says the man who picked up the 21st Tour Card. "It's so much better than winning any tournament."

Paul and Craig are two wonderfully romantic stories of unexpected success and Florian Praegant's is another. The fact that the Austrian managed a place in San Roque was a shock to him because he lost the Second Stage playoff to Euan Little just 10 days earlier. From abject despair, his life has turned all the way around.

Florian played with stunning confidence throughout the six days and looked stronger after each round. His last day 72 and 4th place finish are a testimony to his skill.

"I was a little bit nervous at first today, but I started with two birdies and made a lot of good up-and-downs. Mentally now I am done; I don't want to play here any more," he says. "I can't believe that I finished top 5 and I will only realise it when I play on Tour. After losing the playoff at Second Stage, I thought I would be on the Alps Tour next year. I am so happy to play with the top players in the world from now on; my parents will have a big party for me when I get home."

Pablo Larrazabal of Spain actually hits the very last shot of the 2007 Q School – a 2ft tap-in for 10th place – and Florian's compatriot Martin Wiegele wins the tournament on 11 under despite his last round 76, easily his worst of the week and some 12 shots more than his previous day's 64 total. He finishes just two ahead of Pedro Linhart and Lee Slattery.

Although plenty of players went backwards today (four shot 80 or worse), someone always charges through the pack and Patrik Sjoland of Sweden was this year's last-minute hero. Patrik – a former winner on Tour – was tied 60th before the final 18 holes began and was still one shot outside the cut mark as he stood on the 16th tee. But when a 137yd approach shot dived into the hole for an eagle, the Swede's luck turned around and he would eventually secure the 22nd Card. Thankfully for the sanity of pro golfers, stories of stunning triumph like Patrik's are a balance at Q School to those of pure tragedy.

Six long days have delivered exactly 30 players onto the Main Tour and 126 players are left disappointed, many with their careers in a state of flux. A crowd of about 100 spectators, volunteers, officials, players and caddies applauds as Martin Wiegele receives a silver salver from Mike Stewart in a short ceremony behind the 18th green. Now it is time to head to the airports.

Next year, Final Stage moves to two courses at PGA Golf de Catalunya near Barcelona, a facility operated by the PGA European Tour's courses division. For now, San Roque has provided its final and, perhaps most compelling, last-day Q School dramas. The reputation of the event as one of the most gripping – and often most grotesque – in professional golf has again been enhanced.

The 33rd annual European Tour Qualifying School in 2008 starts in 10 months time and, naturally, most of the 846 pros who failed to secure a Tour Card will again test themselves over one, two or all three stages. You can bet a small fortune that every single one of the failed pros from this year would love to discover another, less stressful way to win a Tour Card. They all hang on to that dream of playing regularly on the European Tour, receiving the keys to a flashy car for tournament week, pocketing the massive prize money cheques, being photographed and interviewed by dozens of media, feeling the warm glow that comes from the prestige of life among the best golfers on the planet.

Only a relative few players ever achieve this level of golfing hierarchy, yet there are many, many tens of thousands who want it, wish for it, even pray for it. Q School is a torture chamber of an event, but it is the quickest pathway to an amazing golfing dream. It will never get easier as the years go by and we can warn the faint-hearted or the obviously untalented to stay away from it because it can break your heart. But, like Everest, Q School exists and can be conquered by a very select band of brave individuals. Who are we to get in their way.

Epilogue

The following 30 players gained their European Tour Cards for full playing privileges for the 2008 season after the Final Stage of the PGA European Tour 2007 Qualifying School.

		R1	R2	R3	R4	R5	R6	Agg
1	Martin WIEGELE (AUT)	71	69	69	72	64	76	421
2	Pedro LINHART (ESP)	71	72	71	69	70	70	423
3	Lee SLATTERY (ENG)	69	76	72	64	70	72	423
4	Florian PRAEGENT (AUT)	73	69	67	72	71	72	424
5	Luis CLAVERIE (ESP)	69	71	68	73	71	72	424
6	François DELAMONTAGNE (FRA)	73	74	72	69	69	68	425
7	Lee S JAMES (ENG)	72	69	74	73	68	69	425
8	Alan MCLEAN (SCO)	71	69	69	74	72	70	425
9	Sion BEBB (WAL)	71	71	69	69	74	71	425
10	Pablo LARRAZABAL (ESP)	71	66	71	70	71	76	425
11	Richard BLAND (ENG)	73	69	71	73	71	70	427
12	Birgir HAFTHORSSON (ISL)	71	70	73	70	71	72	427
13	Joakim BÄCKSTRÖM (SWE)	69	74	68	70	74	72	427
14	Sven STRÜVER (GER)	71	71	68	72	72	73	427
15	Paolo TERRENI (ITA)	72	71	71	67	71	75	427
16	Benoit TEILLERIA (FRA)	76	71	71	69	71	70	428
17	Juan ABBATE (ARG)	74	71	73	70	68	72	428
18	David DRYSDALE (SCO)	70	75	73	70	67	73	428
19	David DIXON (ENG)	70	72	74	68	71	73	428
20	Matthew MILLAR (AUS)	71	73	69	71	71	73	428
21	Craig LEE (SCO)	72	68	75	70	69	74	428
22	Patrik SJÖLAND (SWE)	75	72	73	69	72	68	429
23	Marcel SIEM (GER)	71	72	74	70	71	71	429
24	James KAMTE (RSA)	71	70	73	73	70	72	429
25	Gareth PADDISON (NZL)	74	72	70	73	67	73	429
26	Philip GOLDING (ENG)	75	69	69	69	74	73	429
27	Paul WARING (ENG)	74	70	72	70	68	75	429
28	Jan-Are LARSEN (NOR)	72	70	73	70	69	75	429
29	Ulrich VAN DEN BERG (RSA)	70	71	72	71	70	75	429
30	Thomas AIKEN (RSA)	70	68	72	68	71	80	429

Life after Q School goes on and the few months after November 2007 were an important next chapter in the lives of the players who took part in the tournament.

Sion Bebb – In his very first tournament round of golf after Q School 2007, Sion shot a 7 under par 65 to lead the Alfred Dunhill Championship in South Africa after round one. He would eventually finish 8th and earn more money in one event at the start of the new season than he did in eight months of playing in the previous one. Sion continued to make early season cuts to exactly reverse his form of the previous season and, as spring emerged, he felt he had definitely arrived on the European Tour and was set to take the next step to become a fixture in the top 115 of the money list.

Phil Golding – Phil's euphoria at returning to the Tour lasted well into the New Year and he made an early cut in South Africa. He was also in the mix for the title during the last nine holes in Indonesia in February before finishing tied 13th. The routine of practising, playing and travelling the world as a top professional golfer comes easy to this man. He does miss his wife and son more than ever because of the extra time he spent with them last year, but for now at least, his absence is worth it and he has every chance of staying on Tour for a few more years.

Euan Little – The sunshine of South Africa is where Euan headed directly after leaving San Roque in November 2007. His plan was to play a full season on the Sunshine Tour – for which he was fully exempt – as well as co-sanctioned events which the European Tour also staged on that continent. In his second start of the season, Euan was joint 4th in the South African Airways Open after two rounds and played his third round with one of his heroes, Greg Norman. "One of the highlights of my career," he said. He fell away over the weekend and finished tied 50th, but plied his trade to reasonable effect in the southern hemisphere at the start of the year in preparation for Q School 2008.

Andy Raitt – This man needed a serious break from golf after the continual problems of his hand injury in 2007 and his so-near-but-so-far performance at Q School. Andy's love of golf was being threatened by all the negatives in his life, so he quickly put away his club and tried to construct a "normal" existence. He bought a van and set up an odd-job business just to earn a little money. "I've come to the end of wanting to play on Tour," he said. "I don't want to play golf any more if I can't play at 100%. I've tried to be happy-go-lucky about it, but I've come to the end." However within a few weeks, Andy's decision not to play at all had been broken; he agreed to play in one pro-am as a favour to a friend and, when he began working for a building company full of passionate amateur hackers, he took pleasure in regular fun golf with them. By the spring, he was playing once a week and was taking doing some teaching for clients in Los Angeles and Marbella. The most important thing was that he was loving the feeling of a golf club in his hand again, especially without any pressure. Andy was also meeting another circle of friends including people like Jack Nicklaus's former coach Rick Smith and they were trying to convince him that tournament golf was still possible. However, with Q School 2007 only a few months in the past and with his shoulder still needing plenty of re-hab, a career on Tour was still a long way from Andy's mind.

Guy Woodman – For Guy, the post-Q School period meant a return to working in the pro shop at Stoke Park plus devoting more time to his PGA exams; he also passed his PGA Level One coaching exam. There was a wrist injury to recover from and then another season to plan once the New Year kicked in. There is little time to practice on his own game, but the achievements of others have kept his dream alive even though he has still to make Final Stage of Q School. "Seeing some of the guys who got their Cards this year gives us all hope," he says.

James Conteh – Three days after finishing 14 over par in three disastrous rounds at First Stage of the 2007 Q School, James played in a pro-am at his local club – Moor Park in Hertfordshire – and won the event with a 66. That day he also received £1,000, his biggest cheque of 2007. However, although James also had to return to training bar men and working as a tiler to make ends meet, his Tour Card ambitions remain; this young man is nowhere near giving up.

Martyn Thompson – Life returned to normal for Martin almost as soon as he returned to his club shop after failing at First Stage in September 2007. Every good round of golf Martyn plays fires him up for Q School 2008 and every bad one makes him wonder why he bothers. Somewhere deep in his soul, he wants a Tour Card, but is still unsure how to go about getting it. "Right now, I really think that as long as I am healthy I will give it a try," he says. Martyn is also buoyed by players he knows – like Craig Lee – achieving their European Tour dream. In addition, his wife Sally has finally taken up golf, so life is good.

The stories of many other European golfers on the edge of the Main Tour took significant twists and turns in the months following the 2007 season. England's Richard Finch won his first tournament of the 2008 European Tour, the New Zealand Open, just two months after he almost lost his Card.

Andrew Coltart's Q School disappointment did not hold him back. Thanks to a couple of early season invitations, the Scot found some form and was even in the last group on day four of the Qatar Masters. Also performing well in the Middle East swing was Rory McIlroy who continued to look like Europe's No 1 young prospect by piling up the Euros and will certainly not be thinking of Q School again any time soon.

Pete Baker's year on the Challenge Tour boosted his confidence and by April he had notched up his first top 10 finish on the Main Tour since 2004. However, successful Q School rookies like Craig Lee, Paul Waring and Florian Praegant all found the step up very tough; none of them looked like making a breakthrough in the early months of the season. Even Q School winner in 2007, Martin Wiegele, was only just holding his own on Tour and by April his best finish was 9th in one of the smaller prize money events in Madeira.

And if the likes of Martyn Thompson wanted any more encouragement about a career on Tour, then they can remind themselves of the story of Irishman Damien McGrane (a five time Q Schooler) winning the Volvo China Open in April 2008, just a few short years after he was an ordinary club pro in Wexford.

While those players outside the Tour were all yet again focusing on another Q School, their philosophies were probably best summed up by Romany gypsy Joe Smith whose golf season only began in April with some EuroPro Tour pre-season qualifying events. "See you in September [at Q School]," were his parting words. The dream lives on.

For more information about the PGA European Tour School (Q School) and the golfers featured in this book visit www.golfontheedge.co.uk

Acknowledgements

This book is dedicated to the players who aspire every year to play on the PGA European Tour and, without their help, it would not exist. Obviously, the seven players featured heavily need my first and most warm-hearted thanks. Sion Bebb, James Conteh, Phil Golding, Euan Little, Andy Raitt, Martyn Thompson and Guy Woodman became my 'Magnificent 7' because they were so generous with their thoughts and their time. They allowed me insights into life as a tournament professional that were unique. I wish each of them could have won a Tour Card in 2007, but life is not that fair. Nevertheless, I admire each of them – both as golfers and as men – and hope that their golfing careers are long and successful.

I can also thank all the golfers who are quoted in this book plus some who I talked to who did not make the cut, but their words helped formulate much of the tone of the narrative; special thanks here to David Fisher, Notay Begay, Carl Suneson, Dean Robertson, John E Morgan, Alan McLean, Jamie Little, Sean Whiffen, David Horsey, Jamie Moul, Antti Ahokas, Steve Pullan, David Porter, Paul Grannell, Roy Mugglestone, Mark Searle and Colin Roope. In addition, there were plenty of coaches, caddies, managers and pundits who gave me their thoughts and opinions. Again thanks to those featured in the book but also Pete Coleman, Martin Seddon and Rich Logue. Finally, in this section, my good friend and successful Tour mind guru Nick Hastings was invaluable for his knowledge and support.

At the PGA European Tour office, there are countless people who I have spoken to for assistance and all were extremely helpful, but Mike Stewart who manages the Q School gets a special mention. There were also plenty of helping hands in the various Tournament Offices plus tournament referees, volunteers and various officials who all helped enormously. I am indebted to everyone at the European Tour Media Office, particularly those in San Roque: Roddy Williams, Michael Gibbons, Frances Jennings and Steve Doughty.

Other help came from Huw Owen (who operates www.sionbebb.com), all the members of Hampstead Golf Club who have been so excited about my own excitement and the HGC pros Peter Brown and Tony Sheaff.

In terms of the production of the book, Jonathan Hayden has been a rock with his fabulous advice and confidence in my writing. Ultimate Sports Publications receive thanks for backing the idea of the book. Also thanks to Cat Hollander; Susie & David Novick; Richard Kendal; Vic Robbie; Marcus Nichols at PDQ Digital Media Solutions; and John Harrison for www.golfontheedge.co.uk. Finally, huge thanks and love to my wife Kate for standing so close to me on this journey.